ASSESSING PUBLIC JOURNALISM

ASSESSING PUBLIC JOURNALISM

Edmund B. Lambeth,
Philip E. Meyer,
and Esther Thorson
Editors

University of Missouri Press
Columbia and London

Library of Congress Cataloging-in-Publication Data

Assessing public journalism / Edmund B. Lambeth, Philip E. Meyer, and
    Esther Thorson, editors.
        p.   cm.
    Includes bibliographical references and index.
    ISBN 0-8262-1158-5 (alk. paper)
        1. Journalistic ethics.   2. Journalism—Objectivity.   I. Lambeth,
    Edmund B.   II. Meyer, Philip.   III. Thorson, Esther.
    PN4756.A85   1998
    174'.9097—dc21   98-6621
                                                                 CIP

⊗™ This paper meets the requirements of the
American National Standard for Permanence of Paper
for Printed Library Materials, Z39.48, 1984.
Designer: Stephanie Foley
Typesetter: BookComp, Inc.
Printer and binder: Edwards Brothers, Inc.
Typefaces: New Baskerville and Optima

ED LAMBETH dedicates his contributions to this book to the memory of his colleagues at the *Binghamton Press* and the *Milwaukee Journal,* circa the 1950s and 1960s, for their deep commitment to the craft/profession of journalism and its continuing potential for democratic service.

PHIL MEYER remembers his small-town editors in Kansas, Harry Valentine of the *Clay Center Dispatch* and Bill Colvin of the *Manhattan Mercury,* who did public journalism without even thinking about it.

ESTHER THORSON, for her part, pays respect to the journalists who have been courageous enough to test and apply the concept of public journalism (often in concert with the academy) in search of a more effective way to equip democratic citizens.

CONTENTS

ACKNOWLEDGMENTS

Assistance with the research, writing, or editing of this book has come from many quarters. Among the many individuals to whom we owe thanks are Fran Peterson Lambeth of Columbia, Missouri; David Craig, assistant professor of journalism at the University of Oklahoma–Norman; David Miles, a master's journalism student at the University of Missouri; Virginia Whitehouse, assistant professor of communication at Whitworth College in Spokane, Washington; Shelly Rodgers and Susan Willey, Ph.D. candidates at the University of Missouri; Stacey Oliker, Sheila Webb, Carmen Sirianni, and Jack McLeod, Maier-Bascom professor at the University of Wisconsin–Madison; Professor Jane D. Brown of the University of North Carolina and John R. Dykers, Jr. of Siler City, North Carolina; Michael Finney, Davis Merritt, and Frank Daniels III, editors of the *Omaha World-Herald,* the *Wichita Eagle,* and the *Raleigh News and Observer,* respectively.

The Kettering Foundation, the Pew Center for Civic Journalism, and the Project on Public Life and the Press supplied background information on the origins of their work in the public journalism movement as well as related publications. The Freedom Forum's *Media Studies Journal* and Indiana University's School of Journalism permitted us to republish, respectively, articles by Jennie Buckner and Michael Gartner, and presentations made by Davis Merritt and Jay Rosen, originally presented on April 13, 1995, at the campus in Bloomington, Indiana, as the Roy W. Howard Public Lecture No. 5. The *Charlotte Observer* gave permission to quote extensively from an article in its December 3, 1995, edition. Finally, we thank the Civic Journalism Interest Group, created as a special venue to discuss, debate, and report research on public journalism within the Association for Education in Journalism and Mass Communication.

Finally, we acknowledge the efforts, professionalism, and care of the staff of the University of Missouri Press, especially John Brenner, Jane Lago, and Clair Willcox.

—The Contributors

ASSESSING PUBLIC JOURNALISM

INTRODUCTION

Few controversies in the twentieth century have generated as much division and animus within American journalism as the arrival in the 1990s of "civic" or "public" journalism. Although varied in content and tone, many of the several hundred public journalism experiments spawned in the 1990s shared a tangible concern for the quality of public life and a willingness to push the envelope of journalistic practice to more directly engage their readers and viewers as citizens. Yet those most serious about the enterprise say public journalism is more a constructive attitude change than a radical departure from past practice. Nevertheless, major opponents describe public journalism as thinly disguised commercialism by those willing to traduce the hard-won autonomy, detachment, and objectivity of the American journalist for only marginal gains in public approval. They dispute the extent of the civic maladies the experimenters say they want to help heal.

For the most part, public journalists depict their civic-minded initiatives as a needed corrective to traditional journalism. Most regard mainline news as often overly conflictual and neglectful of community interests or needs. They perceive many mainline journalists as unwilling to innovate in the face of eroding popular support for journalism and reluctant to think seriously about reform amid an endemic antimedia mood of the body politic. Animosity by traditionalists toward public journalism has occasionally abated thanks to entreaties of journalistic moderates. It is their view that, unless public journalism is better understood and rationally discussed, it could permanently sour the internal temper of a craft/profession vital to American democracy. Complicating the dialogue and, ironically, making its outcome more important, are journalism's declining public credibility, growing concentration of media

1

ownership, and a tabloidlike competition for public attention that too often begets "infotainment," voyeurism, or both.

The historically inclined see the divisions over public journalism as a latter-day manifestation of the 1920s debate between educator-philosopher John Dewey and journalist-philosopher Walter Lippmann. Lippmann, with his books *Public Opinion* and *The Phantom Public,* introduced an early modern skepticism over how much journalism could or should shape public judgment. In Lippmann's view, public opinion was so complex that the press would do well if it provided the public with a steady stream of reliable facts and accurately conveyed the best thought of experts to thinking citizens. Although Lippmann later came to publicly admire the democratic role played by the press's professionalism and investigative power, he remained an elitist. By contrast, Dewey, the democratic pragmatist, believed deeply in the capacity of citizens to develop a certain wisdom in public affairs. His work as an educator and his writings as a philosopher testified to his "fighting faith" in the reality of cooperative public intelligence. At different levels and in varying ways, this belief is a premise of public journalism.

Deweyan themes are alive in the world of journalism thanks chiefly to communication scholar James W. Carey, whose career has combined an affection for democratic journalism with a critical intellectual's capacity for parsing its cultural shortcomings as a social practice. In the 1980s, Carey's academic example inspired journalism professor Jay Rosen, whose scholarship also had been influenced earlier by doctoral dissertation supervisor Neil Postman, author of *Amusing Ourselves to Death.* Rosen was to become widely acknowledged as the academy's most influential articulator of public journalism. By the early 1990s, with funding from the John S. and James L. Knight Foundation, Rosen launched the Project on Public Life and the Press. The heart of the project was a series of seminars in which Rosen, media executives, and editors from experimenting newspapers examined how journalism might refresh both itself and public life. The project also enjoyed the intellectual guidance of the Kettering Foundation, the hospitality of the American Press Institute, and support from Rosen's home institution, New York University.

The Kettering Foundation, led by historian David Mathews, brought to the table a commitment to the art and practice of civic discussion—particularly to the framing of public issues—that predated the birth of public journalism. The Knight foundation brought to bear not only funding but also the courage to experiment with new ideas. Not least, it brought the backing, too, of the late James K. Batten, chief executive officer of Knight-Ridder, Inc., the nation's second largest newspaper group. Batten, who began as a *Charlotte Observer* reporter and rose through the ranks, had become deeply worried about declining newspaper circulation and the cloud it cast over the future role of journalism and the health of democratic society. In lectures sponsored by the *Riverside* (Calif.) *Press-Enterprise* on April 3, 1989, and by the William Allen White School of Journalism at the University of Kansas in Lawrence on February 8, 1990, he articulated the economic and civic dimensions of the challenge to American newspapers.

Serendipitously, three years later, Batten, on a civic mission to Philadelphia to seek philanthropic support to rebuild homes decimated by Hurricane Andrew in Florida, met Rebecca W. Rimmel, president of the Pew Charitable Trusts. She had recently become concerned about the alienation of citizens from the news media as well as from American politics. As she discussed her concern with Batten, a seed was planted that led eventually to the creation of the Pew Center for Civic Journalism. One of the most active and influential players, the Pew Center has funded several dozen experiments, emphasizing those that link print and electronic media in civic outreach projects. It underscored its concern by picking veteran Washington and network journalist Ed Fouhy as head of the center and seasoned print journalist Jan Schaffer as executive director. The Pew Trusts also invested in the assessment of Pew Center Projects and made public a summary of its findings.

Not surprisingly, given its lineage as a progressive force in contemporary journalism, the Poynter Institute for Media Studies also contributed to the dialogue on public journalism. It held a conference on "citizen-based" journalism, conducted training workshops on related reporting techniques, and conducted research on the impact of citizen-based journalism projects.

This book brings together a number of different research projects and reflective essays that assess public journalism. They aim to lower the decibel count, modulate the rhetoric, refine and advance the dialogue, and stimulate research. Given the history of public journalism, these goals may seem overly ambitious. Although several of the chapter authors labored in intellectual or geographic proximity to one another, most of us, in fact, did not. Our scholarly approaches, topics, and styles vary—and so, to some degree, do our positions on public journalism.

Some are written by academicians, others by editors. Thus, while we cannot claim unity of voice and certainly have not sought a "unified field theory" of public journalism, most of us did aspire to a collective result. We wanted our work to provide the beginnings of an alternative to at least the most unproductive forms of mud wrestling over public journalism.

More broadly, we hope our chapters will encourage a growth in the systematic assessment of public affairs coverage and of the study of the relationship between journalism and the civic health of North American society. The time is ripe, most of us believe, for the continuous availability of such monograph-length performance assessments for public discussion and professional reflection. They could complement the vital work of contemporary journalism reviews, but with more space and more generous deadlines. For reliability and validity, they would use the advanced analytical methods of the social sciences and the humanities. However, they would need to be much freer of academic jargon than current scholarly publications and should be done with a respect for the freedom and responsibilities of both citizens and journalists as well as the challenges facing democratic institutions. Such performance assessments should be earthy and realistic enough to "shame" when required. Yet their more usual role would be to give reporters, editors, and citizens the deeper, more systematic, and pragmatic feedback they need to improve journalism—and citizenship—as the larger American experiment in democracy enters the twenty-first century.

Sadly, we know of no feedback mechanism that regularly meets all of the above criteria. No doubt this book falls short of the mark. However, we do offer the debate over public journalism and the chapters that follow as an argument for a source of continuing intelligence on the dynamics of the press and public life. If free, independent, and public-service-minded journalism in North America is not an occupation in crisis, it certainly is a severely challenged one that needs all the constructive feedback it can muster, especially from researchers who wish it well. Such is our goal.

Critics and supporters agree that the practitioners of public journalism vary widely in what they mean by the term. Although it is important to avoid premature closure while innovating, public journalism's period of definitional laissez-faire should be coming to a close. In chapter 1, "Public Journalism as Democratic Practice," Ed Lambeth draws on the work of political scientist Charles W. Anderson to interpret public journalism as an expression of the political culture of "pragmatic liberalism." Lambeth offers an operating definition of public journalism that, while it certainly does not bind his collaborators in subsequent chapters, seeks to contextualize some of their work.

That even a cranny of a craft as crusty as journalism should be actively seeking a change in organizational culture may be attributable in no small part to the tandem efforts of Davis Merritt, Jr., the reform-minded *Wichita Eagle* editor (by way of Charlotte, North Carolina, and Washington, D.C.) and Jay Rosen, the professor of journalism and energetic conceptualizer of public journalism. At least to my knowledge, no other duo of editor and academician has had as much impact on the temper and content of debate within contemporary journalism as Merritt and Rosen. Together, in chapter 2, they discuss the origin of the idea of public journalism. The relaxed and attentive venue for their reflections was the fifth annual Roy W. Howard Lecture at Indiana University in Bloomington, delivered on April 13, 1995, under the auspices of IU's School of Journalism. Rosen addresses public journalism, respectively, as an argument, a set of practices, and a movement. Merritt explains why he believes journalism needs cultural change from within. He also articulates the need for "a viable philosophical foundation that could give both new hope and new purpose while protecting the truly essential third-party role of journalism."

Few editors have affected the formation of public journalism more than Merritt, now senior editor of the *Eagle* and the leading advocate and adviser on the subject for the newspapers of Knight-Ridder, Inc. Few, too, have argued more consistently for change in journalism as a democratic practice. In a sense, the evolution of his own thought and experience, though undoubtedly individual and nonreplicable, trace an embrace of change in organizational culture akin to what many other public journalists seek, in different and other ways, for their own newsrooms. In chapter 3, Carol Dykers tells this story by examining what Merritt has spoken and written about the experiments in Wichita. It is a story that has had a major impact on many American newsrooms.

But what do other journalists believe about their profession and its role in today's world? How, if at all, do public journalists of the 1990s differ in their beliefs from those that social scientists such as David Weaver and Cleveland Wilhoit of Indiana University have identified in their studies of newsroom attitudes and beliefs over the past twenty years? In chapter 4, John Bare seeks the answer in a comparative study of the views of the news staffs of the *Eagle*, the *Omaha World-Herald*, and the *Raleigh* (N.C.) *News and Observer.* His findings show both significant differences and continuities among the three newsrooms. They show, among other things, that public journalism is a distinct belief system. But, he concludes, it is one that can either supplement or deemphasize the more traditional beliefs of American journalists.

In chapter 5, Rick Thames, formerly of the *Charlotte Observer* and later Merritt's successor as editor of the *Eagle*, describes and explains how and why the *Observer* changed its 1992 election coverage. The changes emerged during a partnership the newspaper sought and arranged with the Poynter Institute for Media Studies, which has a continuing program of analysis and discussion of citizen-based journalism. Thames is enthusiastic about such new approaches. Reporters at the *Observer* in recent elections have given priority to in-depth coverage of issues identified in polls as most important to voters. They have sought out and printed candidates' written replies to voters' own questions. When such answers have not been forthcoming, they have left embarrassing blank spaces in the public prints.

Ironically, such intensive consultation with voters in choosing content has been criticized as sacrificing journalistic autonomy. Yet *Observer* political reporter Jim Morrill opined, "It was liberating to realize that candidates were no longer the ones who controlled the agenda and pulled our strings." However, Thames's candid account paints a mixed picture of the experimental coverage, yet one promising enough to encourage him to try to perfect the new approach. One warranted inference is that a healthy conversation could and should now ensue between a) critics who say journalists should not set agendas, b) those social scientists who say it is often difficult for the media to avoid doing so, and c) journalists who want to use their talents to equip voters themselves to more effectively influence major issues during and between local, state, and national elections.

In chapter 6, Scott Johnson of the *Columbia* (S.C.) *State* describes the sometimes painful process of not only assimilating the new approaches of public journalism but also marrying them to changes in the basic structure of the newsroom. Under Gil Thelen, executive editor, the top-down, industrial production mode of news definition, gathering, and dissemination was scrapped. In its place, after consultation with the staff, the *State* eliminated traditional "beats" and substituted the issues themselves as the motif for organizing work. One effect was to "flatten the management hierarchy," a move aimed both at improving communication within the newsroom and directing reporters outward to the community.

Johnson's account of how this major restructuring evolved directs attention toward a neglected aspect of public journalism—leadership and management responsibilities for a newsroom structure likely to maximize the chances of a healthy relationship between news staff and the citizenry. In the case of the *State,* published in South Carolina's capital, the leadership appears not the least diffident about the entrepreneurial implications of public journalism. "Setting the Agenda" is one of the titles it gives to periodic public affairs reports that "tell the General Assembly what it should focus on during the coming legislative session based on polling data and interviews with experts and citizens." In addition, the fact that the *State* and other newspapers practicing public journalism continue to conduct investigative reporting argues for public journalism as a companion to rather than a replacement for the interpretive and investigative traditions toward which most American journalists lean.

Journalism's repertoire expanded during the 1990s when public journalists introduced cross-media cooperation as a new means to increase voter knowledge and attention to public issues. One of the earliest of these was in Madison, Wisconsin, a city and state known, in fact, for political experimentation. In chapter 7, media executive Frank Denton and social scientist Esther Thorson report on the impact of coordinated coverage by four different media designed "specifically to empower citizens."

Rather than a laboratory experiment or measurements of existing uncoordinated political coverage, they focus on a 1994 field experiment assessing the effects of planned coverage of the gubernatorial and U.S. senatorial races by the daily and Sunday *Wisconsin State Journal,* statewide Wisconsin Public Television, Wisconsin Public Radio networks, and WISC-TV, a Madison affiliate of CBS. They organized town hall meetings and debates via electronic media and voter education by means of an extensive series in the newspaper called "Armed and Dangerous." The title conveyed the newspaper's attempt to equip voters with the knowledge and civic wisdom they would need to assess the issues as well as the candidates and their campaigns. Using before-and-after telephone surveys, they analyzed responses designed to measure changes in knowledge levels, attitudes, and likelihood of voting. Summarizing, they found that "the public journalism effort achieved widespread public awareness, and most important, the people who knew of the project said that, as a result, they were more interested in and knowledgeable about the election and more encouraged to vote."

To gauge the audience impact of reporting projects that were both cooperative and coordinated across media, the faculty and staff of the teaching news media of the University of Missouri School of Journalism conducted a series of citizen-based initiatives in Columbia, Missouri, during the academic year 1993–1994. The design of their study was influenced, in part, by earlier findings that the differing strengths of print and electronic news media might be usefully combined to improve public knowledge of important public issues and perhaps improve credibility. Using polling data and their own assessments of community priorities, journalists of the daily and Sunday *Missourian,* NBC-affiliate KOMU-TV, and KBIA public radio identified three issues of major concern to their readers, viewers, and listeners. These were neighborhoods and how well equipped they were to cope with urban growth; the status of jobs and the local economy; and, finally, local health care problems, especially issues of equitable access, affordable cost, and quality of service.

Chapter 8 reports the findings from the neighborhood and jobs/ economy stories. Researchers Thorson, Ekaterina Ognianova, James Coyle, and Lambeth sought to discover whether they could detect the effects of "synergy," that is, whether citizens exposed to the above coverage learned more or became more positive toward the media if their exposure came from two or more media rather than one, or none. Earlier studies distinguished between synergy resulting from mere repetition of a message and what is called "Gestalt synergy." The latter occurs when certain elements within the messages combine to increase an effect beyond that caused by repetition alone. In general, the study supported the presence of synergy, although more so from the jobs/economy than from the neighborhood coverage. At least in this study, the most potent combination for synergistic learning and attitude change was newspaper and television. For those two media, measurements showed perceptions of improved accuracy, relevance, and competence of the news media.

These findings, especially if bolstered by the results of additional studies, might imply a heightened role for coordinated, cross-media coverage of public affairs. Concern might be expressed that cooperation could mean a monopoly of public communication in smaller communities. That was not a problem in Columbia, whose trade area is served by two other network television stations as well as a daily and Sunday newspaper, the *Columbia Tribune,* with at least four times the circulation of the *Missourian.* In any event, there are ethical protections available in such initiatives. They are the same cautions that should constrain traditional or investigative reporting—integrity, impartiality, fairness, competence, and a willingness by journalists to publicly explain or justify their reporting methods and to print or broadcast dissenting points of view. Realistically, the future of coordinated, cross-media coverage may be limited by the distinctive cultures of print and electronic news media. Although new technology may have the capacity to blend printed words, audio, video, and archival materials, the differing values and styles of contemporary newspapers and television news have been shown to inhibit and, in some cases, frustrate cooperative attempts.

A question remains how public journalists actually follow up and do for citizens what they say they want to do. This is not so much a test of veracity as it is a matter of journalistic ability to translate the ambitious nomenclature of public journalism into practices that citizens (and researchers!) can recognize. In chapter 9 a team of graduate students at the University of Oregon, advised by veteran researchers James B. Lemert and Janet Wasko, used sophisticated content analysis in an attempt to assess the impact of public journalism on the coverage of elections in the *Wichita Eagle* in 1990 and 1994. Team members were Sally McMillan, Macy Guppy, William M. Kunz, and Raul Reis. As yardsticks for the existence of public journalism, they used a medley of measures. Among them were the presence of background information to help citizens participate in their communities or of stories on major issues or candidates' records; alternately, the degree of emphasis on candidates' character or on the horse race aspects of elections and the extent of reliance on citizen and noninstitutional or nonofficial sources in stories.

Their research leaves us with the question, not infrequent in media research, of whether the cup of democratic journalism in Wichita was half full or half empty. We also have the beginnings of an analytical framework with which to detect and measure the presence of public journalism in nonelection periods (the great majority of the calendar) as well as qualitative insights into the practice.

Both issue- and election-related coverage figure in chapter 10's examination of the critically important idea of "social capital." Researchers

Lewis A. Friedland, Mira Sotirovic, and Katie Daily define it as the "networks of social trust that communities draw on to solve common problems." At first blush, one could conclude from this definition that, in fact, creating social capital is what public journalism does. But the authors argue that public journalism cannot directly create social capital and that the formation of social capital occurs over periods of time longer than most current public journalism projects have existed. However, they believe they have evidence that public journalism can "intensify the connections" between local leadership networks in ways "that may lead to new connections and new forms of trust."

Their analysis of public journalism places in an expanded context the findings of Denton and Thorson as well as those that emerged from the University of Missouri team's experience. It also provides a potentially helpful conceptual prism through which to view the public journalism activities of not only Charlotte and Wichita but also the cities of Columbia in both South Carolina and Missouri. If Friedland et al.'s time horizon is accurate, as it almost certainly is, the change in newsroom culture to which many public journalists aspire may require a patience painful for most reporters and editors to embrace.

The nature of the schism in public journalism is the centerpiece of chapter 11, which pits Jennie Buckner, the editor of the *Charlotte Observer*, against Michael Gartner, onetime head of NBC News and editor-owner of the *Ames* (Iowa) *Tribune*, one of the most vociferous opponents of public journalism. Part of their exchange in the Freedom Forum's *Media Studies Journal* centers on the wisdom of a public journalism–style collaboration between six North Carolina newspapers, six TV organizations, and three radio stations for a portion of their coverage of the 1996 elections.

Their split reflects the intensity and shape of the disagreement ahead for public journalists seeking significant change in the organizational culture of newsrooms. In chapter 12, Ed Lambeth identifies and assesses the possible implications of such a change for newsroom and corporate leadership, ethics and media criticism, and the practice of investigative reporting.

In chapter 13, the concluding chapter, Philip Meyer, a veteran journalist and news media researcher, develops a strategy for a possible future research program on public journalism. He analyzes the mixed blessing of powerful new information technology, reviews strands of research from a variety of scholarly traditions, and, in a synthesis of perspectives, shows how social science can help evaluate whether public journalism can strengthen the political economy of contemporary news media.

Although it is unusually intense and divisive, the dispute over public journalism is far from the first schism in the news business. Muckraking, the crusading exposure of governmental and private corruption, flourished as a popular progressive force in the early 1900s. It collapsed, after an almost two-decade run, as the result of its own excesses, corporate withdrawal of advertising, and the demise of citizen interest.

The passive press of the 1950s made more than a few nostrils quiver in disgust with its deadpan reporting of Red-baiting by Senator Joseph Mc-Carthy and others. Many reputations were unfairly besmirched. Eventually, the press, the public, and a critical mass of moistened civic forefingers in the air gave McCarthy and company a comeuppance. These and other controversies between the press and government of the post World War II era underlined the need of public affairs reporters to provide context and background in their stories. There was, however, no permanent denouement to such controversy.

By the 1960s, a coterie of the Fourth Estate declared the craft's conventions of detachment and objectivity as inadequate to report the tumult of the times—or to take the full measure of social and cultural changes within the country. Tom Wolfe, Gay Talese, Tracy Kidder, and others adapted to journalism such techniques as scene-setting, dialogue, and omniscient narrative voice. Their work is important, not least as contributions to nonfiction books and articles in elite magazines and newspapers. Yet the practice is neither muscular nor popular enough among journalists to carry more than a small part of the load of democratic journalism.

The difference of these "reform" movements from public journalism are evident. To name only a few, the degree of subjectivity, literary imagination, and stylistic control in the "new journalism" is probably too rich for the diet of most civic journalists. The rhetoric that some of the muckrakers used and the values some of them sought to revive bear a family resemblance to the language and goals of public journalism. Many active in public journalism make clear their continuing fealty to investigative reporting. In its interpretive and in-depth, explanatory forms, investigative reporting has played a pivotal role in a number of public journalism initiatives. However, as a reportorial form to find and expose civic wrongdoing it is by no means center stage in public journalism as it certainly was in the crusading, circulation-building style of the early muckrakers.

It is not yet clear what enduring contributions public journalism will make to the economic future and the cultural role of news media in American society. However, the inward reflection and open debate stimulated by Merritt and Rosen should be healthy for American journalism. Yet critics have a point in demanding to know, "What are you doing, and why?" Likewise, public journalists are entitled to ask what the critics and passive traditionalists have done lately to help journalism in its time of need. In the pages that follow, we add our several voices to the conversation.

—Edmund B. Lambeth, for the contributors

I

THE ORIGINS
AND
SIGNIFICANCE
OF PUBLIC
JOURNALISM

1

PUBLIC JOURNALISM AS A DEMOCRATIC PRACTICE

EDMUND B. LAMBETH

If only saying could make it so, "truly democratic journalism" would long since have arrived in North America. For reformers who seek a philosophical counterbalance to classic, laissez-faire liberalism, the Hutchins Commission obliged with *A Free and Responsible Press* as early as 1947. For idealists who want all citizens to have a say and have it said well, the prolific German thinker Jurgen Habermas has since 1960 woven the idea of open and "undistorted communication" into the heart of his vision of democratic society. For the sophisticated who want a good argument for why investigative reporting should be aimed chiefly at helping the neediest, John Rawls's contemporary classic, *A Theory of Justice,* has been available since 1971.[1] Not to mention hundreds of professional skills texts in which the inseparability of a free press and a viable democracy appears as faithfully as the morning sun.

Nevertheless, journalism—though it may be better than ever—is still not what citizens, theorists, or democratic journalists themselves want it to be. Leo Bogart, scholar and former executive vice president of the Newspaper Advertising Bureau, spoke for many when he wrote, "A sober look at how media work in today's world suggests that they

---

1. For the Hutchins Commission report, see Robert D. Leigh, ed., *A Free and Responsible Press: A General Report on Mass Communication.* For an accessible guide to Habermas, see *The Cambridge Companion to Habermas* (New York: Cambridge University Press, 1995). John Rawls, *A Theory of Justice.*

remain vulnerable to manipulation—by political authorities motivated by ideological zeal or crude self-interest, or by economic forces that limit their resources, their variety and their integrity."[2]

Expanding this line of argument, veteran journalist William Greider contends that journalism's own neglect of its First Amendment responsibilities contributed to the capture by special interest groups of many sectors of the U.S. government. In *Who Will Tell the People? The Betrayal of American Democracy*, Greider documented how the press handicaps itself by "alignment with the governing elites."[3] Partly as a result, he said, journalism has lost its ability to relate to a whole generation of citizens, especially the poor and working classes.

In several passages that anticipate the creation of a public journalism movement, Greider writes:

> Like the other primary political institutions, the press has lost viable connections to its own readers and grown more distant from them. Because of this, it speaks less reliably on their behalf. As an institution, the media have gravitated toward the elite interests and converged with those powerful few who already dominate politics. People sense this about the news, even if they are unable to describe how it happened or why they feel so alienated from the newspapers that purport to speak for them . . .
>
> The suggestion that a newspaper ought to accept its own responsibility to democracy would be a radical proposition in any newsroom . . . A newspaper that took responsibility for its readers would assume some of the burden for what they know and understand (and what they don't know and understand). It would undertake to reconnect them with political power and to invent forms of accountability between citizens and those in power that people could use and believe in.[4]

This chapter begins an assessment of the democratic ambitions of the public journalism movement. One goal is to evaluate whether the doing of public journalism represents a radical departure from newsroom practice—and, if so, in what sense. A second objective is to examine the dynamics of journalism as an avowedly democratic social practice and

2. Leo Bogart, "Media and Democracy," *Media Studies Journal* 9, no. 3 (summer 1995): 1–2.

3. William Greider, "Angle of Vision," in *Who Will Tell the People? The Betrayal of American Democracy*, 287–306.

4. Ibid., 288 and 304.

to ask what it would mean for the occupation to assimilate the changes public journalists advocate.

A DEFINITION OF PUBLIC JOURNALISM

Some of the difficulties in the debate over public journalism stem from the lack of an acceptable working definition of the practice. Advocates argue that premature closure on a definition would constrict public journalism's creative possibilities, a posture that may have impeded constructive criticism. For purposes of this essay, I have attempted to distill a definition from the published and spoken ideas and behavior of the practitioners and advocates. It seems to me that public journalism can be viewed as a form of journalism that seeks to:

1) listen systematically to the stories and ideas of citizens even while protecting its freedom to choose what to cover;

2) examine alternative ways to frame stories on important community issues;

3) choose frames that stand the best chance to stimulate citizen deliberation and build public understanding of issues;

4) take the initiative to report on major public problems in a way that advances public knowledge of possible solutions and the values served by alternative courses of action;

5) pay continuing and systematic attention to how well and how credibly it is communicating with the public.

Critics of public journalism say these goals are nothing new. They do, in fact, parallel some of the key passages in the Hutchins Commission report. Hutchins argued that a free press should provide "a truthful, comprehensive account of the day's events in a context which gives them meaning"; serve as a "forum for the exchange of comment and criticism"; offer a "representative picture of the constituent groups of society"; present and clarify the "goals and values of society;" and provide "full access to the day's intelligence."[5]

However, a careful reading will show the form of public journalism defined above would significantly expand and make much more explicit

5. For a discussion of the limitations of the Hutchins Commission Report, see Edmund B. Lambeth, *Committed Journalism: An Ethic for the Profession*, 1–10.

the roles that the Hutchins Commission advanced for the press. It is much more solicitous than traditional journalism of citizen perspectives. It also tries more explicitly to activate and elevate public deliberation on community issues. It is keener on explaining the choices facing the public and, especially, on identifying what values are linked to alternative policies. At its best, it seeks to gain continuing and reliable assessments of its own performance. It also takes more reportorial initiatives aimed at helping the community find ways to solve major public problems.

The greater demands public journalists put on themselves can be seen in the techniques their more ambitious projects deploy. They include, but are not limited to, citizen polling to identify major issues on the public's mind; resource panels of both citizens and specialists to help journalists understand the basics of an issue before they immerse themselves in reporting; focus groups with citizens to deepen and give reporters firsthand knowledge of key facets of an issue; open forums to allow the public to begin to engage and work through public issues; and, finally, studies to discover how well media performed.

These techniques certainly should not and likely cannot become a litmus test of public journalism. They can be expensive, complicated, and time-consuming practices in an industry not noted for its willingness to make such investments, especially not on a long-term basis. The techniques are, however, an important part of a new movement whose range and variety need to be summarized before it can be adequately assessed.

A LOOK AT THE EARLIER EXPERIMENTS

Davis Merritt of the *Wichita Eagle* and his staff pioneered the development of the newsroom use of public journalism techniques, and they were among the first to deploy them in political coverage. They especially wanted to dissolve the "mutual bond of expediency" between politicians and media that led to what seemed like a perpetual focus on the horse race aspects of political campaigns at the expense of voters who preferred substantive information on the issues. Merritt vowed then that the *Eagle* would aggressively report the 1990 campaign to make sure that "candidates talk about the issues in depth."[6] The 1990

6. Davis Merritt, *Public Journalism and Public Life: Why Telling the News Is Not Enough*, 80–81.

coverage stressed in-depth treatment of issues and paid less attention to, though it did not ignore, routine, day-to-day coverage. As an outgrowth of that coverage in 1990, Steven Smith, then managing editor, wrote and later circulated to other newspapers what Merritt described as an "early textbook on reformed campaign coverage."

But citizens also needed better public affairs coverage between elections. Merritt called for "a new purposefulness: revitalizing a moribund public process."[7] The aim was to help Wichita make progress on issues that appeared to yield progress only grudgingly to civic, private, and governmental efforts. In response, the *Eagle* and its lead reporter (and later public journalism editor), Jon Roe, developed an initiative in 1992 that gained national attention: "The People Project: Solving It Ourselves." It applied selected public journalism techniques to community issues such as crime, education, and health. Breaking with tradition, Roe and his colleagues 1) reported success stories; 2) analyzed the core values that defined both the basis of disagreements as well as of possible paths to the solution of public problems; 3) identified ways citizens could act on their own ideas; 4) solicited and published citizens' proposed solutions; and 5) sponsored "agendaless gatherings" in which print and electronic reporters could mix with concerned citizens. There were encouraging hints that these efforts made a difference. Volunteerism in Wichita schools jumped 37 percent in 1992 and reader satisfaction with the newspaper rose by what Merritt called "an unprecedented 10 points—twice the increase among those Knight-Ridder Newspapers whose ratings rose at all." However, he began to argue strongly for a more patient and long-range strategy to change the organizational culture of the American newsroom.

In 1992, reflecting the same values, the *Charlotte Observer,* winner of four Pulitzer Prizes, teamed with the Poynter Institute for Media Studies to assess and revamp its own campaign coverage. The *Observer*'s systematic and innovative use of polling and consistent pursuit of responses by candidates to citizens' questions were imitated by other leading regional newspapers. In a more direct and activist role, the *Observer* used sophisticated computer techniques to identify neighborhoods with the highest crime rates. Then, a foundation-funded community coordinator housed at the newspaper organized solution-oriented discussions in the neighborhoods. The coverage of these sessions and the pinpointing

7. Ibid., 83.

by the *Observer* of specific neighborhood needs generated a strong helping response from the United Way and local citizens. Implicit in many of these projects was the criticism that those public institutions intended to foster safety, health, and education were not working equitably, especially for the poor and middle classes. The projects demonstrated, with varying degrees of success, the efficacy of public participation. It appeared that established institutions—both public and private—could themselves benefit by becoming more accessible to citizens.

If Merritt served as the journalistic progenitor of public journalism, then Jay Rosen played a pivotal and even novel role as the leading public intellectual of the movement.[8] In seminars with journalists and academicians, to those opposed as well as those already persuaded by public journalism, Rosen invited journalists to adapt for their own purposes the pragmatic democracy of John Dewey. Thus, in a characteristic Deweyan description of how public journalism got started, Rosen said:

> The do-ers gave the talkers new things to talk about while the talkers gave the do-ers a language to describe their doings. This is still how we operate, and if public journalism succeeds as a "movement" it will succeed precisely this way: Practice inspires theory, so that theory informs practice.[9]

Practice varies widely. Thus, the *Norfolk Virginian-Pilot* emphasizes not projects but day-to-day public framing of issues and storytelling. The focus is on people as citizens and as human beings trying to make civic sense of their public involvements. To meet these goals, the newspaper management created a special "Public Life Team" of reporters and editors. In Spokane, Washington, the *Spokesman-Review,* to broaden the mix of community conversation, used journalists to assist readers in writing letters to the editor. The *New Orleans Times-Picayune* added to its year-long series on race relations an internal newsroom discussion of differences on race. In South Carolina, editor Gil Thelen of the *Columbia State* reconfigured traditional beats into new "interdisciplinary" teams

8. See Rosen's account of his experience, "Making Things More Public: On the Political Responsibility of the Media Intellectual," 363–88.

9. Jay Rosen, "Public Journalism as a Democratic Art," opening presentation at a seminar of the Project on Public Life and the Press, November 11, 1994, 1.

such as "governance," "quality of life," "community roots," and "leisure." As Scott Johnson explains in more detail later in this book, the new approach seeks a shorter and flatter table of organization and a more collaborative and deliberative newsroom.[10]

The *Akron Beacon Journal,* which won a Pulitzer for its public journalism–style coverage of race, generated twenty-two thousand signature pledges by citizens to work toward better race relations. Assisted by the Kettering Foundation, the *Dayton Daily News* generated new civic attention and action to curb teenage crime and then shifted its focus to the related issues of the health of Dayton family life. Gannett, the nation's largest publicly owned newspaper group, issued a company-wide mandate that each of its news media outlets look outward and attempt projects that make a difference in Gannett communities.[11]

The debate these initiatives triggered over the ethics and efficacy of public journalism suggests that some represent significant departures from journalistic but not necessarily from democratic traditions. None of the goals or techniques of public journalism appear inherently or flagrantly at odds with the classical liberal or enlightenment ideals intended to protect individual rights by the rule of law, government by consent of the governed, freedom of expression, rationality in decision making, individual initiative, and institutional efficiency.

HABERMAS TO THE RESCUE?

Were public journalism to require a philosophical patron saint, Habermas, arguably, would appear to be a logical nominee.[12] His still-continuing life's work emphasizes the impartial public discourse of an "ideal speech situation" in which citizens and factions have equal access to a noncoercive public sphere in which contending arguments are equally well expressed.

Like Immanuel Kant, Habermas is concerned with tests of consistency and due process. But rather than a Kantian individual's affirmation of a universal moral rule that he or she could embrace without contradiction, Habermas accepts as morally valid only those norms affirmed

10. Arthur Charity, *Doing Public Journalism,* 93.
11. See for example "Newspapers Must Make a Difference," a front-page advertisement of *Editor and Publisher,* November 18, 1995.
12. See Carol Reese Dykers, "A Critical Review: Re-Conceptualizing the Relation of 'Democracy' to 'News.'"

through the rational, consensual, and impartial judgments of all moral agents affected by the norm who are equally well equipped to articulate their interests.

When thus briefly and bluntly stated, Habermas's position may seem hopelessly unrealistic. However, the Habermasian ideal appears more relevant when one considers that many contemporary societies have failed to solve their major problems by relying on either societal custom, extreme laissez-faire economics, or the various species of authoritarianism. Freshly, if with seeming naïveté, the followers of Habermas argue that his work can re-create genuine faith in rational democratic discourse that has eroded in the twentieth century. They also believe Habermas, despite the density of his writings, offers concrete possibilities. Done well, they say, discourse by Habermasian design can create an energetic public sphere with intelligence and direction.[13]

Habermasians also believe that their ideas of democratic discourse can, in turn, generate both sorely needed political legitimacy and collective will. These are no small assets, whether the community is a village, a medium-sized city, a metropolis, a nation, or a planet.[14] But few persons have been able to take the germinal insights of Habermasian theory and transmute their potential into practical procedures that benefit public life.

However, American political scientist James Fishkin has led an indefatigable effort to establish the usefulness of what he calls a deliberative public opinion poll. Although Fishkin describes Habermas's "ideal speech situation" as "utterly Utopian," he pays Habermas the respect of inventing a pragmatic tool for small-"d" democrats. In England in 1994 and in the United States in 1996, Fishkin organized a demonstration

13. Such an interpretation of Habermas, although with qualifications, is apparent in Daniel Yankelovich, *Coming to Public Judgment: Making Democracy Work in a Complex World,* 215–19.

14. Some of the most important of Habermas's works have been translated by the M.I.T. Press. The works and their translators are *Structural Transformation of the Public Sphere: An Inquiry into a Category of Bourgeois Society,* translated by Thomas Burger; *Moral Consciousness and Communicative Action,* translated by Christian Lenhardt and Shierry Weber Nicholsen; and *Justification and Application: Remarks on Discourse Ethics,* translated by Ciaran Cronin. This chapter also draws upon Jane Braaten, *Habermas's Critical Theory of Society* (Albany: State University of New York Press, 1991); Habermas's *Communication and the Evolution of Society* (Boston: Beacon Press, 1979); and Stephen K. White, ed., *The Cambridge Companion to Habermas* (New York and Melbourne: Cambridge University Press, 1995), especially Mark Warren's "The Self in Discursive Democracy," 167–200, and Simone Chambers, "Discourse and Democratic Practices," 233–59.

of what the public would think were it exposed to a systematic and model debate of the issues. A deliberative poll records the views of a representative sample of an electorate, and gathers a cross-section of respondents for a weekend of deliberation, followed by a second poll. The results and any changes are then presented and discussed on national television. Fishkin's experiments in deliberative democracy and the better public journalism initiatives raise the hope that the currently sour civic dialogue in North America can again be made fresh and effective.[15]

The most extensive study of public journalism's possible effects on voters began to emerge in a report by Philip Meyer and Deborah Potter on the 1996 election project of the Poynter Institute for Media Studies.[16] It examined print and broadcast coverage in twenty markets and scaled the communities according to the extent to which they intended to practice "citizen-based journalism (CBJ)" in covering the campaign. Content analysis of newspapers and TV stations was done for seven weeks before the election. Panel surveys of 1,012 citizens (50 in each market) were conducted before and after the election to gauge media effects. Among the highlights of the findings:

• Newspapers were more CBJ-oriented than television.

• Newspapers intending to practice CBJ carried significantly more issues stories and significantly fewer "horse-race" polls than non-CBJ newspapers. Thus, many media practiced what they preached.

• Citizens in the top ten CBJ markets "learned more in the course of the campaign than citizens in the low-CBJ markets," even though citizens at both ends of the CBJ scale grew in their knowledge of politics.

• Mistrust of the media is high across the twenty markets, with 58 percent blaming the media for the way the political process works and 62 percent saying the media are "run by a few big interests."

• Citizens in communities where newspapers were high in their intent to practice CBJ knew significantly more about candidate stands on the issues and they trusted the media more.

15. James Fishkin, *Democracy and Deliberation: New Directions for Democratic Reform,* 36. James Fishkin, "Ideal Citizens Give a Considered Judgement," *The Independent* (London), May 9, 1994, and Fishkin, *The Voice of the People: Public Opinion and Democracy.* See E. J. Dionne, Jr., *Why Americans Hate Politics* and Thomas Patterson, *Out of Order* (New York: Knopf, 1993).

16. Philip Meyer and Deborah Potter, "Effects of Citizen-Based Journalism in the 1996 Election," Poynter Institute for Media Studies, St. Petersburg, Fla., March 17, 1996.

• However, contrary to what public journalists hoped would be the case, citizens in high-CBJ markets were not more likely to participate in the political process—that is, to vote, follow the campaign closely, talk with friends about politics, or attend political meetings. Nor did they express more trust in government.

• The superiority some citizen-based journalists place in issue coverage versus poll-based stories did not hold up. "Polls, by providing context for and arousing interest in the campaign, appear to help voters focus on the candidate issue positions," Meyer and Potter reported.

But Meyer and Potter were not ready to close the book on the complex research questions to which their 1996 study gave only partial and incomplete answers. They concluded that "citizen-based journalism involves a basic cultural change that affects both content and a newspaper's relationship to its community in ways that we have not yet learned how to conceptualize, much less measure. The idea offers a fertile field for further research."[17]

FRAMEWORKS FOR QUALITATIVE ASSESSMENT

But journalists must first step back and gain a perspective on how they might assimilate the best features of the idealistic, prickly, and ambitious public journalism movement. They need a framework of analysis in keeping with the earthy, practical, and heavily tradition-bound nature of their craft. One such framework is Charles W. Anderson's attempt to blend two American perspectives—liberalism and pragmatism.[18] Anderson's *Pragmatic Liberalism* is distinctive, in part, for its attempt to examine the usefulness of specific forms of reasoning and deliberation at the level of corporate profit-making and nonprofit enterprises in a democratic society. He identifies these types of deliberation as "reasons of trusteeship, critical reason, entrepreneurial reason and meliorative reason." Anderson, although he specifically mentions news media only in passing, has occupations such as journalism in mind in his theory and analysis.

The "trusteeship" of pragmatic liberalism is a form of reasoning that puts innovations to the caliper of custom and tradition. "Especially when criticism of dominant institutions is widespread, it is important that the

17. Ibid., 14.
18. Charles W. Anderson, *Pragmatic Liberalism*.

rationale for the going concern be fully appreciated before reform is attempted," Anderson writes. Geneva Overholser, the ombudsperson of the *Washington Post,* spoke with the voice of a "trustee" when she wrote:

> The problems that gave rise to civic journalism lie not in journalism's principles but in its practice. If we have been concentrating overmuch on the negative, then we must renew our commitment to tell the whole story, to be accurate and comprehensive. If we are turning too often to inside sources, we must bring back the time-honored practice of journalism that runs on shoe leather and send the troops out to talk to people . . .
>
> Moreover, presenting civic journalism's good questions as ideas with venerable antecedents rather than as shiny new notions, and casting the movement in the light of refurbishing traditional journalism rather than replacing it, would provide a resonance and grounding that is now noticeably lacking.[19]

But civic or public journalism is posing more than "good questions," and most of its practitioners believe conditions in journalism require major behavioral change, not merely fresh commitment to past practice. Even so, most of the leaders of public journalism say they do not wish to replace either traditional storytelling or investigative reporting but to supplement both with new approaches. They argue, but have not yet convincingly persuaded their peers, that the best work done so far builds on the best of both the narrative and investigative traditions. But that linkage may have been lost in what *Boston Globe* editor Tom Winship, who supports civic journalism, calls its frequently "overblown rhetoric."[20]

Overholser, former editor of the *Des Moines Register,* does have a point. Anderson, the pragmatic liberal, himself insists that "the case for prevailing practice (needs to be) heard" and even serve "as a basing point for reform." But Anderson also argues for an in-depth understanding by practitioners both of how problems developed within current practice and precisely why it might need to change, perhaps even change substantially. Unless practitioners understand this and have the freedom to invent new approaches to meet current needs, journalism may not be able to evolve in healthy directions. Anderson writes:

19. Geneva Overholser, "Learning from 'Civic Journalism,' " *Washington Post,* September 17, 1995.
20. Tom Winship, "Civic Journalism: A Steroid for the Press," 5, 37.

> The point now is that we are capable of stepping back from inherited custom and usage, and reexamining how well suited existing practice is to our purposes. Such liberalism teaches that the perspective of the detached individual, who can contemplate fundamental questions of aim and purpose without preconception, is better than that of the experienced but unreflective master of an inherited body of technique.[21]

OBJECTIONS BASED ON PRINCIPLE

To use critical reason, Anderson says, is to invoke principle to "point to some disparity between theory and practice," in effect, "to trigger an alarm," adding:

> Principled criticism is an essential part of reasoned political deliberation. Without it, the claims of trusteeship go uncontested, and prevailing usage, tradition and technique are not questioned. Liberal tradition, again, requires that detachment from existing practice which it is the function of the critic to provide . . . Someone must speak for the rationale of the going concern, and someone must propose alternatives to it if we are to create more serviceable designs for action.[22]

An objection on principle bubbled up slowly—in retrospect, perhaps too slowly—within Knight-Ridder, Inc., during what, arguably, was the very first exercise in public journalism.

In the late 1980s, publisher Jack Swift of the *Columbus* (Ga.) *Ledger-Enquirer* went beyond customary journalistic limits by including action recommendations in the newspaper's "Columbus Beyond 2000," based on extended coverage of the community's long-term problems. Rather than stand aloof from follow-up civic action, Swift (whose suicide later hastened the demise of the project) helped lead the formation of a Columbus improvement task force as well as the selection of its members, including reporter Billy Winn. Barbecues to meld the disparate leadership elements within Columbus were held by Swift at his home.

Winn himself said that the extensive coverage and action helped improve race relations, groom community leadership, and renew hope with $170 million in municipal improvements. However, he concluded that the newspaper's staff "probably should not have become so involved." Criticism to that effect had circulated in Knight-Ridder, Inc. Reflecting on the experience, Winn wrote:

21. Anderson, *Pragmatic Journalism,* 170.
22. Ibid., 172.

> . . . it could be argued that our greatest failing was in not learning to say "no" when community leaders asked us to help them with a project. When we said yes it inevitably expanded our activist role. As already stated, we were aware of this and yet we seemed powerless to stop ourselves. Once you admit that you are part of a community, saying no to that community is like saying no to yourself.[23]

Winn seems to foreclose the possibility that a newsroom's entrepreneurial reporting on alternative solutions to community problems can coincide with journalism's independent reportorial role. Building newsroom cultures able to sustain such independence is a key task for public journalism. But independence need not imply indifference.

THE REASONS OF DEMOCRATIC ENTERPRISE

To use the phrase "First Amendment enterprise" is to implicate Charles Anderson's third form of deliberative reasoning—the "entrepreneurial" mode. Its goal is to discover "a better way of doing things." The editor, Merritt, the intellectual, Rosen, and the reporter, Greider, are quintessential First Amendment entrepreneurs. In their parallel but different domains, they freely express, develop, or propose ideas that attempt to improve journalism as a social practice.

But their critics differ with them in at least two ways. First, they question whether the civic ethic is sickly or failing—whether the entrepreneurship of public journalism is really necessary. Second, they argue that the institutions of the press are either ill equipped or too powerful to engage in the kind of entrepreneurship public journalism represents.

At a symposium honoring the late James K. Batten, the Knight-Ridder chair and chief executive officer, Everette Dennis, then executive director of the Freedom Forum's Media Studies Center, argued against the pessimists. "While civic life and democracy itself are always in play, perhaps always at risk, I see no evidence of corrosive decay that should sound an alarm throughout the land. Do we need a new journalistic faith to arrest problems and put America on the straight and narrow? No, I don't think so."[24]

Among those on Dennis's side of the argument are lifelong public activists, such as Frances Moore Lappe and Paul Martin DuBois, whose

23. Billy Winn, "Public Journalism—An Early Attempt," 54–56.
24. In Winship, "Civic Journalism."

recent compendium of civic initiatives depicts a nation whose grassroots communities are flourishing.[25] Almost a decade earlier, thoughtful commentators such as Elaine Spitz could write:

> In the United States people devote astonishing amounts of time and energy to public service—coaching sandlot ball clubs, serving as docents in museums, planting bulbs in public parks, raising money for community projects. A society that starts its children out selling Girl Scout cookies and graduates them to pro bono work as lawyers may be the most participatory the world has ever known.[26]

Ultimately, the most creative and pragmatic result of Dennis's point could be to challenge the leaders of public journalism to examine their assumptions about the extent and quality of civic participation, issue by issue, community by community. The American civic culture may look less like a thick carpet, coast-to-coast, and more like a speckled Jackson Pollock painting, region by region.

Another test—at least partially met in Wichita, Dayton, and Charlotte —is whether public journalism initiatives actually generate and focus the intelligence and energy of the citizenry on a community's most serious problems. Such assessments require a quality of judgment, media criticism, and public scholarship not now found in most local and metropolitan communities.

Then, do public journalists expect too much of themselves? "The elemental tasks of describing events and discerning their causes are already beyond the skills and budgets of many newsrooms," wrote Max Frankel, former managing editor of the *New York Times* and now media columnist for its magazine. Stick to one's traditional knitting, Frankel implored.[27]

Writing several years before the public journalism movement, political scientist Daniel Hallin questioned an assumption by the press of a concerted role in generating public participation. As early as the 1980s he wrote:

> What the modern mass media cannot do is to play the role of sparking active public participation in deciding the role of public policy. I use the

25. Frances Moore Lappe and Paul Martin DuBois, *The Quickening of America*.
26. Elaine Spitz, "Citizenship and Liberal Institutions," in *Liberals on Liberalism,* edited by Alfonso Damico (Totawa, N.J.: Rowman and Littlefield, 1986), 198.
27. Max Frankel, "Fix-It Journalism," 28.

word cannot deliberately. Individual journalists working in established news organizations can certainly from time to time break out of the focus on technique and strategy to raise the direction of public policy as an issue; they can be sensitive to the underlying message their reporting conveys about politics and the citizen's relation to it; they can give a hearing to those who do seek to play a mobilizing role. But all of this must remain within relatively narrow limits . . . It is not a role appropriate to institutions with such massive social power.[28]

If one scans the literature that links press and public philosophy, Greider, in fact, may be the respondent who speaks most cogently to both Frankel's minimalism and Hallin's fear of the power of the press. Greider argued:

> To take responsibility would mean to rethink nearly everything they (newspapers) do, the presumptions of autonomy that protect them from criticism and the self-esteem that is based on prestigious feedback from elites. Reporters would have to reexamine their own methods for defining the content of news as well as their reliance on those in power. Editors would have to throw out some of the inherited rules for producing news . . . in order to overcome the political inertia of their readers.
> . . . I imagine a newspaper that is both loyal and smart, that approaches daily reality from the perspective of its readers, then uses its new sophistication to examine power in their behalf. A newspaper with those qualities would not solve the democratic problem, but it could begin to rebuild the connective tissue that is missing.[29]

Public journalists say, mostly in unison, that they do not intend to either advocate policy positions or jettison the ideal of objectivity. However, they are proposing a significant change by insisting that journalism accept more responsibility for trying to stimulate and raise the quality of public deliberation. They can do so by accepting as standards of excellence 1) in-depth reporting on alternative solutions to public problems; 2) campaign coverage that asks elected officials to address key issues on the mind of the public; and 3) coverage designed to actively foster citizen participation and deliberation. These standards are consistent with Daniel Yankelovich's argument that journalists need

28. Daniel Hallin, "The American News Media," in *Critical Theory and Public Life*, edited by John Forester (Cambridge: MIT Press, 1985).
29. Greider, "Angle of Vision," 305.

to do better in their responsibility to help the public think through the major judgments it must make.[30]

But, we might fairly ask, how can we know that the news media are not already accepting such responsibility? At the most fundamental level, not accepting responsibility for local democracy might show up in ignorance by journalists of how or whether the information they are dispensing for citizens' sake is actually registering with readers, listeners, and viewers. Precisely this condition was encountered among journalists by W. Russell Neuman, Marion R. Just, and Ann N. Crigler in an extensive study comparing the effectiveness of print and electronic media: "When first asked what people learned from their stories, they responded with variations on a theme of 'how would I know?' "[31]

The point is not that every edition of a publication or broadcast requires its own survey of how well the local media communicate the knowledge people need to make their communities work democratically. However, for journalism to truly connect with the public, periodic studies of communication effectiveness need to be conducted, published, and publicly discussed. At most media conglomerates, where profit margins can be twice as high as firms in other industries, investments in such research and in related continuing education of journalistic staff are meager at best, and fall far short of what their potential would justify.[32] In short, a continuing assessment of performance needs to be built into the doing of journalism itself.

THE LEADER AS "MELIORATOR"

If Anderson's democratic trustee emphasizes "tradition," his rational critic "principles," and his entrepreneur "projects," his final democratic reasoner seeks agreement. He or she exercises what Anderson calls "meliorative reason." It is brought into play "when the problem is to decide what is to be done when entrepreneurial visions, principled objections and the prudent counsels of trustees are in contention." An Andersonian "meliorator" labors to bring forth not necessarily a hidden

---

30. Yankelovich, *Coming to Public Judgment,* 64–65.

31. See W. Russell Neuman et al., *Common Knowledge: News and the Construction of Political Meaning,* 93, and Jolene Kiolbassa, "Covering Political Issues: The Closed Loop of Political Communication," master's thesis, Massachusetts Institute of Technology, 1989.

32. An illustration of such research can be found in John P. Robinson and Mark R. Levy, *The Main Source: Learning from Television News.*

or self-evident solution but an argument for a course of action around which the differing views of the parties can congeal. In Anderson's words:

> In the end, meliorative reason is a form of pragmatic analysis. It is, again, the search for means to accommodate principle to practice, for advancing the course of liberal democracy without impairing the integrity or efficiency of vital institutions. The search, always, is a suggestive fit between theory and practice.[33]

Thus, understandably, journalists in the "Taking Back Our Neighborhoods" project at the *Charlotte Observer* were uncomfortable with arranging and conducting discussions of possible crime prevention and abatement proposals about which they would be reporting. The problem was resolved by relying upon a community coordinator, paid through a nonprofit foundation, with a desk in the newsroom. Whether or not it is the best resolution, it illustrates the process of melioration. The *Akron Beacon Journal,* whose series "A Question of Race" won a Pulitzer, hired facilitators from outside the newsroom to conduct community discussions of race relations.

Lou Ureneck, editor of the *Maine Sunday Telegram* and the *Portland Press Herald,* wanted to help foster intensive discussion of public issues in Maine, but, at first, had difficulty seeing how he could act on that interest in concert with the Maine Council of Churches. A nearby foundation, the Study Circles Resource Center (SCRC), had developed a discussion technique and a study manual. Both the council and Ureneck were eager to find a proper way to proceed. Ecumenical and secular discussion leaders were recruited. Education reform emerged as the topic of dialogue. The newspaper retained control of the coverage and worked with educators and the council to define perspectives that would be debated. Some twelve hundred Maine citizens turned out for two series of the forums.[34]

Such are the uses of "melioration."

JOURNALISM AS A SOCIAL PRACTICE

Anderson concludes that it takes all four of these modes of reasoning for the practitioners of democratic enterprise to move forward.

---

33. Anderson, *Pragmatic Journalism,* 176.
34. Charity, *Doing Public Journalism,* 108–9.

His articulation of the process of pragmatic liberalism brings to mind the work of someone who is Anderson's philosophic polar opposite—Alasdair MacIntyre, an Aristotelian moral philosopher. To Anderson, MacIntyre's view of a social practice is implacably traditionalist, with occupations sealed hermetically in custom.[35] Yet, in so classifying Mac-Intyre, Anderson ignores the strengths of MacIntyre's discussion of the dynamics of social practices. One need not accept MacIntyre's conservatism or his gloomy philosophical outlook to appreciate his model of how social practices can renew and uplift themselves. At a minimum, MacIntyre's argument can rivet the attention of journalists on their own behavior, their own relationship with news media management, and the adequacy of corporate investment in the quality of journalism practiced in the nation's communities.

I believe that Anderson's four forms of deliberative reasoning can be put to work—to some extent, already are at work—within journalism defined as a social practice.

To MacIntyre, a social practice is a complex, interactive human activity that pursues certain ends or "goods." For medicine, cure is an end; for teaching, learning; for research, knowledge; for journalism, news. To achieve these goods, in whole or in part, practitioners strive to meet certain standards of excellence. These standards partially define the practice. To meet them, one must often exercise the virtues—courage, honesty, a sense of justice. The more one blends these central virtues with the competencies required by the practice, the more likely—circumstances permitting—are its ends or goods to be achieved.

"Goods" of a practice are of two kinds—those internal to a practice and those external goods bestowed by the institutions that carry the practice. These latter include wealth, prestige, money, and standing in society. Yet, it is the level of excellence achieved in reaching internal goods that propels the practice forward through time.

In journalism's case, these internal goods include successful exercise of the complex abilities by which journalists discover and effectively convey the data, narratives, and insights that the public wants and needs,

35. See especially Alasdair MacIntyre, "The Nature of the Virtues," in *After Virtue* (Notre Dame, Ind.: University of Notre Dame Press), 181–203. For a more extended application of MacIntyre's concept of social practice to journalism, see Lambeth, *Committed Journalism*, chapter 7, "Ethics and Standards of Excellence," 72–82. Anderson, *Pragmatic Liberalism*, 169.

especially those it needs. In a complex, pluralistic, and democratic society, these needs include the mundane information and stories of daily life (interest rates, retail prices, and human triumphs over adversity). More critically, they also include in-depth stories and interpretations that help citizens oversee, nourish, and criticize the institutions of a democratic society and thereby help keep them free and viable.

Pragmatic liberalism is itself a product of such a free society, and the forms of reasoning it requires—trusteeship, critical reason, entrepreneurship, and honest compromise—can increasingly become internal goods of the practice of journalism. Yet, journalism and other social practices (medicine, law enforcement, business, religion, etc.) can be corrupted when the institutions that carry them lose their balance and become preoccupied with pursuit of external goods—with profits, prestige, or power and position within society.[36] In this sense, the institutions of the press include not only the large, publicly traded media corporations and their management and stockholders but also the professional journalistic associations and the educational institutions that serve the press. In Leo Bogart's words, "Mass media can serve democracy only when those who manage them feel passionate responsibility to create and maintain it."[37]

In a fundamental sense, then, the issue raised by the research in this book is whether the free press can or should embrace the more ambitious goals of public journalism. Those who answer affirmatively argue that the practice would thereby put itself in a position to systematically elevate and extend the "goods" it can achieve. The press's own good as well as the public good would be served. An opposing view is that public journalism is merely a promotional and commercial ploy invented by management to maximize the external goods of the marketplace. Thus, Michael Hoyt, senior editor of the *Columbia Journalism Review,* said the "best argument against public journalism, perhaps, is that its rhetoric makes such excellent cover for pandering." He added that "a newsroom that would seek to market itself as the community's pal, meanwhile, is the kind that could reflexively refrain from doing anything that might offend that community."[38]

36. This theme is developed in different ways in Ben Bagdikian, *The Media Monopoly,* John H. McManus, *Market-Driven Journalism: Let the Citizen Beware?,* and Doug Underwood, *When MBAs Rule the Newsroom.*
37. Bogart, "Media and Democracy," note 4, 10.
38. Michael Hoyt, "Are You Now, or Will You Ever Be, a Civic Journalist?" 29.

With other critics, Max Frankel of the *New York Times* worries that public journalism's "emphasis on 'solutions' and 'connections' will inevitably distort the news agenda and end up compromising the paper's independence." Howard Schneider, managing editor of *Newsday*, said flatly that by such in-depth involvement a newspaper "loses its credibility."[39]

Surveys show, however, that the press has relatively little credibility to lose. Revisiting a problem with origins in the late 1970s, Daniel Yankelovich and his colleagues showed major shifts of public opinion in a recent five-year period. When asked, "In which of these do you find that you have great confidence?" a representative sample of Americans answered dramatically:[40]

	1988	1993
Doctors	71%	63%
Religious leaders	38	26
Federal government	18	12
State government	12	9
Local government	15	10
News reports on TV	55	25
News reports in newspapers	50	20
News in magazines	38	12

Even though journalism engendered more confidence than government, journalists could hardly be reassured. Thus, in 1994, the Times-Mirror Center for The People and The Press found that 71 percent of the citizens in a national poll agreed that "the news media gets [*sic*] in the way of society solving its problems."[41] This cuts to the marrow of journalism's self-image as an occupation protected by the First Amendment of the U.S. Constitution for the very purpose of informing and empowering the people.

Evidence points not merely to the pessimism of the public but also to increasing constraints on the ability of the press, in fact, to perform what

39. Frankel, "Fix-It Journalism." Schneider's comment appears in Walter Cronkite's documentary on the Discovery Channel, "Is That the Way It Is?" March 22, 1995.

40. Yankelovich Monitor, Yankelovich Partners, 1993, 20.

41. The Times-Mirror Center for The People and The Press, *The People, the Press and Politics: The New Political Landscape*, Washington, D.C., 1994, 121.

has been widely taken to be its constitutional role. Despite consistent increases in profits, media conglomerates continue to cut news editorial jobs. John Morton, an analyst with Lynch, Jones and Ryan, documents and laments continued shrinking of the space devoted to news and cutbacks in research. They suggest, he said, that the industry is eating its own "seed corn." Bogart, the scholar and veteran of the newspaper industry, sees a commercial culture that has eroded the nation's communication environment to a point that parallels the condition of the physical environment thirty years ago.[42] If corporate investment in the human capital and physical product of journalism is seriously disproportionate to what it should be, how would the public know unless journalists themselves document the case for the public and insist, with the public, that management and stockholders listen and respond? Many seasoned journalists argue that some media corporations are beginning to understand that, done in a way that seeks to raise the quality of public life, public journalism is expensive and could negatively affect the bottom line. If that proves to be the case, it could be the chief impediment to the healthy evolution of public journalism, despite the fact that news media corporations regularly register profit margins that are among the highest in American industry.

The chapters that follow seek to assess the record of public journalism as a fledgling democratic practice within journalism. They are written in the belief that, as theologian Robert McAfee Brown argued, social movements must encourage "a critique from within as well as a critique from outside." He concluded:

> No movement can ever be so pure that it does not need this. Indeed, the movement that looks suspiciously at inner critique will by that very fact have forfeited playing a creative role in the future.[43]

42. Ed Avis, "Where's the Money Going? Bigger Newspaper Profits Don't Mean More Jobs," 20–22. John Morton, "When Newspapers Eat Their Seed Corn," 52. Leo Bogart, "The American Media System and Its Commercial Culture," 33.

43. Robert McAfee Brown, "Toward a Just and Compassionate Society: A Christian View," *CrossCurrents* 45, no. 2 (summer 1995): 171.

2

IMAGINING PUBLIC JOURNALISM

An Editor and Scholar Reflect on the Birth of an Idea

DAVIS MERRITT AND JAY ROSEN

AN EDITOR'S PERSPECTIVE,
BY DAVIS MERRITT

Not very many years ago, the thought of sharing a podium with an academic such as Jay Rosen would have stirred in me a swarm of grumpy ghosts and weary journalistic shibboleths.

Doing . . . and teaching; town and gown; practice and theory; the array of slogans we use to express the supposedly conflicting aims and ideas of journalism and academia. At best, I would have anticipated an hour or so of talking at cross-purposes; at worst, a time of total incoherence.

But here we are.

Me, a reporter and editor with thirty-eight years in the trenches of daily journalism and, like most of my shrinking clan, a pragmatist; a mere escapee from a journalism school whose ultimate sustenance comes from those rare and electric moments when "stop the press!" and "baby, get me rewrite!" make sense.

And Jay, in my mind a lettered, thoughtful theorist; in the minds of some of my peers a near anarchistic tosser of thought-bombs into the

This chapter was originally presented under this title on April 13, 1995, as the fifth annual Roy. W. Howard Public Lecture in Journalism and Mass Communication Research, published at the Indiana University School of Journalism and edited there by David H. Weaver, Roy W. Howard Research Professor. It is reprinted here with permission.

peaceable if not somnambulant kingdom of American journalism; a denizen of the deepest pools of academic obfuscation.

What could one possibly have to say that would interest the other?

Jay and I have been saying things to each other, off and on, for almost four years, since we first encountered one another in September of 1991.

Despite our differences of age, background, geography, and inclination, détente was almost instantaneous. The meeting occurred when the Newhouse School at Syracuse and the Kettering Foundation mounted a seminar in New York and invited me to talk about a modest election project that the *Eagle* had done in 1990 and was planning to expand in 1992.

What we called "Your Vote Counts" had gained some attention nationally because it was an unabashed and activist effort to restore some role for citizens in the election process. Doing so meant, for the *Eagle* and its staff, stepping over "The Line," that quasi-mystical Rubicon separating "Good Journalism" done by "Real Journalists" in a mind-set of determined detachment from, well, something else. That something else, intimidating for traditionalists to contemplate, was a mind-set of caring whether our constitutional democracy could work well enough to fulfill its promise.

I had decided, after the tragic presidential campaign of 1988, that something had to change in the triangle of politics, public, and press that defines modern election campaigns. I so declared in an op-ed column the week after election day.

It was clear to me that politics wasn't going to change on its own. The armies of handlers, consultants, and theorists who for decades had been relentlessly distorting campaigns into empty contests liked what they had wrought. It suited their narrow purposes. Half of them won every election day, and half lost, and fifty-fifty odds at success in any venture aren't too discouraging. Besides, win or lose, the handlers were paid. And, of course, they learned. Everyone replicated next time what had won last time, making the process a death-spiral for democracy.

It was equally clear to me that the public couldn't change on its own, being merely a victim of the incestuous partnership of politics and the political press.

Which left only us, the press, to change, to try to halt the devastating spiral.

That first Voter Project, in Kansas's 1990 gubernatorial election, produced some tantalizing signs of hope. Voter turnout in areas we reached was measurably higher than in other areas of the state. Voters within the *Eagle*'s reach felt that they understood the issues at a measurably higher level than did voters outside our area. But, most satisfyingly to me, an acquaintance whose intellect I respect commented during our Voter Project, "You're trying to save democracy, aren't you?" I modestly agreed.

Her perception was the most satisfying result for me because it was a strong signal that people will correctly recognize and appreciate a newspaper's efforts to move beyond telling the news.

That 1991 gathering at Lubin House in New York consisted of some of journalism's reigning lions, a couple of young tigers, an assortment of old war horses like me, and, as it developed, at least one representative of a species given to digging in its heels.

About thirty minutes into the session, a voice, its origin hidden from my line of sight down the long table, began a liturgy. It spoke of newspapers' loss of readers, the decline in voting, the national loss of a sense of place, declining civic membership, the rising disgust with politics, the decay of public discourse.

The so-far-disembodied voice suggested that these are related problems, that if public life does not remain viable newspapers cannot remain valuable, and of finding a way to conceive of the newspaper as a support system for citizens.

Clearly the mind behind those words—Jay Rosen's—and my thoughts were coming from the same place and headed, albeit separately, toward something unknown though, perhaps, discoverable.

It became clear during that morning, as others spoke, that most of the people around the table, despite their differing backgrounds, shared pieces of the same concerns and that most of them were driven to forge some change in those threatening circumstances.

I deal to this extent with this bit of history about public journalism for several reasons:

1) It demonstrates that the idea of public journalism did not arise in a marketing context; that it is not, as some critics contend, a new color weather map or other superficial ploy.

2) It illustrates the interdisciplinary origins of public journalism, marking a point at which working professionals, concerned academics, and people from public-interest foundations realized they held common concerns and aspired to a common cause.

3) It set me, personally, on a search for new meaning after (at that point) thirty-four years of telling the news in a culture that, in a significant way, had lost its bearings.

In 1988, thirteen of those thirty-four years had been spent telling the news in Wichita. Like many "good" newspapers, we had been the watchdog; we had afflicted the comfortable and comforted the afflicted; we had printed the news and raised hell; we had let the chips fall where they may. We had followed all the shibboleths and rousing slogans of our tradition. In the process, we had filled the walls of a large conference room with the plaudits of our peers: awards in every national and regional and state category by which our profession measures itself.

From a strictly internal standpoint, in the narrow intellectual and spiritual confines of the newsroom, there was no apparent reason why that could not and should not continue.

But: Public life, in Wichita and elsewhere in the country, was not getting noticeably better, for all our journalistic effort.

But: The *Eagle*, like other newspapers, was experiencing soft circulation and declines in readership, and our credibility was increasingly in question.

But: The idea of another thirteen years of that hard—and necessary—work seemed likely only to fill more walls in that conference room at the *Eagle*. If simply telling the news wasn't working either for us OR society, then we clearly needed a more useful purpose.

It was apparent that the decline in public life and the decline in the efficacy of journalism were tracking closely.

Was that mere coincidence?

If it was more than coincidence, what, if anything, could be done about it?

Was it journalism's duty to do more than tell the news?

What in our behavior, our very culture, would have to change in order to define a more useful role?

Where could we find the ideas to build a viable intellectual foundation to bring both new hope and new purpose to journalism?

The answers assuredly were not available in the traditional culture of the profession. Doing daily journalism is a demanding task. Journalists, pinched for time, increasingly drowning in more and more information, must act out of a set of ingrained reflexes. As Yogi Berra querulously asked of Casey Stengel when Stengel admonished him to "Use your head up there at the plate"—"How can you think and hit at the same time?"

Further, those well-developed reflexes were tied to an operating axiom: detachment. We persuaded ourselves that our credibility springs from our detachment; that a studied lack of concern for outcomes is mandatory for us to maintain our place.

As with many parts of our prevailing philosophy, we manufactured that one to meet our own perceived and narrow needs. It is, in fact, a debilitating concept for reasons I will deal with shortly.

But first, let's consider the origins of our culture. Before there were deadlines, or city editors, or county commissioners to catch in some moldy taxpayer rip-off, there was the First Amendment.

The chronology is crucial. It helps account for journalism's fundamental toughness; a congenital, sleeves-rolled-up aggressiveness; a snarly conviction that nice guys don't get newspapers out.

The culture of toughness has more beneath it than the inevitability that many stories, by their nature, are going to make one person or another unhappy. And there's more beneath it than the pervasive maleness of the profession that persists even into the equal-opportunity nineties. While such realities have helped form the cultural trait of toughness, they alone cannot explain it.

History can. The reality is that the free press was born in a defensive crouch. Its birth certificate was a declaration—significantly, an affirmative negative—that "Congress shall make no law. . . ."

The First Amendment was written to ensure that individual Americans' rights were specific and absolute in the face of the establishment of a central government. So long as citizens could gather, talk, write, petition, and be free of an established religion, they could be free to determine how that central government functioned and their lives were led.

It could not have been contemplated, but probably was inevitable, that a large and powerful subculture would grow up around those four words, "and of the press." So potent a prohibition as "Congress shall make no law," consistently buttressed by court decisions, could hardly have resulted in anything else; the vacuum was too great, the opportunity too unfettered.

As the central government grew more powerful, fought wars, passed laws, instituted taxes, controlled the economy, the proscription against its incursion on individual freedoms became more meaningful.

The growing stakes involved in big government made the arguments about its direction louder and more contentious, the temptations on officialdom's part to mute the criticism grew more appealing, and the journalistic defenses became more fierce.

The First Amendment became a glowing crucifix thrust arms-length against any would-be devil's approach. Aggressive assertion of the right was the prime directive, the source of all else. "Don't tread on me?" Don't even think about it.

Of course, the amendment does not guarantee that "the press" be fair, or accurate, or honest, or profitable, or, of course, paid attention to. Only that it be free to be none or all of those things, just as can any citizen who picks up pen and paper.

While the amendment was written to empower people rather than any institution, it has become, for the organized "press," a license to self-define unique among American institutions. Neither clergy nor bar nor medicine nor academe can claim, and have validated by the courts, more latitude in action and deed. That enormous latitude is a mixed blessing.

Alexis de Tocqueville recognized and sardonically reflected upon the uniquely free status of America's press early in his writings about his 1832 journey: "I confess that I do not entertain that firm and complete attachment to the liberty of the press which is wont to be excited by things that are supremely good in their very nature. I approve of it from a consideration more of the evils it prevents than of the advantages it ensures." But he recognized also the absolute necessity of that liberty. "In this question . . . there is no medium between servitude and license; in order to enjoy the inestimable benefits that the liberty of the press ensures, it is necessary to submit to the inevitable evils that it creates."

Such singular latitude can be uncomfortable in a nation of laws. When every other institution's or profession's activities are to a lesser or greater extent limited, journalism faces constant challenge and questioning about its standing to be thus unfettered.

Small wonder, then, that the defensive crouch not only remains a part of the culture but virtually defines it.

Given that historic and unique difference from all other institutions, it is not surprising—and perhaps unavoidable—that a guiding axiom of modern journalism is determined detachment.

But that trait has unfortunate consequences today, for both public life and journalism.

Among them:

• Allowing determined detachment to set us apart from the consequences of choices—ours or the public's—breeds a dangerous arrogance, a self-granted immunity that smacks of a priesthood.

• Detachment encourages us to ignore or demean outside criticism, which in turn means that we lose the potential benefits of outside help and advice. This trait is particularly unappealing to people at large and is in fact built on inconsistent logic.

On the one hand, we reject much outside criticism on the grounds that our critics, being outsiders, don't understand or at best underappreciate how we must operate. You're not involved in journalism, we say, so your criticism is invalid. You just don't get it.

But, on the other hand, we insist that it is precisely our detachment, our noninvolvement, that validates our own criticism of other institutions, such as government. We look with suspicion or concern upon the few journalists who are allowed to move into the field after careers in government or business. They are somehow tainted by their past insider status and thus unlikely to be able to perform honestly the arcane rituals of true journalism.

We further ensure that no serious challenges can be mounted to our guiding axioms by talking only to ourselves when faced with a dilemma. When journalism faces some important issue, journalists invariably call a meeting of other journalists. We may invite some outsiders to offer their suggestions, but they are not involved in the actual deliberation, the working out of the dilemma. That must be reserved for the priesthood, lest some wildly unjournalistic notions become part of the discussion. Only members of the tribe can think usefully about the tribe's problems.

As I sat and thought about these things last year, it became clear, to me at least, that for anything important to change about my profession—and about public life—that core idea of determined detachment needed rethinking. We needed a viable philosophical foundation that could give both new hope and new purpose while protecting the truly essential third-party role of journalism.

And that base could not be found in the ingrown culture of my newsroom, or the panel discussions at the American Society of Newspaper Editors, or the plenary and concurrent sessions of the Associated Press Managing Editors.

But what about de Tocqueville? And Toffler? Garreau and Bellah? Putnam and Dionne and Yankelovich and Neumann and Iyengar?

Did these people have anything to say to journalists? Did the concerns they dealt with, the insights they developed, the research they carried out, present some new ways for journalists to think about the essential but ignored connection between journalism and public life?

My early association with Jay Rosen and David Mathews of the Kettering Foundation and others concerned about the state of public life suggested that they did. In the fall of 1993, almost on impulse, I sought a year's leave of absence so I could, removed from the pressures of the daily task, think and read and talk and perhaps write about all of this.

It's revealing to note that my journalism colleagues were astonished. A sabbatical practice that is well understood and routinely used in academics was virtually unheard of in corporate journalism, which illustrates yet another gap between my profession and academia. Other than the nine months of the Nieman program at Harvard University, six weeks or so of corporate-sponsored and narrowly framed attendance at a university was the only sabbatical territory that had been explored.

That my request to be left totally free for a full year was promptly approved by Knight-Ridder demonstrated the growing concern within that company about the future of newspapers and their communities.

So I set out in search of nonjournalistic bricks that might be used to build a viable philosophical foundation that could support a different concept of the role of journalism in our democracy.

And I found it in some nonjournalistic places. Here was Daniel Yankelovich with insights about how people actually come to public judgment on issues. There was Robert Putnam making the case for civic capital—and newspapers—as essential to a successful society. Over here was Russell Neuman and colleagues exploring the dangerous waters of issue-framing as done in modern media. And, of course, back there was Alexis de Tocqueville explaining the vigor of early American democracy as a function of people's deep involvement in civic associational affairs.

The bricks they brought to the construction site were useful because they shared some characteristics. The basic material was the fine sand of good research. But grains of statistical and observational sand don't make a brick. Their bricks were not theoretical, but real. They were formed in the heat of real life, shaped to be handled by real people. In short, they were made to be applied to a purpose beyond themselves. They were, in a word, useful.

Here's what I made of the work of those people and many others:

1) The viability of public life and the value of journalism are inextricably bound together.

2) Public life cannot regain its vitality on a diet of information alone, for there's far too much of it for even the most well-intentioned citizen to digest. If journalists view their job as merely providing information—simply telling the news in a detached way—they will not be particularly helpful to public life or to their profession.

3) The objective of our journalism must be to reengage citizens in public life. To make that shift, we must take two steps: add to the definition of our job the *additional* objective of helping public life go well, and then develop the journalistic tools and reflexes necessary to reach that objective.

That means reexamining some of our existing reflexes and, where appropriate and protective of our core values, altering those reflexes. For instance, we need to reevaluate the usefulness of conflict as the highest coin in the journalistic realm. We need to understand balance not as contrasting polar extremes expressed by absolutists and experts but as a continuum with myriad points between the extremes. We need to see people not as readers, nonreaders, endangered readers; not as customers to be wooed or an audience to be entertained but as a public, citizens capable of action.

Of course, doing those things requires that we move away from detachment as a guiding axiom; that we embrace and announce certain values that underlie our journalism. This can only be done if journalists think of the people reached by their efforts not as readers or nonreaders, not as spectators, not as an audience to be entertained, but as a public, as citizens capable of action. That unavoidable juncture is where many traditionalists raise alarms. They insist that our credibility stems from our detachment. I contend quite the opposite.

Picture in your mind someone—not a journalist—who has credibility with you. That person has certain characteristics: he or she is probably honest, intelligent, well-intentioned, trustworthy—you can make your own list. But somewhere on that list will be the recognition that you and he or she share some basic values about life, some common ground about common good. Without that foundation, there can be no credibility.

Now consider journalism. We say that we are honest, intelligent, trustworthy, well-intentioned; that we have all of those traits. But we insist that we don't share values, with anyone; that we are value-neutral.

And, not surprisingly, we have little credibility.

Those are the elements of my public journalism philosophy. But here's a reality that comes packaged with the philosophy: melding those ideas and reflexes into the traditional culture of newsrooms cannot be accomplished by fiat or memo or inoculation. Training additional reflexes will take thought and development, and thus can only be accomplished through determined and focused attention over time.

I have collided with that reality in the three months since I returned to the *Eagle* newsroom after that marvelous year on leave. It did not take very long to confirm what I suspected: thinking and writing about this idea is much easier than doing it.

This is, indeed, generational cultural change, and we must not surrender to unreasonable expectations. I continually get inquiries and challenges to display "results, accomplishments, differences" that public journalism has made. There are very few because public journalism is cultural change. Most of what can be accomplished lies ahead. We know, at this point, precious little about how to start turning a hopeful philosophy into the stuff of news stories and broadcasts.

I have a thoughtful friend, Balbir Mathur, who has been involved in various worldwide efforts to effect real change. At lunch recently, he asked how things were going with public journalism.

"OK," I said. "Not bad."

"You've been at this a few years, are you seeing any results?" he asked.

"Oh, sure, we're seeing some things here and there . . ."

"That's too bad," he said.

"What do you mean?"

"If this is true change, if it is really fundamental and you're seeing results after only a few years," he said, "you're not doing enough, you're not asking all the right questions."

He's right, of course. But at this point in the development of public journalism, these things are clear:

• Journalism must develop a long-term response to the pathologies of public life and journalism.

• We must start now, and persevere until we get there.
• Journalists need not, in fact cannot, do it in isolation.

Changing the culture of journalism will require the best and most earnest efforts of journalists, academics, philosophers, conscientious citizens—everyone who cares about the future of our society.

IMAGINING PUBLIC JOURNALISM, BY JAY ROSEN

Let me begin by noting that Buzz Merritt and I have been doing public journalism by appearing on many platforms together as an editor and a scholar equally concerned about the press and public life. Public journalism is public. It's an open dialogue about where journalism should be going, and it has just as much to do with thinking, talking, and writing—in public—as it does with doing journalism in a more "public" way.

In fact, when people criticize public journalism—as they often do—they are actually contributing to it because part of the "it" is the discussion and debate the idea has provoked. Similarly, when journalists do journalism about public journalism—trend pieces, for example—they are in a sense doing what they think they're observing: they're contributing to the natural history of the idea.

We're here to reflect on the birth of a notion, but perhaps I should say what the notion is before explaining how it came about. What exactly is public journalism? Well, it's at least three things: First, it's an argument about the proper task of the press. Second, it's a set of practices—experiments, really—that are slowly spreading through American journalism. Third, it's a movement of people and institutions. I suppose its fourth dimension is as a debate or controversy, but since every article in the trade press about public journalism is actually about the controversy—not the idea—I will not dwell on that here.

What the argument says is this: Journalism cannot remain valuable unless public life remains viable. Public life is in trouble in the United States. Therefore, journalism is in trouble. Fortunately, there is something the press can do—or rather, many things. It can help citizens participate and take them seriously when they do. It can nourish or even create the sort of public talk that might get us somewhere, what some of us would call a deliberative dialogue. The press can change its lens on the public world so that citizens aren't reduced to spectators in a drama dominated by professionals and technicians. Most important, perhaps, journalists can learn to see hope as an essential resource which they cannot deplete indefinitely without tremendous costs to us and them.

Even if they do these things, they won't save democracy or solve all their community's problems. But they will put themselves on the side of those seeking answers to a genuine difficulty: how to make democracy work for citizens, and how to engage citizens in the real work of democracy.

Public journalism is also a set of practices, most of them experiments by local newspapers trying to connect with citizens in a more useful way. For example, following an approach pioneered by Buzz in 1990, the *Charlotte Observer* in 1992 abandoned the approach to election coverage known as the horse race angle. Instead, it sought to ground its coverage in what it called a "citizen's agenda," meaning a list of discussion priorities identified by area residents through the paper's own research. When candidates gave an important speech during the campaign, the contents were "mapped" against the citizen's agenda, so that it was easy to tell what was said about those concerns that ranked highest with citizens.

This may seem like a modest reform, but it involved a fundamental shift in the mission of campaign journalism. The master narrative changed from something like, "Candidates maneuver and manipulate in search of votes" to something like, "Citizens of Charlotte demand serious discussion." The Charlotte approach has become widely known and widely copied because it addresses long-standing frustrations with a campaign dialogue dominated by political professionals and the cynicism they engender.

A second kind of public journalism initiative is underway at the *Norfolk Virginian-Pilot*. There, the editors have created something called the public life team, which is a group of reporters assigned to cover politics and government in a "more public" way. Among the techniques they employ is the use of small deliberative forums, what they call "community conversations," not to ask people what they want to read, or to survey their opinions, but to discover how nonprofessionals name and frame issues. This then becomes the starting point for the paper's political reporting, replacing the usual sources—the machinations of insiders or the maneuvering of public officials.

Earlier this month, I assisted the editors of the *Virginian-Pilot* in a weekend retreat intended to jump-start the process of changing routines. Fifty participants devoted three days to thinking through the shift in consciousness and technique that public journalism demands. The editors and I agreed on a price of admission to this retreat: a rather lengthy reading list of works in democratic theory and press scholarship—including essays by political scientist Robert Putnam of Harvard, along with excerpts from Daniel Yankelovich's important work, *Coming to Public Judgment,* and de Tocqueville's *Democracy in America.* Officials of Landmark Communications, the company that owns the newspaper, invited themselves to the retreat. They too had to do the reading.

When fifty working journalists take time out to spend the weekend struggling with the implications of democratic theory and press criticism for their own work, when they do so under the expectation that they will reform their routines accordingly, when the executives within their company are joining them in this adventure, I hope you can see how a new kind of space has been opened up within journalism. By the way, the Norfolk retreat was on the record because, as I said, public journalism is public. There was a community representative there who later wrote about what she saw—in the newspaper.

Other public journalism practices have involved creating public forums that show citizens engaged in deliberative dialogue, sponsored by a media partnership in Madison, Wisconsin, in order to model democratic habits of mind and talk. There have been several interventions in a lethargic public climate in places like Boulder, Colorado, and Olympia, Washington. These bring together civic leaders, experts, and groups of citizens to chart a long-term vision for a community, which is then published and debated in the newspaper. There have been various efforts to focus political reporting on the search for solutions to public problems and a variety of measures to heighten the visibility of citizens in the news by, for example, telling the story of individuals who got involved and made a difference. There have been campaigns to get people to vote, including some that allowed people to register in the lobby of the newspaper. There have been other efforts to engage citizens as participants—for example, a "Neighborhood Repair Kit" published by the *Star Tribune* in Minneapolis, which sought to give residents the information and incentive they needed to improve their neighborhoods.

The third form public journalism takes is as a movement. In the classic American tradition of public-spirited reform, this movement is trying to recall journalism to its deepest mission of public service.

The movement is primarily drawn from professionals within the press, along with a smaller number from the academic world, and several institutional players. I would estimate its core membership at perhaps two hundred or so, with several hundred others expressing sympathy with the general aims.

Most (but not all) are daily newspaper journalists, typically from small- and medium-sized cities like Charlotte, North Carolina, or Wilmington, Delaware, although we do have a tiny foothold in larger precincts, like the *Boston Globe*. The institutional support comes from projects like mine, funded by the Knight Foundation, from the Pew Center for Civic Journalism, supported by the Pew Charitable Trusts, from the Poynter Institute for Media Studies, and especially from the Kettering Foundation, a think tank in Dayton, Ohio, which was the incubator of the idea.

At this stage, public journalism is very much a minority impulse, rooted primarily in the regional press. But it is on the radar screen of the entire press, and has been debated everywhere. The practices that correspond to the argument are not very far advanced; they are experiments at best, and it will be five to ten years before we know what their real potential is. We are just at the beginning of a long process of cultural change within journalism, and there is every chance that the movement will be marginalized, defeated by the forces of reaction, or by its own failure to grow and mature.

So that's what public journalism is. How it was born is a slightly longer tale, and for me a personal one. My portion of it began when I encountered a debate that took place during the 1920s, which still fascinates scholars of the press. At issue then was how to describe this "thing" we call the public, and how much respect to give to that mysterious force called public opinion.

The last great exchange on these subjects involved two famous names, Walter Lippmann and John Dewey. Lippmann was on his way to becoming the most renowned journalist of his time. Dewey was already the nation's senior philosopher. Even more interesting is that Dewey, the philosopher, had a strong interest in journalism and had experimented briefly with his own newspaper, called "Thought News," while Lippmann, the journalist, wrote several works of political philosophy that are still read today. These two men were extremely qualified, then, to debate the big subjects that concern us today: the press, the public, and the nature of American democracy.

In 1922, Lippmann wrote his classic work, called *Public Opinion*. His main point was that an informed and engaged public—the kind we expect to have—is more or less an illusion. The world is huge, it's complicated, and it's largely inaccessible. People lack the time or motivation to study it in depth. So they rely on hazy impressions and half-conscious stereotypes in forming their views. The press was supposed to correct for these defects, but it had to compete for attention against all the other arts of persuasion. Besides, the press was a commercial venture, dedicated as much to profit as it was to public service.

Lippmann declared the whole thing unworkable. It was foolish to expect average citizens to have a reliable opinion on every public issue. Citizens did have a place in modern democracy, but it was a limited one. The most we could expect is an occasional yes/no or up/down verdict—as in "throw the bums out." But even these simple decisions could be manipulated, and often were. Against the soaring rhetoric of American democracy, Lippmann placed the limitations of the average citizen, the stubborn realities of human nature, the daunting complexity of modern life. He put his faith elsewhere, in well-informed experts, those who might provide leaders with better and better facts on which to base their decisions.

John Dewey drew a very different conclusion because he started in a different place. The reason we have governments at all is that we live in an interdependent world, he said. A public is simply a name for people who realize they share common problems. Democracy demands that these problems be discussed and understood. And to give up on this hope is to give up on democracy itself. Dewey agreed that citizens had a difficult time in a complex world where they were blitzed with misleading messages. The public, he agreed, was in deep trouble. He described it as "inchoate," unformed. It was potentially there, potentially real. But it would emerge only if politics, culture, education, and journalism did their jobs well. Democracy for Dewey was not a system of government, but an entire way of life. And it was up to us to create a way of life that gave the public a fighting chance.

In 1925, Lippmann went even further in his skepticism. He wrote another book, the *Phantom Public*, in which he argued that on most issues there is no public at all. There is only manipulated opinion and the maneuvering of insiders. Dewey did not dispute this point. But he refused to accept it as the way things must be. At stake, he believed, was a fundamental principle of democracy, which is that people know best what is best for them. Experts, no matter how well-informed they are, can't substitute for the public's best judgment. How can experts know what the rest of us want? And how can we ourselves know unless we have a chance to think, talk, and deliberate? Besides, said Dewey, democracy is not just self-government; it also involves self-development. The notion of a participating, deliberating, learning public expressed a moral demand: that everyone have a chance to develop into a better citizen. People have better things to do, Lippmann said; citizenship is a tiny portion of their lives.

Back and forth this argument went. When I discovered it as a graduate student it seemed highly relevant to our problems today—so relevant that I did my dissertation on it. The odd thing was that people in the press didn't seem troubled at all by the questions that had vexed Dewey and Lippmann. What could we reasonably expect of citizens? Yes/no decisions at election time or participation in a fuller and richer public life? Was the public an illusion, an impossibility, or was it merely inchoate, unformed? If we want democracy to improve, should we focus on government and its decisions, as Lippmann did, or should we emphasize the civic climate in which people become a public, as Dewey did? These, it seemed, were fundamental questions. They determined your approach to everything, including your approach to journalism. But journalists weren't having these debates over the nature of the public, nor were they learning about the problem in journalism schools.

Of course, there were reasons for this silence: One reason is the rise of opinion polling, which began in the 1930s. The polls give us the illusion that there's a fully formed public on virtually every question. Commission a poll and "public opinion" springs magically to life. When polling became standard practice in journalism, the questions raised by Lippmann and Dewey seemed to fade away. At the same time, the commercial thrust of the news media suppressed debate about the nature of "the public." Clearly there were readers and viewers on the other end of the news: didn't they constitute the public? Why worry about it, as long as you're selling papers?

Finally, there was the doctrine of objectivity, which became the official philosophy of the press just about the time Lippmann and Dewey were writing. Objectivity is about informing the public; it tells us to worry about things like accuracy, balance, and fairness. But Lippmann's concern wasn't how to "inform" the public. It was whether a public could be *formed* at all in a busy society with a commercial culture. That question faded from view when objectivity became the professional stance of the journalist. So opinion polling, the commercial success of the news media, and the professionalization of journalism all conspired to bury the issue of how we imagine, how we create this "thing" we call the public.

The more I thought about it, the more dangerous this silence in journalism seemed. For it really does matter whose view you adopt: Lippmann's or Dewey's. My own view was this: Lippmann's analysis was compelling, but also a dead end. Once you persuaded yourself of the public's limitations, you had only one choice: hand over most decisions to the professionals, as we did, for example, in Vietnam with very dubious results. Or take the current issue of health care reform. Unless you have faith in the experts, in the professionalization of politics, you have to go back to the drawing board and try to imagine how people might form themselves into a public capable of grappling with the issue—just as Dewey suggested.

By 1988, I was convinced that Dewey was much closer to being right. And James Carey is the one who helped convince me. More than any other scholar, it was Carey who brought this debate from the 1920s forward into our own time. But journalists didn't read Carey, or any other communication scholar, so I began to wonder: what if they did? What if they began wrestling with the problem of how to understand the public, and what if they saw the implications for their own work?

Around the same time, there were some big developments in journalism that made the ghosts of Dewey and Lippmann rise. For example: Circulation declines and competition from new media forced journalists to examine their faltering connection to the audience. If readers and viewers are disappearing, perhaps there's something wrong in the way the audience is being imagined. Meanwhile, the critique of horse race coverage and the insider mentality in Washington journalism brought the excessive dependence on polling to light. Maybe the polls were part of the problem. Finally, after Watergate, especially, objectivity made less and less sense. For the news media had grown more and more adversarial, and more and more interpretive in response to the tactics of officials and handlers.

By 1988, disgust with the way things were going reached a momentary peak with a single image from the campaign trail. Remember that footage of Michael Dukakis, his tiny head bobbing in the turret of a tank as he tried to parade before us his concern for national defense? For many of us that image stands out as a kind of symbolic low point, a ploy so transparent that when we saw it, we saw through more than the sad and ineffective candidate who staged it. We saw through the entire system that permitted Dukakis to think he was saying something useful by climbing aboard that tank.

According to many people in the press—and Buzz Merritt was one—journalists were inescapably a part of that system. By continually showing up for this kind of "media" event, they helped consecrate it as a legitimate form of political communication; by interpreting a photo opportunity as an opportunity to do their journalism, they became a party to the emptying out of political discourse; by jeering at such events even as they tried to cover them, they joined in a culture of cynicism that remains with us today. All of this was evident to those in the press who were disturbed by the 1988 campaign.

In our recent history, there have been other moments of shared disgust as journalists contemplated their perplexing relationship to public officials. Think, for example, of the "Five O'clock Follies" during Vietnam, the briefings where Pentagon officials would leave reporters incredulous. What distinguished the Dukakis tank ride was that the shared disgust was also self-disgust. Many people in the press felt implicated in what campaigning had become. For a moment, at least, they dropped the illusion of the observer's innocence, the fantasy of a knower without responsibility for the known.

Public journalism really began with this moment, with this feeling of being implicated in the disintegration of politics. One of its inspirations was David Broder of the *Washington Post,* probably the most respected political reporter in America. In January of 1990, Broder used his weekly column to address his colleagues in the national press. Here's what he wrote: "We cannot allow the [November] elections to be another exercise in public disillusionment and political cynicism."

This was a startling thought, for Broder saw journalists as responsible, not only for the reports they produce, but for the realities they report. He went on: "It is time for those of us in the world's freest press to become activists, not on behalf of a particular party or politician, but on behalf of the process of self-government," Broder wrote. Note the language here. Journalists "cannot allow" the 1990 elections to become another fount of cynicism. They must become "activists" and take the campaign momentum away from the hired guns who profit from the disillusionment they help create. These are the words of someone who feels himself implicated.

Buzz Merritt was feeling the same way. In 1990 he decided that the *Wichita Eagle* would not be a party to another exercise in political cynicism. In his newspaper, the governor's campaign would be a discussion of issues of concern to Kansans. What the candidates said about those issues would be highlighted; whatever else they were saying would be downplayed or ignored. People would be urged to vote, and the *Eagle* would make it as easy as possible for them to register.

When I met Buzz in 1991 a number of things started to come together. Broder had made his provocative statements. Meanwhile, Jim Batten, the CEO of Knight-Ridder, had been urging journalists to worry about the unraveling of community life, the withdrawal of citizens from public affairs. Dewey would have enjoyed Batten's speeches and Broder's columns, for they seemed to suggest a profound connection between journalism and the health of our civic climate. This was exactly the point he was making in the 1920s.

Buzz Merritt, as far as I know, had not read my dissertation. But here was a journalist who took the issues involved seriously. He understood that his challenge as a journalist was to help *form* as well as inform the public. His voter project in 1990 tried to motivate people to behave like citizens. So he was willing to experiment with his newspaper in devising a different approach. Even more important, he was willing to stand up in front of his colleagues and tell them that they had gotten off track. This was a difficult message to ignore for all the reasons I mentioned earlier: the loss of readers, the dissatisfaction with the horse race, the growing inadequacy of objectivity as philosophy.

So the timing was right and Buzz and I joined forces. I got a grant to start the Project on Public Life and the Press. He got a year off from Knight-Ridder. We set out to create public journalism in those three dimensions: as an argument, a practice, and a movement. Public journalism also became our way of working together, an attempt at overcoming the divide between doing and thinking. There is one sense in which I am willing to pronounce our effort a success, all others being premature. I've succeeded in devising a new method for studying the press, one that works much better for me.

I used to be a media critic, and here's how I worked: I would observe what the press does, filter it through my theoretical framework—essentially, my dissertation—and then write about the results. You can discover a lot that way, but there's a problem. Journalists haven't read your dissertation; they don't share your framework. So whatever you discover is of little interest to them. They can't be blamed for this; after all, they have deadlines to meet.

In my partnerships with Buzz and other journalists around the country I employ another method: I operate almost completely through the medium of conversation. My theoretical framework becomes whatever is needed in order to keep the conversation progressing. Public journalism is something journalists themselves must carry forward. Therefore, what I think it should be doesn't matter as much as the version of it that I can share with reporters, editors, and news executives around the country. What *we* think it should be—that's what counts.

And that's why Buzz and I wrote a joint manifesto together. Actually, it's two manifestos—one by me, one by him. We tried to compose a single essay but the strain of our different starting places was too great. So we settled for a joint introduction. I'm rather proud of that piece. It's comparable to a literature professor and a novelist creating a joint statement about where contemporary fiction needs to go. Of course, the statement is significant only to the degree that it resonates with others. If public journalism doesn't resonate, then it doesn't really exist.

What I'm constantly trying to discover, then, is the language that permits me to join with journalists in searching for the next stage in this movement's development. The only way to discover this shared vocabulary is to try it out with people like Buzz and his colleagues, and this is the sort of "research" I now conduct. The kind of discoveries you make are political as much as intellectual. They have to do with the language or, if you will, the platform on which I can stand with a lot of others in journalism who are struggling to revise their assumptions and routines.

A big portion of this platform is designated by the term "public life." In the argument we've been developing, public life is what journalists are allowed to be in favor of; it is something they can stand on and stand for. By "public life" we mean everything from bowling leagues that draw people out of the home to political debates that draw leaders together with citizens. Public life has to go well if people are to form themselves into a public. Or, as I frequently put it, journalism cannot remain valuable unless public life remains viable. In this sense, public journalism is a translation into the 1990s of Dewey's concern during the 1920s. It's a way to put journalists on the right side of that debate, where Dewey was straining to see how the public might emerge.

It is also my way of overcoming the breach between academic studies of the press and the practice of journalism. There's an analog to public journalism in what we might call public scholarship. That's what I think I'm doing, but actually I'm not sure. In public journalism we frequently have to realize that we don't know what we're doing. We're making it up as we go along. That's why we try to take our critics seriously, and we have plenty of those.

I want to close by addressing the young journalists who may be out there. Most of you have probably heard about the "New Journalism" that arose during the 1960s. One of the finest examples is Michael Herr's intense and exciting book, called *Dispatches*. Herr went to Vietnam to write about it, but Vietnam confounded his plans. Early in the book he writes as follows: "I went [to Vietnam] behind the crude but serious belief that you had to be able to look at anything, serious because I acted on it and went, crude because I didn't know, it took the war to teach it, that you were as responsible for everything you saw as you were for everything you did."

For some time this passage has disturbed and fascinated me. What gets me is the line, "You were as responsible for everything you saw as you were for everything you did." What can it possibly mean? Herr, after all, was a reporter in Vietnam, not a combatant. What he saw was the product of other men's actions, not his own. For telling us what he saw, for reporting the facts, he was clearly responsible. But that is a conventional thought, and not the one Herr wants to relay. Listen again to what he says: "you were as responsible for everything you saw as you were for everything you did." In what sense is a reporter "responsible" for the scene that unfolds in front of him?

Well, there is this sense, a universal law of observation that not everyone chooses to observe: What you see depends on where you go. The decision to place yourself at a certain spot makes you responsible, in a way, for what you see from that spot; and if this decision is not made freely, then there is no such thing as a free press—and no such thing as academic freedom, either. So my universal law of observation, which is also Michael Herr's law, states that you position yourself first, and then you begin to observe. Your responsibility begins with the positioning part.

I close with these thoughts because they offer a roundabout way of explaining how Buzz and I find ourselves in this position, equally invested in an idea that came from two directions at once. I think we both wanted to observe a scene that would give us some reason to hope. Public journalism has been the result. You must decide what you think of it, but when you do decide, ask yourself a simple question: where do I want to place myself, and from there can I find some reason to hope?

3

ASSESSING DAVIS MERRITT'S "PUBLIC JOURNALISM" THROUGH HIS LANGUAGE

CAROL REESE DYKERS

When Davis Merritt, editor of the *Wichita Eagle* in Kansas, became the central journalistic figure of a movement—arguing that journalists should facilitate rather than aggravate American public life—he had given his cause neither a name nor a definition. Only in December 1993, on his newspaper's op-ed page, did he first call his upstart idea "public journalism."

The movement generated a great deal of bad press, leading to complaints from Merritt that his ideas were unfairly characterized by journalists with axes to grind and preconceptions about his goals.[1] This chapter's contribution is to assess Merritt's developing ideas about public journalism by tracing their evolution in his own words, found in his newspaper columns published from 1984 through 1996, and then by critically evaluating those columns. This method is based on the idea that journalism *is* using language, particularly in what Habermas has called the "public sphere."[2] So, to assess "public journalism," an analyst must examine public journalists' published language. The effort benefited from Merritt's cooperation and full access to his newspaper's library and newsroom.

1. Merritt told journalism educators at a seminar on public journalism at the Poynter Institute in St. Petersburg, Florida, in February 1995 that since journalists had been interviewing him about his ideas and misunderstanding him, he had begun to understand how angry citizens and politicians felt about having journalism "done" to them.
2. Habermas, *Structural Transformation of the Public Sphere,* trans. Thomas Burger.

Merritt's ideas may seem to have burst onto the public stage in the early 1990s merely because newspapers everywhere were experiencing a recession and at the same time fighting a longtime free fall in circulation numbers, with some publishers willing to try just about anything to stop the circulation losses. And if these weren't troubles enough, a parallel concern—among both journalists and academics—was the news media's penchant to cover national elections using a "horse race" model, and, in both 1984 and 1988, cryptic television sound bites.[3]

But Merritt's advocacy of public journalism is not merely a reaction to such phenomena. It reflects a personal intellectual journey. The concerns he raised publicly in 1990 about his newspaper's election coverage were part of a series of steps that moved him slowly in the mid-1990s to advocate and foster change. The public articulation of his ideas emerged piecemeal in his newspaper columns since the mid-1980s. These ideas in turn bubbled up from interaction of Merritt's experiences in the news culture of Knight-Ridder Inc., owner of the *Wichita Eagle,* against his upbringing in the small North Carolina city of Hickory; his stint as a teenage sports editor at Hickory's daily newspaper, whose readers found sports news valuable; and the humanities courses he took as a journalism major and holder of a prestigious Morehead Scholarship at the University of North Carolina at Chapel Hill in the late 1950s. Professors there entranced him with philosophical discussions of democracy's origins and newspapers' necessary role in public life.[4]

Among Merritt's insights as a would-be public journalist, one of the most important lessons for journalists, and for journalism educators,

---

James Carey, "Journalism and Criticism: The Case of an Undeveloped Profession," *The Review of Politics* 36, no. 2 (1974): 227–49. Carol R. Dykers, *Making Journalism "Public": A Case Study of Change at the* Wichita Eagle, Ph.D. diss., University of North Carolina at Chapel Hill, 1995. The dissertation was a case study examining whether public journalism, as articulated by Merritt, is a practical application of Habermasian "discourse ethics."

3. See for example Leo Bogart, *Press and Public: Who Reads What, When, Where, and Why in American Newspapers* (Hillsdale, N.J.: Lawrence Erlbaum, 1989); Frank Denton, "Old Newspapers and New Realities: The Promise of the Marketing of Journalism," *Reinventing the Newspaper* (Washington, D.C.: Twentieth Century Fund, 1993): 1–58; Howard Kurtz, "Yesterday's News: Why Newspapers Are Losing Their Franchise," *Reinventing the Newspaper,* 59–117; Stephen Lacy, "Ideas for Prospering in a Changing Market," *Newspaper Research Journal* 13, no. 3 (1992): 85–94. Guido H. Stempel III and John W. Windhauser, *The Media in the 1984 and 1988 Presidential Campaigns* (New York: Greenwood Press, 1991).

4. Davis Merritt, interviews with the author, March 22, 1994, and October 14, 1993.

is a very simple one: Journalists' values and practices do not easily mutate, especially when the practitioner has learned them well enough to function capably at the highest levels of salary and prestige. So even change-advocate Merritt has found it difficult to consistently alter his journalistic values and practices.[5] Davis "Buzz" Merritt is hardly a heretic, and never would advocate dumbing down American journalism to provide slack-jawed TV-addicted spectators with a voyeur's view of life in these United States. Merritt is an intellectual, and just a tad too stuffy to become the pied piper of pop journalism.

For more than twenty years in Wichita, Merritt has written consistently about public affairs. The values that he held dear in 1976 as he began his first full calendar year in Wichita remain essentially unchanged from those he espoused in his columns in 1996. That was the year he stepped away from daily editing duties to become a public journalism advocate for his Knight-Ridder employers.

What has changed most in Merritt's columns are not his basic journalistic values, but a few beliefs about how journalists behave toward news "consumers"—reflected particularly in how he addresses readers and explains the newspaper's role in Wichita. But these few changes sufficiently questioned journalist-traditionalists' taken-for-granted sense of how to relate to audiences that they attacked Merritt, presuming that he had gone "soft." They didn't appreciate that his idea could help them remain independent while dealing with competing new technologies and financial belt-tightening to maintain newspapers' high profit margins. Merritt appreciated his idea's potential role, even if he couldn't succinctly express it in a way to help traditionalists grasp it, for he asserted several times during 1995 and 1996 that "public journalism doesn't cost anything. More than anything, it's a change in attitude."[6] Such a remark seemed curious, given the thousands of dollars of foundation grant money and newspaper operating budgets that paid to poll citizens or to create citizen panels during several years of public journalism experimentation.

---

5. This is a key point. Its importance can be clarified through an anecdote: As I embarked on an earlier, but similar, project at another newspaper, I described plans not only to interview journalists at that newspaper but also to analyze the newspaper's content over time. A former newspaper executive retained to analyze that paper's change efforts rejected my plan, writing me that content analysis was "not needed." He said journalists planned changes; therefore, content would change. As I researched Merritt's efforts, on the other hand, he talked of the difficulty of changing his journalistic habits even after he decided to change.

6. Davis Merritt, telephone interview with author, August 7, 1996.

A "change of attitude" is, in fact, vital to the ability to "do" public journalism. For more than twenty years in Wichita, Merritt has written about upholding American democracy's First Amendment ideal. The "change in attitude" he pushes requires journalists to make that ideal a touchstone, not an afterthought invoked to fend off would-be censors. Public journalism asks journalists to focus on *how* they might improve public discussion and enlarge citizens' sense of themselves as a public, despite the news media's changing economic and technological patterns. The shift is hugely important at a time when Americans are mourning the loss of civility in public life. Ritually, many journalists insist that Americans' current contempt for them is no different from a thousand-year-old tradition of killing the messenger of bad tidings. This overlooks the fact that as this century closes, computer technology makes it easier than ever before for citizens to simply ignore the messenger. As Merritt rightly argues, journalists need to focus on repairing citizens' low regard for journalism. That, he believes, is more urgent than their companies' need to throw up a site on the World Wide Web or try to sell their stories through online databases. The tone of the words that journalists write and speak matters more than the venue in which journalism is displayed.

Examining Merritt's published discourse in chronological order and in its social and historical context reveals crucial changes in his thinking.[7] The columns show how he has struggled with his and other journalists' ignorance of their publics. In that twisting, nonlinear struggle over a twelve-year period, Merritt's vocabulary and the syntax by which he positioned himself in relation to readers changed. He stopped viewing himself as a detached, aloof observer and began to identify himself as *one* with readers in a democratic public.

The change was clear after I examined columns published during Merritt's first decade in Kansas from 1975 through 1983. The attitude that journalists need only give readers "facts" permeated his early

7. The theory underpinning this kind of "developmental" or "genetic" analysis has been developed by cognitive anthropologists and sociocultural psychologists, including Dorothy Holland and Jaan Valsiner, "Cognition, Symbols, and Vygotsky's Developmental Psychology," *Ethos* 16 (1988): 247–72; Lev Vygotsky, "Problems of Method," in *Mind in Society: The Development of Higher Psychological Processes,* edited by Michael Cole, Vera John-Steiner, Sylvia Scribner, and Ellen Souberman, 58–75; James Wertsch, *Voices of the Mind: A Sociocultural Approach to Mediated Action* (Cambridge: Harvard University Press, 1991).

ASSESSING DAVIS MERRITT'S "PUBLIC JOURNALISM"

Wichita columns, including one published on September 26, 1976. It began:

> You don't fail to let us know when you are disturbed by what you see and read. And that feedback is important to us, as part of the calculations we make in putting out each day's editions. It isn't, of course, the decisive factor. Our obligation as an institution is to tell the news even if it afflicts or disturbs all of us.

Reader feedback, Merritt's language implied, could not be allowed to supersede journalistic judgment. Today's public journalists reject such self-serving attitudes, insisting that they must care how events turn out, must acknowledge that readers and viewers often see "truth" differently than do journalists, and that the way journalists ask questions and the questions that they choose affect our civic life. Merritt now understands that journalists abrogate their First Amendment role by simply claiming to give "facts," then ignoring how they decided which facts to present, whether the "facts" are understood, and how they are acted upon.

But Merritt wasn't fully aware of his intellectual journey's tortuous path when he told me during our first phone conversation in mid-August 1992, and in a subsequent interview in Wichita on August 20, 1992, that he had begun his drive to "change the culture of the newsroom" during fall 1990 when he became irritated with the Kansas gubernatorial primary campaign. Candidates talked in shorthand images and refused to explain what they would do if elected governor. In a September 9, 1990, column, he had announced that the *Eagle* would cover the fall campaign differently. His push for change, he told me, had begun then.

But the next day, after reading microfilm for several hours in the newspaper library, I found contrary evidence: Merritt's November 13, 1988, column, "A new political contract must restore meaning to election campaigns." It was one of three fall columns critiquing 1988 presidential politics. His November 13 column criticized 1988 election coverage, then asserted that journalists' way of covering elections would have to change "before the next time." When I showed Merritt that 1988 column, he didn't recall having written it—yet in 1992, he was acting in its spirit.[8]

8. I had planned to do a standard quantitative content analysis, comparing 1988 election stories and commentary with 1992 election stories and commentary; the 1988

In my quest for the origin of Merritt's ideas about public journalism, I relearned serendipitously what most journalists know by experience and most historians know from their training: Even with excellent interviewing skills and honest respondents, a researcher should look at every available contemporary document to accurately reconstruct the past.

Merritt's November 13 column vividly reminded me of journalism's past. He described the then-just-concluded Bush-Dukakis presidential race as a "shambles" and charged that both journalists and candidates had performed poorly. He argued that resolving the failure "will require a total rearranging of the contract between candidates and journalists." In fact, he added midway through the column, "the campaign people aren't going to change simply because it would be right to do so. . . . So changing the contract is up to the media."

To whom was Merritt talking? Ostensibly, he spoke to all his readers. But his vocabulary, his arguments' assertive force and their framing, suggest little that an ordinary citizen could do. Indeed, he wrote, "It is inescapable fact that journalists stand between candidates and the voters." In fact, Merritt's initial wording and arguments showed little respect for citizens: He noted that despite the prevalence of inadequate "sound bite" TV journalism, people said that they got most of their news from television. He described journalists feeding the "lowest common appetite among the voters." He said people were uncritical, would accept unquestioningly the distorted numbers of horse race polling. Then his arguments began to contradict themselves: He wrote that both politicians and the media "have become terms of reprobation" among citizens, thus suggesting that citizens knew what was going on but were powerless to change the game.

Merritt suggested four remedies: (a) let "candidates bore readers and viewers" by giving them longer sound bites and stories relating exactly what candidates said, for it is journalists' duty "to portray reality, not to entertain"; (b) don't cover the "so-called debates" until "candidates agree to unfettered, focused debates on issues"; (c) tell the voters about candidates' position papers; (d) report public opinion polls accurately, explaining each poll's margin of error to voters, and admit that when

news content and Merritt's election columns were to be pre-change, while 1992 content and columns were to be post-change. Merritt's memory lapse turned my attention instead to investigating when and how his thinking evolved.

percentages for each candidate fall within the margin of error, the winner is too close to call. This was four years before such practices were tried in the 1992 election and touted as just invented by newspapers like the *Charlotte Observer.* It was two years before syndicated columnist David Broder made similar suggestions in a 1990 column and in a speech at Riverside, California.[9]

Merritt's language suggested uncertainty about whether reader-voters would appreciate the difference in journalists' stories if such changes were made, a sort of love/hate relationship with his reader/public. But like many journalists with doubts about citizens, he did have faith in the democratic process, so long as the voting public is "well-informed." With this 1988 column, Merritt began defining what "well-informed" might mean. Two previous October columns had disparaged both politicians' and journalists' performance during the 1988 campaign but appreciated readers' need for a role beyond voting. One column even suggested how voters could protest: His October 9, 1988, column, "Packaged politics: Candidates show contempt for voters," slammed the imbecilic 1988 vice-presidential debate and advised readers, "You should be insulted by it and mad as hell that it occurred and you should let the people responsible know about it." Foreshadowing 1990s public journalism, he included names and addresses of chairmen of both the Republican and Democratic national committees so that people could vent their anger to officials.

Later in 1988 and in 1989, Merritt apparently had no ideas for acting consistently on such ideals; my reading of his columns from then until fall 1990 found no further refinement of his 1988 suggestions. But the pivotal 1988 moment was clear as I read and reread all 179 newspaper texts that he had written from 1984 through 1994, and then his 1995 book. I was looking for patterns, those that continued or that took surprising jumps forward or backward.[10] In the October and November 1988 columns, an objective expert patiently advising outsiders transformed into a citizen-editor who felt betrayed by both journalists and politicians. His 1988 columns predicted that journalists would have to change how they covered elections, because politicians

9. David Broder, "Democracy and the Press," *Washington Post,* January 3, 1990.
10. This method is described in Norman Denzin, *The Research Act: A Theoretical Introduction to Sociological Methods* (Englewood Cliffs, N.J.: Prentice Hall, 1989), and Catherine Marshall and Gretchen B. Rossman, *Designing Qualitative Research* (Newbury Park, Calif.: Sage, 1989).

CAROL REESE DYKERS

wouldn't change their democratically dysfunctional but politically effective mudslinging.

Still, public journalism is about more than covering elections. It is simply the case that Merritt, who covered government for the *Charlotte Observer* as a young reporter and then spent two tours in Knight-Ridder's Washington bureau before being sent to Kansas, is very comfortable with the journalistic genre of political coverage and journalists' taken-for-granted role as watchdogs of the political process. Because he had been a Washington insider and found it unsatisfying, he had the confidence to break the rules for covering politics.[11] And he fired an interesting salvo in the battle to make public journalism respectable when he wrote in his September 9, 1990, *Eagle* column:

> In the interest of disclosure as the 1990 Kansas gubernatorial campaign begins, I announce that The Wichita Eagle has a strong bias. The bias is that we believe the voters are entitled to have the candidates talk about the issues in depth.[12]

A journalist admitting to "bias" is a journalist waving a red flag at his brethren. A citizen-reader also might be startled, or simply happy that one journalist finally had admitted to having values. Indeed, Merritt's 108 editor's notes, book reviews, and columns published in the six previous years consistently had presented him as a journalist who believed journalists' role is to report the news and not to promote outcomes or values. The magnitude of this simple change is most clear if it is contrasted with a typical journalistic rationale, like that in Merritt's December 16, 1984, column explaining why his newspapers covered the arts in Wichita, pointing out differences between critics' reviews of arts performances and the newspaper's standard arts news coverage:

> . . . [C]overage of the arts in the news columns is the same as coverage of sports, of government, of any aspect of life: we apply high priority and considerable resources of time and space to . . . telling readers what is going on, and we leave it to readers to form opinions and, if they wish, to take action. If people do not support a baseball team, it is not our job in the sports news columns to exhort them to do so. If a business is failing or a political campaign is succeeding, it is our job to report that.

11. Davis Merritt, interviews with author, March 8, 22, 1994.
12. Davis Merritt, "Up Front, Here's Our Election Bias," *Wichita Eagle,* September 9, 1990.

> It is not the news department's job to attempt to affect the outcome. That's the business of the editorial pages.[13]

Such rhetoric reflects the coupling of two journalistic norms, objectivity and detachment. Merritt's language shows that in 1984, he took as immutable the connection between the concepts of objectivity and detachment, making it difficult for him to redefine that norm until he acquired another way of thinking about journalist practice, a thinking device.[14] By 1994, Merritt had found such a device to aid his effort to modify his profession's objectivity model. His new term, "public journalism," helped him to struggle against his trained inclination to employ, without critically examining its implications, the idea that one cannot be objective unless one is also detached from one's community. For many journalists, detachment is how objectivity is operationalized. With his November 1988 columns, Merritt began thinking about the perils of such traditional notions of detachment; with his September 1990 column, he began publicly to modify the detachment norm.

In his book *Discovering the News,* Michael Schudson saw objectivity as journalism's vital core ideal, helping journalists understand what they do and how they should do it. Merritt now argues that being objective does not require being detached, in the sense of journalists not caring whether what they do serves their profession's objective of supporting public discourse. Merritt now urges journalists to be "fair" and "balanced," another way of discussing the impartiality goal at objectivity's core.[15] To take Merritt's ideas one step further, I would argue that we journalists urgently must reflect upon the question, "Are we helping people to listen to one another and giving them an opportunity to be heard?" This implies more than giving citizens an opportunity "to have their say." Habermasian-influenced public journalism would help people to use language so that those with different viewpoints may "hear" rather than only argue. This kind of facilitating is reciprocal and thus it is "balanced," "fair," and "objective"—without being "detached."

13. Davis Merritt, "Newspaper's Reviews Aim to Inform, Not to Promote," *Wichita Eagle,* December 16, 1984.

14. Holland and Valsiner, "Cognition, Symbols, and Vygotsky's Developmental Psychology."

15. Michael Schudson, *Discovering the News: A Social History of American Newspapers* (New York: Basic Books, 1978). Davis Merritt, interviews by author, October 14, 1993, and March 22, 1994.

Merritt's past columns suggest that his struggle over what "objectivity" requires became necessary as he repositioned himself in relation to his readers. Journalistic objectivity was affected by the repositioning *only* if one assumes that truth cannot be found by journalists who care whether public life works in communities they serve. That, of course, is what some critics claim when they critique public journalism. While Merritt continues to espouse fair and balanced reporting, he has changed his insistence that the newspaper should be aloof and detached.

In print, Merritt first described that change in his September 1990 column. He pledged that his newspaper would work to affect the Kansas governor's race. Two candidates, Democrat Joan Finney and Republican Mike Hayden, wouldn't talk about issues. The newspaper was obliged, Merritt concluded, "to do everything we can to induce the candidates to address the issues rather than skim over them." It was a principled change, consistent with the rationale for a free press in a democracy. In the fall 1990 column, Merritt redrew the boundary between good and bad journalistic practice:

> . . . [O]ur reporters will be operating under express directions to get to the [candidates'] answers, and, if there are no answers, to report that, pointedly.

That has not always been the case with our and other reporters, and American democracy has been the loser. Voter participation is falling rapidly; voter interest in candidates and campaigns is flagging even more.

The newspaper's reporters, Merritt added, would seek direct answers but would be fair and balanced. His posture toward reader-voters had improved since his November 1988 linguistic disrespect. However, he still addressed readers as mere *voters* who "have the right to know what the candidates intend to do once in office." Reader-voters wait while journalists act in the political sphere; they consume what journalists give them, then vote. Merritt's chief 1990 innovation was to urge people to accept a basic citizen's role: to vote—not to be active citizens.

Wichita's hot summer of 1991 provided the next catalyst for Merritt's intellectual grappling with objectivity's boundaries. Wichita was the site of a national anti-abortion protest by Operation Rescue. A residue of polarization and anger remained when the protest officially ended in late summer. However, Merritt's column, "How we cover abortion protests," does not mark an accomplishment on the public journalism journey. It signifies a missed opportunity in a circumstance that, in retrospect, would have benefited from a focus on the role of Habermasian deliberation in American political life, so it, too, aids in understanding what changes public journalism requires. The August 11, 1991, column defended a typical journalistic response to crisis and controversy. It noted that national opinion polls showed that most Americans weren't extremists on abortion—always for, or always against. Most Americans, he said, approved of abortion *sometimes:* Wichita was polarized, but the newspaper wouldn't facilitate discussion:

> The diversity of opinion . . . means that the issue is not going to be settled quickly if ever. And it certainly means that it cannot be settled in a few weeks of demonstrations. . . . Within that realistic context, about four weeks ago as the Operation Rescue demonstrations were announced, the editors who direct our news coverage reached a fundamental operating decision. Within our resources of staff and space, we would cover the news events surrounding the demonstrations as fully as warranted. But we could not do that and also conduct a forum on the whole issue of abortion, pro and con.

Merritt thus described a decision to produce event-oriented coverage, and to ignore an opportunity to explore the core values of a major social issue. Merritt has said that he didn't consciously recognize connections between the abortion protest and his developing ideas about public journalism.[16] But Wichita's polarizing abortion summer seems pivotal in Merritt's eventual decision to act on a concern that he had expressed almost five years earlier. In a column published August 3, 1986, "Seeking sense amidst the clamor of the 'Casuists,' " Merritt had asked:

> Could it have been only a decade or so ago that social commentators were bemoaning the lack of involvement by Americans? . . . Now the mid-1980s finds us awash in causes, from Anti-Abortion to Zero Population and the whole alphabet that lies between.

Journalists, Merritt said, "thrive on action, on multiple opinions and even raucous debate." But Merritt feared trends he was observing might hold public life hostage to "excessive zeal, even mindless cant." Such an outcome, he predicted, would affect both journalists and "you, the

16. Davis Merritt, statement faxed to author, April 29, 1995.

consumers of the news that we collect and print." Most importantly, he wrote:

> . . . all the shouting and closed-mindedness damages communication, which is the purpose of news. No resonance can occur when information, such as a news story, bounces against concrete preconceptions. The information is lost because resonance—at least some glimmer of sympathetic vibration—is essential to communication.

This is a nascent understanding of Habermas's concept of "communicative action," social interaction in which conversants are oriented toward understanding, dialogue focused on finding out what another person means or intends, rather than to win a language battle.[17] The encounter that spurred Merritt to write that August 1986 column was with a reader who chastised him for printing a story about a Wichita doctor who performed abortions. The woman's accusation, that the newspaper was approving and supporting the man by interviewing him after his clinic was bombed, spurred Merritt's lecture to readers on a fundamental journalistic value that inspires his change effort:

> When the news story is about an issue that the reader feels intensely, an intellectual obligation arises. He or she must be willing to suspend, at least temporarily, some intensity of feeling and substitute a bit of open-mindedness. It is painless; and for those truly secure in their beliefs, it's a simple exercise.

But too often that doesn't happen.

Merritt noted the closed minds, the raised voices, the outrage simmering in public life. He was worried. Society needed more listening, less shouting. He saw implications for news media:

> In our news pages, we try to be the honest broker of information, passing along what we can discover that is applicable to resolution of public issues. When the climate of reception is so passionate and loud, casuists spend more time and energy trying to decide what our position is vis-à-vis theirs than they spend analyzing and absorbing the information itself.

17. Jurgen Habermas, *The Theory of Communicative Action, Volume Two,* trans. Thomas McCarthy (Boston: Beacon Press, 1987), 389–403, and *Moral Consciousness,* trans. Lenhardt and Nicholsen; C. Calhoun, "Introduction," *Habermas and the Public Sphere* (Cambridge: MIT Press, 1992), 1–48.

> This is not a new development in human nature; slaying the mes-
> senger is an ancient human foible. But 10 and 20 years ago it did not
> exist in its present depth and extent. Newspapers have not changed
> that much in what we do and how we do it during that period. Large
> groups of reader-casuists have.

Ten years later, after his circuitous intellectual journey, Merritt recognizes that he can't simply blame readers-as-zealots for his industry's
findings of a credibility gap between newspapers and their readers.
He understands how newspapers' approach to news contributed to
a gap—and perhaps even manufactured some zealots. But in 1986,
Merritt concluded that journalists could not affect that aspect of society
"because it would require abandonment of our basic role." That role was
his solid belief, in both 1986 and, apparently, still in summer 1991, that
good journalism was reporting, not being concerned about outcomes.

But in 1992, when he wrote "Breaking the Cycle of Political Cynicism"
and published it on February 23, Merritt began a sustained period of
changed approach to the *Eagle*'s audience and to its task. He chose a
comfortable topic—the 1992 presidential campaign—to announce the
change. In his February column, Merritt focused on election coverage.
The research mentioned in the column had been commissioned originally for a broader effort, the not-yet-published summer 1992 "People
Project." His February column reminded readers of his dislike of ma-
nipulative political campaigns. He began by sounding like an editorial
writer endorsing a candidate, then qualified his language. He was not
endorsing Paul Tsongas.[18]

> Paul Tsongas should be elected president. . . . I don't care about him
> actually being president; he could resign the day after the election. . . .

18. In my 1995 draft of this as a dissertation chapter, which I sent to Merritt for
comment, he questioned this quote that I chose to illustrate my point. He was concerned
because I had omitted what is *now* the second sentence of the quote's first paragraph.
My omission was to speed the reader to the last sentence of the *second* paragraph,
upon which I was focused. But Merritt's solid sense of objectivity caused him to worry
that someone reading only this fragment of his column might think he personally
had endorsed candidate Paul Tsongas in print—a terrible transgression for an editor
oriented to traditional news values. In practice, Merritt carefully separates actions
of reporters and news editors from the opinions of columnists and editorial writers.
Traditionalists who denigrate Merritt's public journalism must understand this. Those
of us who admire Merritt's willingness to discuss values must appreciate his continuing
concern that journalists be detached from political partisanship.

CAROL REESE DYKERS

> Just by actually winning the election, he would accomplish what the nation so badly needs: a rejection of the packaged, blow-dried, media-driven, manipulated, sound-bite campaign. Such campaigns feed Americans' suicidal cynicism about the political process and thus are the seeds of destruction of the democratic process.
>
> Mr. Tsongas talks about issues. Softly, sometimes hesitantly, and always bereft of the inflated coin called "charisma," he tells people what they know, deep down, is the truth: There are no easy answers. Substance and truth . . . matter.

Merritt's liking for Tsongas resulted not from his politics, but from his descriptions of problems and invitation to Americans to help resolve them. Here, Merritt in effect suggested a new campaign model: Candidates' capacity to publicly work out plans to address voters' perceived concerns should determine which candidate is elected. In this column, Merritt reminded readers of their newspaper's 1990 election coverage and explained that the paper's post-election research had found that "people are in fact interested in the real issues." Merritt noted that in 1990 the paper had provided "mobilizing information," and would do so again in 1992. This would give readers information on how to register, analyze campaign ads, and write stories about issues.

It was an interesting word choice for a tough-guy journalist: "mobilizing information" is an academic term.[19] It is information that helps citizens to act; for example, information about the place and time of a future meeting. Such information enables news "audience" members to behave as "citizens"—to attend a meeting, for example—and providing that information is a key aspect of Merritt's public journalism.

Merritt's use of the academic term signals a new stage of consciousness. In fall 1991, the Kettering Foundation had invited him to a New York City seminar on newspapers and public life. The invitation came because foundation officials liked the *Wichita Eagle*'s 1990 Voter Project, and wanted him to join a group of journalists and media scholars to discuss newspapers' role in public life. At that meeting, Merritt met Jay Rosen, the New York University professor who argues that news media should help public life go well.[20]

19. James Lemert, *Does Mass Communication Change Public Opinion After All? A New Approach to Effects Analysis* (Chicago: Nelson-Hall, 1981).

20. Kettering Foundation, "Squaring with the Reader: A Seminar on Journalism," *Kettering Review* (winter 1992): 33–51. Jay Rosen, "Making Journalism More Public," 267–84; "Politics, Vision and the Press: Toward a Public Agenda for Journalism," *The New News*

Merritt could not recall the chronology of his exposure to academic research, but sometime during this period, he took an academic turn as he searched for a way to help his newspaper "connect with the community."[21] He described "struggling through" a 1985 academic work by Keith Stamm, *Newspaper Use and Community Ties*, then sailing through a much less difficult to read but provocative 1991 work by pollster Daniel Yankelovich, *Coming to Public Judgment: Making Democracy Work in a Complex World.*

Yankelovich's book and the meeting with Rosen have shaped Merritt's ideas about changing the practice of journalism. Both these influences deserve brief discussion:

1. Rosen's contribution is more obvious because Rosen and Merritt have lectured together. Rosen coined the term "public politics" and became coauthor, with Merritt, of a monograph describing "public journalism." Indeed, Rosen's article, "Making Journalism More Public," described thinking about journalistic practice as focused on an existing public, an idea that fits with Merritt's long-held ideals of officials as merely custodians of the public's business and newspapers as a forum where people can see how their business is being conducted.[22]

2. Yankelovich's *Coming to Public Judgment* is a well-written and easily absorbed argument by a top public opinion researcher who clearly had thought about his research findings and synthesized them over a period of years. Yankelovich argued for bridging an expert-versus-public dichotomy in American public life and advocated introducing citizens to information that helps them make good judgments, an approach compatible with Merritt's journalistic ideals.

Such academic orientations were fresh when Merritt wrote his February 1992 column to tell readers that the newspaper was reviving its 1990 "Your Vote Counts" style of campaign coverage—providing periodic updates on presidential candidates' stands on issues. Merritt then announced a startling way of deciding what issues should be covered—

---

vs. The Old News: The Press and Politics in the 1990s, vol. 1 (Washington, D.C.: Twentieth Century Fund, 1992), 3–33 (1993a, winter). "Beyond Objectivity," 48–53; "Community Connectedness," paper presented at the Community Connectedness: Passwords for Public Journalism Conference (St. Petersburg, Fla., 1993); and "Making Things More Public: On the Political Responsibility of the Media Intellectual," 363–88.

21. Davis Merritt, interviews with author, August 20, 1992, and October 14, 1993.

22. Rosen, "Politics, Vision and the Press"; Jay Rosen and Davis Merritt, Jr., *Public Journalism: Theory and Practice;* Rosen, "Making Journalism More Public," 267–84.

startling, at least, to traditional journalists whose method for devising an election coverage plan has been to schedule, before primary campaigns begin, a meeting of political reporters and editors to decide which issues should be covered. Merritt found a different way to set an agenda:

> For the past few months, as a continuing part of the "Your Vote Counts" project, our research department has done in-depth interviews with almost 200 of you. These were interviews of a minimum of 30 minutes, face-to-face, to learn about what troubles Kansans about their lives. We'll base our issues coverage on what we discovered in those interviews. We'll be asking candidates . . . how they intend to address those . . . issues, and, if they don't want to address them, we'll want to know why so that we can tell you.

For traditionalists, Merritt said the plan would be flexible. He wrote, "Other subjects will undoubtedly insert themselves into campaigns, and those will be covered." But the focus was on getting answers from candidates to citizens' concerns, not journalists' concerns. Merritt was inviting active citizens into the political process.

Those two hundred interviews mentioned in Merritt's February column took on a new life and much greater importance during summer 1992. The innovative summer project was originally called "The List Project" because of plans to publish extensive lists of community resources available to citizens. The two hundred face-to-face interviews, whose collateral duty became to focus 1992 election coverage, were done by communication researchers and graduate students at Wichita State University.

"We just wanted to find out what was on people's minds," Merritt says. Admitting that the abortion protests in summer 1991 had startled his staff, he said that the interviews were planned even before the abortion protests. The interviews became the basis for an unusual project: a series of major stories about political life in Wichita, published over ten weeks from late June through late August, featuring ordinary citizens talking about issues they cared about. The pieces launching coverage on each issue in a package of seemingly traditional concerns—education, crime, families, political gridlock—quoted no political candidates. An academic was heard from here or there, but mostly, the stories featured ordinary people discussing ideas and issues. Merritt's front-page column of June 21, 1992, announced the series would begin the next Sunday and that his newspaper had a goal: rebuilding people's sense of community and getting them involved in that community. He explained why:

> The mood of the Nineties is frustration. In interview after interview, survey after survey, we complain that schools aren't doing the job, that crime is beyond known remedies, that the political system is unresponsive and in gridlock. And that we, busy with challenging personal lives, feel unable to do anything about any of that.
>
> Our reaction up to now has been to disconnect. We disparaged, and dropped out of, the political system . . . ; we retreated into . . . narrowly-defined interest groups. In an act of sure civic suicide, we abandoned the broad concept of community in favor of something we felt we could control: We retreated into determined individualism.
>
> Individualism is an admirable trait, but when it is the primary thrust of lives, the idea of community dies. And without . . . the realization that we must act together if we're going to exist together, common problems simply cannot be solved.

Merritt was including journalists when he wrote "we must act together." He then came to the project's core—the paper would provide a place for people to have a mediated conversation within a summer-long feature series called "The People Project":

> The People Project . . . is a collaborative effort to give shape and momentum to your voices and ideas, with the goal of reasserting personal power and responsibility for what goes on around us.
>
> It breaks new ground in the relationship between a newspaper and its readers and community.

The newspaper, a television station, and a radio station would give "the space and time for an informed community discussion of crucial issues." From "broad, open discussions," Merritt said, "ideas about solutions can arise, as well as the commitment to carry out the solutions; to solve it ourselves." The theoretical ideal of citizens talking to understand one another better was being tried in Wichita.[23] And in the process, the *Eagle* was attempting to transform people whom its editor had addressed a few years before as merely voters into active citizens who can find truth by talking to one another and trying to understand one another. The forum's authenticity was problematic: Unelected people's

23. Rosen and Merritt, eds., *Public Journalism;* Habermas, *Moral Consciousness,* trans. Lenhardt and Nicholsen, and Habermas, *Justification and Application,* trans. Cronin.

words were picked from transcripts of interviews or produced during new interviews by Jon Roe, a reporter. Roe then organized the words into a journalistic genre—a series of feature stories. Still, top billing went to *unelected people*'s words—not to experts, candidates, or aloof journalists. And lay citizens' newspaper speech was authentic enough that hundreds of Wichitans turned out after reading Roe's stories. They conversed in face-to-face discussions three times that summer. It was, Merritt suggested,

> a huge and accessible marketplace where ideas can form and be exchanged. Not simply ideas about what's wrong, but ideas about solutions. . . . At the end of it, we'll know an important thing about ourselves: whether we have the will, given the opportunity, to take responsibility for our lives and our community.

This was a forceful statement from a journalist who seemed to have convinced himself while writing his column that it would be OK if this experiment mobilized the community. Lots of "mobilizing information" was included so that the stories wouldn't be, Merritt hoped, "passive reading." Sunday issue packages on July 5, July 19, and August 2 included, in Merritt's words,

• A discussion of the problem and what you have said about it, based on surveys and extensive interviews with a broad range of residents.

• A look at why the issue is so difficult to resolve. The reason is that, in each case, people hold conflicting core values that they are unwilling to compromise. The exploration of those values is designed to encourage a search for solutions among people with differing ideas.

• A comprehensive list of organizations and agencies that are working toward solutions, with phone numbers and addresses so you can get involved or use their services.

• An invitation for you to brainstorm, along with everyone else, in a variety of ways, by telephone, fax, in person and in writing, on the air and in the newspaper.

• Information about a series of special community events where you can meet with people who share your interests in the problem, to begin to solve it ourselves.

Merritt's old ideas about journalists as required surrogates for citizens in the public sphere had vanished. A journalist's discursive practice—his columns—created opportunities for real-life acts, something beyond words in the newspaper.

ASSESSING DAVIS MERRITT'S "PUBLIC JOURNALISM"

In late August 1992, a picture accompanied Merritt's Sunday column wrapping up his newspaper's summer experiment. The picture's caption read, "Volunteer workers align the rafters atop the new Augusta Community Center, which was built in a single day Saturday." So much for negative news and lazy spectators. The editor acknowledged:

> When some of us at *The Eagle* started thinking about The People Project back in June, we were fueled by concern and hope.
> Concern that answers to the problems that plague our society were not being found in the usual places.
> Hope that ordinary people had some answers within themselves.
> The 10 weeks of the project produced electrifying affirmation of our hopes. Otherwise ordinary-seeming citizens by the hundreds are both thoughtful and activist in their approach to what bothers them about their lives and surroundings.

Merritt showed respect for readers as citizens. But how can a journalist who has lived in a community since 1975 describe as "electrifying" the discovery that "ordinary-seeming citizens . . . are both thoughtful and activist"? That language suggests that the change was not in the citizens but in the journalist, who had a new view of people. As Merritt wrote in this column ending the initial People Project, *"The Eagle* is a different newspaper in some important and interesting ways, as are most of the people who work here." One difference was providing citizens ways to act: Writing about solutions rather than only problems, and including in public affairs stories some mobilizing information, so citizens easily could tell public officials what they thought. These are important, but frequently neglected, aspects of journalistic practice.[24]

In his column, Merritt complimented the "array and significance of ideas" provided by "ordinary folks." Providing ideas that can be acted upon and relevant insights from lay people are two fundamental differences between the People Project stories and most traditional news stories. The latter tend to be filled with ideas and opinions from experts and public officials, filtered through the knowledge and preconceptions of journalists. Coverage of the ideas and concerns of lay citizens about public affairs is the chief means by which journalists can make real the ideal of the "public sphere," where no issue is unworthy of discussion, nor settled by means other than the power of a better argument to convince its hearers that it contains "truth" after it has been fully

24. Joseph Keefer, "The News Media's Failure to Facilitate Citizen Participation in the Congressional Policymaking Process," *Journalism Quarterly* 70, no. 2 (1993): 412–24.

considered in a rational manner. The difficulty for journalists, as Merritt and his staff recognized during a discussion on August 20, 1992, as the first People Project ended, is that journalists have trouble "covering" something as diffuse as "people's ideas." The *Eagle* did it in its People Project.[25]

But Merritt still didn't "get it," still couldn't consistently change his stance toward readers. After its summer 1992 People Project, the news pages of the *Wichita Eagle* periodically displayed smaller-scale versions of the paper's pioneering coverage. In late 1993, Merritt used his term "public journalism" in his newspaper's pages for the first time. His December 26 column said that the paper's People Project and Voter Project efforts "are at the heart of a potentially important change in the field of journalism." The paper, he wrote, had been experimenting, while "a few people in other parts of the country and in other fields were also worrying about the deterioration of public life." He described as a common concern that "the way journalism has been practiced in the last 20 or so years has contributed substantially" to public life's problems. He wrote that he agreed with such civic leaders as David Mathews of the Kettering Foundation, Jay Rosen of New York University, Ed Fouhy of the Pew Charitable Trusts, and David Rubin of Syracuse University, that public life must be revived:

> By reviving public life, we mean several things, primarily the re-accep-
> tance by all citizens of personal responsibility for what goes on in
> our neighborhoods and schools and cities; we mean restoring the
> importance of rational public debate on issues; we mean re-invigorating
> a political system that has been captured by the insiders and profes-
> sionals.

Yet despite the successes of the summer 1992 People Project and what Merritt had then described as the journalists' new respect for readers, the editor fell back on a traditional assumption. Merritt wrote that his newspaper's public journalism project aimed to convince citizens to "re-accept" personal responsibility. He therefore accused *citizens* of refusing responsibility "for what goes on in our neighborhoods and

25. Keefer, "The News Media's Failure"; Habermas, *Moral Consciousness* (1990) and *Justification and Application* (1993); Yankelovich, *Coming to Public Judgment*. Davis Merritt, from discussion with *Eagle* editors taped by author during a newsroom meeting on August 20, 1992.

schools and cities." But in making that statement, Merritt was ignoring his own criticism of media coverage of politics and the idea that the mass media have deprived citizens of their ability to take part in public life by usurping the public sphere and standing between citizens and elected officials. The announcement of the invention of "public journalism" continued, in a subconscious way, to blame citizens for journalistic conventions that disconnected citizens from public life. In Wichita, citizens acted when provided information and a forum for acting, according to Merritt's own assessment of his newspaper's projects. Merritt had much to ponder, and he announced that he was taking a year's leave from his editor's post to read and think about changing how journalists do their jobs.

Ten months later, in late October 1994, he tried again to define public journalism. Still on leave and just after he had cowritten with Rosen a monograph discussing public journalism, and as he worked on the final draft of a 1995 book describing his thinking to that point about public journalism, Merritt commandeered his newspaper's entire op-ed page. The ideas and language in the monograph, in his 1995 book, and in the three articles that filled the October 1994 op-ed page all reflect similar ideas about and descriptions of public journalism. All were written during 1994. The 1995 book appropriately adds some background about Merritt's career and thinking that help to validate him as someone whose ideas should be taken seriously. But Merritt already had credibility on his own newspaper's op-ed pages, for he had the editor's title and longevity of nineteen years in Wichita that had produced a relationship with *Eagle* readers.

With that relationship in mind, he wrote the centerpiece column of that October 30, 1994, op-ed page, "Public Journalism: A Movement toward Fundamental Cultural Change." In it, Merritt said he was "trying to articulate a philosophy about the appropriate role of newspapers in a democracy and trying to persuade my fellow journalists around the country to at least think hard about it." In explaining his ideas, Merritt addressed readers personally, writing, "I want to take you down the roads my mind has traveled, . . . giving you an understanding of the philosophy and how it is affecting, and will continue to affect, The Eagle and, I hope, our community."

Merritt's use of the term "our community" put him in solidarity with other citizens. He signaled his concern that his ideas should be clear not *just* to journalists or to political leaders but also to Wichitans and

Kansans. But as he explained public journalism's basic propositions, he wrote that "public journalism adopts a purpose beyond merely 'telling the news.' It accepts as a fundamental mission helping public life go well." In that sentence, he created a problematic view of the term "news." Merritt's 1995 book is subtitled "Why Telling the News Is Not Enough."[26] But why imagine public journalism as going *beyond* "telling the news" rather than imagine that news now *includes* topics valued by public journalists? Merritt's conversations with journalism educators at the Poynter Institute in February 1995 suggested that he could imagine "news" differently. For the Poynter audience, Merritt had described a 1994 meeting he attended:

> There was some conversation about . . . getting citizens together, a part of planning to create some new coverage for the '96 campaign. I had to bite my tongue because the person talking said, "Yeah, well, those citizens talking to each other, that's page 33 stuff." . . . He said if you don't have the candidates, it's page 33 stuff! I didn't say anything, but I just about went through the ceiling. If our notion is that citizens talking to each other about important issues is [not important], then you have to ask . . . WHY is it page 33 stuff? Because the newspaper SAYS it's page 33 stuff, that's the only reason.[27]

Yet in his October 1994 column and in his 1995 book, Merritt apparently could not yet imagine *consistently* that "news" includes the citizen conversations that many journalists believe are unimportant.

Another key issue raised in his October 1994 column resulted from his urging public journalists to imagine themselves as "fair-minded participants." Reassuringly for traditional journalists, Merritt asserted that public journalists should practice good judgment, be fair, do balanced reporting, work to be accurate, and write the truth. But those "journalistic virtues" should be used *on the field of play*. Like a good umpire or referee, public journalists help resolve conflicts. Journalists need only move far enough beyond detachment to care whether "this becomes a better place to live through democratic decision-making." Other than that, he wrote,

26. Merritt, *Public Journalism and Public Life*.
27. Davis Merritt, February 24, 1995, from transcribed discussion with members of the Civic Journalism Interest Group of the Association for Education in Journalism and Mass Communication (AEJMC), at the Poynter Institute in St. Petersburg, Florida. In transcribing all conversations, when a word or phrase was heavily emphasized by the speaker, I have placed the emphasized word(s) in all capital letters.

> Ideally, the official never impinges on the game. . . . But his presence as a fair-minded participant is necessary in order for an equitable decision to be reached.
>
> What he brings to the arena is knowledge of the agreed-upon rules, the willingness to contribute that knowledge, and authority . . . the right to be attended to.

The problem with the concept of "democracy," however, is that it lacks one clear-cut "rule book" for its practice. Thus, Merritt's sports metaphor breaks down, pointing to a legitimate concern among journalist-traditionalists uncomfortable with becoming a "participant." They imagine themselves and other journalists "participating" *without* a rule book, unable to maintain credibility or to apply properly their concepts of fairness or balance. Merritt rightly argues, however, that traditional investigative stories reflect unstated assumptions about how public officials should behave and how public life should go.[28] Thus, although the boundaries of his practice were not worked out by late 1994, a pivotal difference between "public journalism" and good traditional reporting is that public journalists are encouraged to address readers as citizens and to invite them to be active in the public sphere. This is an important outlook that might overcome the public's distrust of journalists' habitual focus on differences to the point of perpetuating incivility and thereby driving thoughtful citizens out of the public sphere, just as flame wars within Internet chat groups drive out civil discussion (and discussants).

Examining Davis Merritt's columns underscores an important fact about using language in public. By our choices of particular words and topics, we give away our secret beliefs and dreams. Merritt's language reveals a transition from a time when he imagined unelected citizens to be merely passive "readers" to his current thinking that unelected citizens have a role in public life beyond merely voting, and that journalists have a duty to help reader-citizens pursue that role. Reader-citizens must discuss issues and make good judgments before voting, so good journalism focuses on making accessible the process of "coming to public judgment." Public journalists make clear such values about public life, while good traditional investigative reporters seem to ignore their implicit values, taking for granted the rightness of their own outrage.[29]

---

28. Eric Voegelin, "Liberal Democracy," *Review of Politics* 36, no. 2 (1974): 250–73. Davis Merritt, interview with author, February 23, 1995.

29. Merritt, interview with author, February 23, 1995. Yankelovich, *Coming to Public Judgment.* Theodore L. Glasser and James S. Ettema, "Investigative Journalism and the

Such thinking underpinned an April 14, 1996, front-page note from Merritt about his newspaper's 1996 election coverage. One section addressed "citizens" (not readers); another section addressed "candidates." He told citizens, "We will take not just your issues to the candidates, but your questions. . . . Your questions are different from those journalists generally ask. Rather than . . . strategies and personalities, you tend to ask about problems and solutions."

Two months later, in columns published on June 30 and July 1, Merritt explained better than he had in his 1995 book or in previous columns public journalism's fundamental quarrel with conflict-driven journalism. After reading about a speech by Republican presidential candidate Bob Dole, Merritt attacked his own and other newspapers' and broadcasters' coverage. He wrote:

> Bob Dole's speech Tuesday at the Philadelphia World Affairs Council had been billed as a "major foreign policy" statement. So as I opened my Wednesday *Eagle* and tuned in the morning news, I hoped to find out what President Dole was planning to do about world affairs once in office.

Such substance wasn't in his newspaper's story. So, Merritt explained, he rummaged through the newspaper's wires, finding stories by such major services as Knight-Ridder's Washington bureau and the Associated Press; all merely repeated charges Dole made against President Bill Clinton, with one or two paragraphs about initiatives Dole said he would undertake. Fearing that journalists were just emphasizing conflict, Merritt got a copy of Dole's speech; on reviewing that, he wrote, he found among its eight, single-spaced pages much "crackling rhetoric" calling Clinton names, then on page six, "Finally . . . some affirmative statements about what President Dole would do" in office. "Why must I wade through pages and paragraphs and headlines of stormy rhetoric to get to the precious little substance that's there?" Merritt asked.

In his following Monday, July 1, column, he responded: Both journalists and politicians continued to make voters into spectators "at a popularity contest rather than a participant in a decision." He fumed that the 1996 campaign must not be about "confrontational rhetoric

Moral Order," in R. K. Avery and D. Eason, eds., *Critical Perspectives on Media and Society* (New York: Guilford, 1991): 203–25.

or political strategizing." Instead, it should be a "national discussion" about how government should work.

To fully appreciate the change of attitude required for journalists to emphasize discussion, not conflict, it's helpful to examine one final column, published on August 4, 1996.[30] There, Merritt denounced two candidates who were vying to replace Bob Dole in the U.S. Senate. Other Wichita news outlets had quoted the two squabbling over whether one candidate had suggested abolishing a home mortgage tax deduction or had been misquoted by a reporter. Merritt blasted both reporters and candidates for wasting space and time arguing whether the candidate had committed a gaffe rather than clarifying what he really believed. Then, Merritt wrote, "You didn't read about the flap in *The Eagle,* nor will you, except here, because we're not playing that game anymore." Merritt could now decide openly what was *important* for citizens to know about a candidate. He wrote:

> For too many decades, journalists—for their own complex reasons—combined with political campaigns to demean and nearly destroy the American electoral system. You've borne witness to that destruction by failing to go to the polls in large numbers and by expressing, righteously, your disgust and cynicism about politicians and journalists.
>
> We at *The Eagle* decided five years ago that we could no longer be a part of the systematic dismantling of democracy, and we changed how we define our role in campaigns. . . .
>
> . . . [W]e use our limited time and space to report about things that matter, such as where the candidates stand on issues . . . , such as who is providing the money for candidates, such as useful discussions of policy issues.

The column was, in one sense, a breathtaking move: A journalist admitted publicly that his newspaper ignored a story that other media covered. *Eagle* editors decided to only mention the flap in Merritt's column as an example of what Kansas's largest newspaper wouldn't report in the 1996 campaign. The decision, as Merritt wrote near his column's end, acknowledged that the *Eagle* based election coverage on "values. . . . We think they are the right values: put emphasis on information that helps you make a judgment about real things, not the ephemeral, fabricated, manipulated things that constitute modern political campaigning."

30. Davis Merritt, "Let's talk about some issues that matter," *Wichita Eagle,* August 4, 1996.

Such a statement causes journalist-traditionalists to invoke notions of a "slippery slope" that appears when journalists openly decide which "events" to leave uncovered and which to ignore. But traditionalists do not now cover all "events" in their communities; they use subconscious routines to decide which events are "news" and which are not—ignoring that such routines *are* based on values. In contrast, public journalism practitioners try to articulate and thereby acknowledge their values. Public journalism values, such as those Merritt described in his August 1996 column, are articulated in public so that citizens can understand and comment upon coverage decisions based upon them. If observed consistently, the practice forces journalists to demystify traditional values by discussing them with others, thereby moving journalists from their assumed perch above the linguistic battles of American public life and helping them to see that every choice—of a word to describe an event, or to cover one event but to ignore another—is underpinned by values. It's an initially uncomfortable, inward-looking regimen for traditionalist-journalists accustomed to seeing themselves as one-way mirrors reflecting something called facts.

Davis Merritt's "change of attitude" helped him to recognize such realities. To arrive at his new attitude, Merritt endured a long, twisting intellectual journey that, by its conclusion, helped him identify with other citizens and allowed him to discuss his values with his readers. But such a torturous journey won't be necessary for others if journalists and journalism educators can help new and aspiring journalists to see their role in public life as facilitating citizens' conversations—with one another and with political candidates and other would-be leaders—about public issues and public choices. Public journalism helps journalists understand that they can be more than an enlightened few who are privileged to engage politicians and other officials on an imaginary stage of public life while clueless citizen-voters spectate in a darkened audience. Such journalists can appreciate that just as they grew in wisdom while acting in public, unelected citizens can be transformed by talking in public. Not all, perhaps not even most, citizens will choose to join the debate, but it is not journalists' place to deny entrance to public conversation. It is a journalist's highest calling to facilitate a public role for all citizens. That facilitation is public journalism.

4

A NEW STRATEGY

JOHN BARE

As public journalism grows as a concept and spreads as a practice, it is generating debates but precious little empirical research. Advocates tend to present public journalism as a solution to several of the newspaper industry's problems, while critics offer a variety of reasons to reject it. Neither side presents much scientific research to bolster its case. Steering public journalism issues away from this arena of cheerleading—what Everette Dennis calls the "evangelical road shows"[1]—and into an accepted area of research will resolve many questions.

Advocates tout public journalism as a cure for many ills—declining market penetration, disintegrating communities, and dwindling social capital—while at the same time arguing that public journalism itself cannot be reduced to a concrete definition. It is, they say, more an art or philosophy. Jay Rosen explains the theories behind the break from traditional journalism, and media organizations hold up examples of past content as evidence that their organizations committed public journalism. Others define public journalism by detailing how to practice it.[2]

1. Everette E. Dennis, "On People and the Media: Raising Questions about Public Journalism," 2.

The cooperation of Michael Finney, Buzz Merritt, and Frank Daniels III, editors of the *World-Herald*, the *Eagle*, and the *News and Observer*, respectively, helped make research for this project possible. Thanks also go to my doctoral adviser, Phil Meyer, and members of the dissertation committee.

2. Jay Rosen, "Getting the Connections Right: What Public Journalism Might Be." Presentation to Project on Public Life and the Press First Summer Institute, American

Only recently have headlines called for the emotional debate to give way to more systematic evaluations. Thanks to research showing that journalists' traditional belief systems have remained remarkably consistent over recent decades,[3] much of what the newspaper industry knows about itself is documented by measures of journalists' attitudes. So instead of producing how-to lists, advocates of public journalism should study the innovation the same way researchers have always assessed traditional journalistic ideals.

Critics often wonder whether public journalism merits any discussion at all, with many asking: "Is this really journalism?" The idea of applying public journalism ideals to the editorial pages has been greeted just as sourly. "If being an editorial page editor is the print equivalent of talk radio, and I'm not saying that's not a worthy activity, it's not something that engages me intellectually or will serve longtime interests," said *New York Times* Editorial Page Editor Howell Raines.[4]

Yet critics also offer muddled arguments. On the one hand, critics charge, public journalism is nothing new because good newspapers have always delivered community-oriented information. They are quick with a caveat, however, claiming public journalism is new—and unwelcome—because it crosses the line that separates journalism from advocacy; public journalism, followed to its inevitable end point, will force practitioners to argue in favor of particular policy outcomes.

Critics are correct in noting that advocates have been overly reluctant to fix their position with a concrete definition of public journalism, but the critics go too far in demanding a definition that is both precise and universal. Devising a single public journalism definition for all U.S. dailies would be as impractical as trying to create a single definition

Press Institute, June 13, 1994; Unsigned, paid Gannett advertisement, "We Believe in 'Public Journalism'—And Have Done It for Years," *American Journalism Review* (April 1995): 16–19; Lisa Austin, "Public Journalism: A Progress Report"; Arthur Charity, Jr., "Doing Public Journalism," manuscript (New York: New York University's Project on Public Life and the Press, 1994), vi.

3. Rem Rieder, "Public Journalism: Stop the Shooting," *American Journalism Review* (December 1995): 6; David H. Weaver and G. Cleveland Wilhoit, *The American Journalist;* John W. C. Johnstone, Edward J. Slawski, and William W. Bowman, *The News People: A Sociological Portrait of American Journalists and Their Work* (Urbana, Ill.: University of Illinois Press, 1976); and David Weaver and G. Cleveland Wilhoit, "Daily Newspaper Journalists in the 1990s," 2–21.

4. Hoyt, "Are You Now, or Will You Ever Be, a Civic Journalist?" 27–33. Judith Sheppard, "Climbing Down from the Ivory Tower," *American Journalism Review* (May 1995): 18–25.

of investigative journalism for all newspapers. Investigative reporting differs from the *Washington Post* to the *Charlotte Observer* to the *Berkshire Eagle,* and so on. It is the same with public journalism. What works—and what is necessary—in one community may not be suitable for another community, so any universal definition would have to be too general to provide meaningful guidance.

Instead of following the ideological fault lines separating fans and critics, public journalism research should employ scientific measures to assess public journalism and its potential impact. In examining newspapers, researchers should measure the impact of public journalism three ways. One, public journalism can manifest itself in editorial content. Two, public journalism can change the practices and behaviors newspaper staff members use to gather and report the news. Three, public journalism can affect the attitudes and beliefs of the reporters and editors.

So far, public journalism commentators have highlighted anecdotal examples of innovative editorial content ("look what we did") and novel newsroom practices ("look how we did it").[5] The third area, attitudes and beliefs of the reporters and editors who create the content and carry out the practices, has been largely ignored. As a result, there is no indication whether the reporters practicing public journalism hold beliefs that are any different from the beliefs of the most traditional, change-averse reporters.

It is ironic that researchers have so thoroughly neglected assessments of the beliefs of news staff members. In fact, public journalism research efforts should focus first and foremost on beliefs of editors and reporters, for they are the individuals who must turn the idea into a hands-on practice and create the editorial content.

It is proper to examine attitudes first because changes in content and practices should occur after changes in beliefs. Put another way, news staff members who adopt public journalism as their dominant belief must first modify their attitudes regarding journalism and community. Once these beliefs are altered, the attitude changes should reveal themselves in two ways: new types of editorial content and new

5. For example, the Pew Center for Civic Journalism and the Poynter Institute for Media Studies have published a paper, "Civic Journalism: Six Case Studies" (Staci D. Kramer, author). See also "We Believe in 'Public Journalism,' " 16–19; Austin, "Public Journalism: A Progress Report"; and Charity, "Doing Public Journalism."

types of newsroom practices. For journalists who consider and reject public journalism edicts, this reaffirmation of their traditional beliefs also should affect attitudes in a way that is measurable. Armed with an empirical measure of public journalism beliefs, researchers can determine whether journalists have adopted this new ideology.

Framing the public journalism debate in terms of belief systems also makes it possible to build on the widely recognized methods established by Weaver and Wilhoit, who found evidence of three traditional "belief systems" among U.S. newspaper staff members, and the classic research of Converse, whose definition of constrained belief systems is well suited to the study of journalism attitudes.[6]

Journalists' attitudes, not the content they produce or the practices they employ, merits attention from public journalism investigators, based on previous research showing that investigative/interpretive ideals have long dominated the newspaper industry. If public journalists are, in fact, really doing something new, it follows that they should adopt a new dominant belief, one not in conflict with public journalism tenets. That would mark a dramatic break from tradition. After journalists' beliefs are documented, the research agenda should move on to the question of a relationship between staff beliefs and content, and between staff beliefs and newsroom practices.

Focusing on the beliefs of reporters and editors is really a simple idea, one that never should have been overlooked for so long. In order to alter news content and journalistic practices, which is the aim of public journalists, innovators must first modify the beliefs held by the practitioners. Using survey measures like those Weaver and Wilhoit developed, it is possible to determine which news staffs have made public journalism their top priority, and which ones have not. Here, this initial measure of public journalism attitudes is based on self-administered mail surveys of 426 editorial staff members of the (Raleigh, N.C.) *News and Observer;* the *Wichita Eagle;* and the *Omaha World-Herald.* The *Eagle* is a Knight-Ridder-owned paper that has been pursuing public journalism for more than six years. The *News and Observer,* at the time of data collection, was a family-owned newspaper experimenting with ways to use new technologies to deliver information

6. Weaver and Wilhoit, *The American Journalist;* Johnstone, Slawski, and Bowman, *The News People;* and Philip E. Converse, "The Nature of Belief Systems in Mass Publics," in *Ideology and Discontent,* edited by David Apter (New York: Wiley, 1964), 206.

to readers. The *World-Herald* is an employee-owned newspaper that follows traditional, detached journalism practices.

Public journalism fits nicely alongside the traditional journalistic roles: investigative reporting, information dissemination journalism, and adversarial journalism. Each is a label for an ideal that guides journalists. For the most part, newspapers successfully pursue all three objectives simultaneously. Only when two or more of the ideals come into conflict are editors forced to make value judgments as to which ideal is most important. When this occurs, the most developed ideal is the one that will win out, according to Converse.

Converse uses the term "attitude constraint" to describe the degree to which the components of a belief system are internally consistent and well developed. Determining which one of a news staff's beliefs is most important is a vital step because the dominant belief system will prevail when newsroom ideals come into conflict. For instance, an editor with limited resources may be forced to decide whether to pursue a strategy that promotes the information dissemination function of journalism or the investigative journalism function. The decision will hinge on which ideal is most central to the editor's professional ideology.

PUBLIC JOURNALISM

The cultural, economic, and technological changes sweeping across all media have forced publishers and editors to fight for their position in the media marketplace, and newspapers have seen their readership and profit margins dwindle.[7] The traditional basic function of U.S. daily newspapers—providing citizens with information they need to function in a democracy—is now performed more efficiently by electronic media.

As many newspapers experimented with redesign and marketing efforts, in Wichita another answer emerged: public journalism. Stated generally, public journalism involves a shift in a newspaper staff's professional values designed to give the community a greater voice and presence in the newspaper and to help the newspaper put itself forth

7. Robert L. Stevenson, "The Disappearing Reader," 22–31. The 1993 General Social Survey revealed that only 46.2 percent of U.S. adults read a newspaper daily, the first time in that survey's history that the daily readership measure had dipped below 50 percent. The GSS daily readership measure jumped to 49.6 percent in 1994; that still represents an 11 percent drop from the daily readership figure of a decade earlier.

as an agent to achieve positive change in the community. In 1988, *Eagle* editor Davis Merritt, Jr., began exploring new methods of covering public affairs and new techniques the newspaper could use to produce grassroots solutions to community problems.

Merritt has emerged as one of the most notable practitioners of public journalism, but he was not the first to recognize the need for newspapers to secure their position in the community. In 1962, journalists said opportunities to "contribute something of value" to their communities rated below other functions. Two years later, Leo Bogart argued that the "advertising health" of newspapers was tied to the "state of downtown urban retailing and the changing racial composition of the cities," but Bogart failed to convince newspaper executives to address the growing problem. The Burgoons found evidence supporting the notion that journalists were out of touch with citizens of the communities they covered and held a "patronizing and unflattering view of their readers."[8] Suggestions that newspapers should fashion their coverage to the needs of their communities were met with warnings such as the *Quill* headline: "Beware the Market Thinkers."

For the *Eagle's* Merritt, the key moment came in late 1988. That year, after suffering through an exasperating election, he decided the old ways of journalism had failed. Merritt suggested new ways of covering elections, and the paper changed course in 1989. Others, including the late Knight-Ridder CEO James Batten and Common Cause founder John Gardner, began urging newspapers to function as "an instrument of community and potentially a generator of community." The move toward public journalism suffered after the suicide of an executive editor deeply involved in a controversial public journalism project.[9]

Still, the call for change grew louder, drawing energy from commentators such as John Herbers and David Broder. Soon more newspapers around the country embarked on innovative projects, and the experiments began to take on the names of hometowns or labels such as

8. Merrill Samuelson, "A Standardized Test to Measure Job Satisfaction in the Newsroom," *Journalism Quarterly* 39 (summer 1962): 285–91; Leo Bogart, *Preserving the Press: How Daily Newspapers Mobilized to Keep their Readers,* 41; Judee K. Burgoon, Michael Burgoon, and Charles K. Atkin, *The World of the Working Journalist* (New York: Newspaper Advertising Bureau, Inc., 1962), 80.

9. Davis Merritt, Jr., "A New Political Contract Must Restore Meaning to Election Campaigns," *Wichita Eagle,* November 13, 1988; "Newspapers, Community and Leadership: A Symposium on Editorial Pages" (Key Biscayne, Fla.: Knight-Ridder, Inc., 1989); Alicia Shepard, "The Death of a Pioneer," *American Journalism Review* (September 1994): 35.

"press activism." Yankelovich's *Coming to Public Judgment,* from which public journalists borrowed heavily, helped affix the "public" label to the movement. After Rosen and Batten called for "public journalism" to replace the discredited objectivity ideal as the new dominant model, trade magazines soon heralded the arrival of "public journalism."[10] In 1994 Rosen's Project on Public Life and the Press drew many of the nation's top journalists, newspaper executives, and scholars to a public journalism conference. More recently, scholars have adopted the term "civic journalism" as a label.

Despite public journalism's surge, critics have held firm. The *New York Times*'s Eugene Roberts and *Newsday*'s Howard Schneider argue that good newspapers have always provided readers with information they need to function effectively in their communities. Leonard Downie, Jr., of the *Washington Post* voices another common objection: "No matter how strongly I feel about something that's going on out there, my job is not to try to influence the outcome. I just don't want to cross that line." Merritt acknowledges that some newspapers have "crossed lines of involvement that I would not," in the name of public journalism. For his part, he contends that public journalism "does not mean trying to determine outcomes, but it does mean accepting the obligation to help the process of public life determine the outcomes."[11]

10. John Herbers, "Forcing the Issues," *Nieman Reports* (spring 1991): 14; and David Broder, "A New Assignment for the Press," *Press-Enterprise* (Riverside, Calif.) Lecture Series, February 12, 1991. Along with the work taking place in Wichita, which moved forward with the Voter Project and the People Project: Solving It Ourselves, similar experiments were ongoing in Columbus, Ga., Charlotte, N.C., Columbia, S.C., Norfolk, Va., and Des Moines, Iowa, among other places. In another company-sanctioned effort, the Gannett chain in 1991 established its NEWS 2000 program to encourage public journalism and "community leadership projects." In 1994 alone, thirty-eight of the company's newspapers carried out fifty public journalism projects. For examples see Edward D. Miller, *The Charlotte Project: Helping Citizens Take Back Democracy;* Unsigned, paid Gannett advertisement, "We Believe in 'Public Journalism,' " 16–19; and Austin, "Public Journalism: A Progress Report." Michael Hoyt, "The Wichita Experiment: What Happens When a Newspaper Tries to Connect Readers and Citizenship?" *Columbia Journalism Review* (July/August 1992): 43–47; John Bare, "Case Study—Wichita and Charlotte: The Leap of a Passive Press to Activism," 149–60; Yankelovich, *Coming to Public Judgment;* Rosen, "Beyond Objectivity"; James Batten, "Public Journalism: Fulfilling Our Responsibility"; Sheppard, "Climbing Down," 18–25; Alicia C. Shepard, "The Gospel of Public Journalism," *American Journalism Review* (September 1994): 28–34; and Rebecca Ross Albers, "Going Public: Going Public Unites Some Publishers and Newsrooms in a Controversial Mission," 38–40.

11. Shepard, "The Gospel of Public Journalism," 30. Davis Merritt, Jr., "Public Journalism and Public Life: Why Telling the News Is Not Enough," manuscript (New Jersey: Lawrence Erlbaum Associates, 1995), 16.

In this debate, Merritt and other public journalists choose their words carefully and slice arguments finely. The same holds when it comes to defining public journalism. Rosen admitted in 1994 that "we're still inventing it. And because we're still inventing it, we don't really know what 'it' is." Rosen has, however, tried to distinguish public journalism from traditional journalism: "Traditional journalism worries about remaining properly detached. Public journalism worries about becoming properly attached. So: public journalism becomes the undeveloped art of attachment to the communities in which journalists do their work." Rosen says journalists must strive toward some larger goal, something he labels "spiritual."[12]

While Merritt explains that public journalism "means separating the canons of journalism—objectivity, for instance—from some of the silly axioms that have grown up around those canons, such as not caring," he also hedges by saying, "Nobody knows how to do public journalism yet." He defines it by what it is not—a formula, a new weather map, advocacy journalism, nostalgia for the old days of newspapering. But he offers in the affirmative only that public journalism is "a pragmatic recognition that people flooded with contextless, fragmentary, episodic, value-neutral information can't make effective work of their decision making."[13]

In his most useful explanation, Merritt says journalists must move away from simply "telling the news" to communicate a more thorough explanation of public life to their communities. For this to occur, Merritt says, journalists must undergo a "mental shift."[14] This mental shift requires a change in core beliefs, which adds support to the argument that researchers should study public journalism as a belief system.

Attitude changes such as Merritt describes can be detected with the public opinion measures employed here. Based on the innovations Merritt and the *Eagle* have adopted, staff attitudes toward public journalism ideals should be more highly organized and more internally consistent, when compared with staff attitudes at newspapers where public journalism has been ignored or wholeheartedly discouraged. Compared to the news staffs of nonpublic journalism papers, the *Eagle*

12. Rosen, "Getting the Connections Right."

13. Davis Merritt, Jr., excerpt of comments from Panel Discussion on "The Emerging Electronic Democracy," *Nieman Reports* (summer 1994): 54; Rosen, "Making Things More Public," 26.

14. Merritt, "Public Journalism and Public Life," 114.

staff also should rate public journalism ideals as more important. Adopting public journalism as its dominant belief will require the *Eagle* staff to make a compensating change in its overall ideology by reducing in relative importance the traditional beliefs likely to conflict with public journalism ideals. In addition, attitudes of the *Eagle* staff should differ from the long-standing industry norms Weaver and Wilhoit have documented.

BELIEF SYSTEMS

A belief system is "a configuration of ideas and attitudes in which the elements are bound together by some form of constraint or functional interdependence." Constraint, the term describing the internal consistency of the various elements of a belief system, is evident when knowledge of a person's standing on one particular issue makes it possible to predict that the person also holds other specific beliefs. Strong intercorrelation between a set of variables stands as evidence of internal consistency and constraint.

Researchers look for evidence of relationships within and between belief systems. There is constraint, or strong internal consistency, *within* a belief system when there is a strong intercorrelation between a set of points related to a single ideal, such as freedom of expression. A strong belief in each individual item predicts a strong belief in the others.

Also, there are strong relationships *between* multiple complementary and competing belief systems. As Converse explains, consistency between belief systems "may be taken to mean the success we would have in predicting, given initial knowledge that an individual holds a specific attitude, that he holds certain further ideas and attitudes." The idea that two competing belief systems are constrained "refers to the probability that a change in the perceived status (truth, desirability, and so forth) of one idea-element would *psychologically* require, from the point of view of the actor, some compensating change(s) in the status of idea-elements elsewhere in the configuration."[15]

For instance, a person's views on the freedom of expression ideal may predict views on educational philosophy. If so, changes in attitudes toward freedom of expression would necessitate some corresponding change in attitudes toward education. The belief that is more central

15. Converse, "The Nature of Belief Systems," 206.

to the individual's overall ideology is the one likely to force the change. This controlling belief "constrains" the others.

Converse's explanation is important here because strong intercorrelation among a set of public journalism measures may be taken as evidence that the measures comprise a well-developed public journalism belief system. If such a public journalism belief system exists, it would be just one part of a newspaper's overall ideology.[16] Just as a person's overall ideology is made up of several interdependent belief systems, a news organization's overall ideology also consists of many interdependent belief systems.

Further, Converse explains, belief systems are "bound together" functionally, which means that when new information alters one part of the overall ideology, then some compensating change is expected to occur in other parts as well. Here, Converse's theory is helpful in a second way. It not only allows for the recognition of a public journalism belief system but also holds that the adoption of a public journalism belief system is likely to produce corresponding changes in other elements of a newspaper's overall ideology.

Here is how Converse explains it:

> Let us imagine, for example, that a person strongly favors a particular policy; is very favorably inclined toward a given political party; and recognizes with gratification that the party's stand and his own are congruent. . . . Let us further imagine that the party then changes its position to the opposing side of the issue. Once the information about the change reaching the actor has become so unequivocal that he can no longer deny that the change has occurred, he has several further choices. Two of the more important ones involve either a change in attitude toward the party or more likely a change in position on the issue. In such an instance, the element more likely to change is defined as less central to the overall ideology . . . [17]

In the same way, consider a reporter who favors the traditional journalism model. The reporter is satisfied as long as the newspaper for which she works favors those same values. But if management moves the paper away from the detached model toward a public journalism

16. In the way that Converse uses the term "belief system," it can be a bit confusing. A single public journalism belief system may exist, but it may stand as only one component of an overall belief system. This overall belief system will be referred to here as ideology in order to avoid confusion.

17. Converse, "The Nature of Belief Systems," 208.

model, the reporter may make any of several decisions. She may quit and search for a newspaper with an ideology that matches her own. Or, she may follow her employer's lead and embrace public journalism beliefs. The latter option would require "some compensating change" in her professional ideology. The change might occur in the form of decreased appreciation of traditional journalism, because the nature of the new values would be inconsistent with those of the old model.[18] It is in this manner that the adoption of public journalism beliefs is most likely to affect traditional newsroom beliefs.

To establish links between abstract beliefs of individuals and their specific policy positions, researchers have adopted hierarchical models of ideological consistency. Also, researchers have offered theories to explain how one belief system becomes dominant in a person's ideology. Nie and Andersen found that "increased salience (of the belief system) leads to increased attitude constraint"—not the education or sophistication of individuals, as Converse proposed. Or, the centrality of the belief system—the "intensity with which the individual holds a given belief"[19]—may determine which attitudes become dominant. Beliefs held closest to the "central core" of an individual's ideology are more stable, consistent, and well formed.

Other research findings indicate that beliefs developed only recently are more likely to be weakly formed and in risk of being pushed aside in favor of competing beliefs. Newcomers to a profession, in other words, are more apt to adopt innovative attitudes. Or, attitude changes could be driven solely by psychology. Internal motivations—psychological predispositions formed during childhood—may determine how successfully individuals reconcile traditional beliefs with new, competing beliefs.[20]

18. For research that documents cynicism as a traditional value, see Burgoon, Burgoon, and Atkin, *The World of the Working Journalist.*

19. Mark A. Peffley and Jon Hurwitz, "A Hierarchical Model of Attitude Constraint," *American Journal of Political Science* 29 (November 1985): 871–90; Mark Peffley and Jon Hurwitz, "Models of Attitude Constraint in Foreign Affairs," *Political Behavior* 15 (March 1993): 61–90; Robert Rohrschneider, "Environmental Belief Systems in Western Europe: A Hierarchical Model of Constraint," *Comparative Political Studies* 26 (April 1993): 3–29; Norman H. Nie, "Mass Belief Systems Revisited: Political Change and Attitude Structure," *Journal of Politics* 36 (August 1974): 540–91; and Norman R. Luttbeg, "The Structure of Beliefs among Leaders and the Public," 398–409.

20. Herbert F. Weisberg and Jerrold G. Rusk, "Dimensions of Candidate Evaluation," *American Political Science Review* 64 (December 1970): 1168–85; and Rohrschneider, "Environmental Belief Systems," 3–29.

Peffley and Hurwitz confirm that scholars still accept Converse's original concept of belief systems and internal consistency. For that reason, and because the instrument employed here was not designed to yield data suitable for the hierarchical modeling, Converse's original work will serve as a guide. Finally, the language of public journalists supports the decision to study public journalism as a belief system.[21]

JOURNALISM BELIEF SYSTEMS

Weaver and Wilhoit, building on the research of Johnstone, Slawski, and Bowman, found that three "distinct belief systems dominate journalists' attitudes about press functions." First, the "investigative/interpretive" belief has long been dominant.[22] Journalists believe it is most important for reporters to investigate government claims, analyze complex problems, and discuss national policy. Next, the "information dissemination" belief system recognizes the importance of getting information to the public quickly and concentrating on the widest audience possible. The second most dominant belief system, the information dissemination function is central to detached, objective journalism. Third, Weaver and Wilhoit describe the "adversary" function of the press as a "minority view" of journalists. This belief system recognizes the importance of serving as an adversary to government officials and to business.

21. Peffley and Hurwitz, "A Hierarchical Model of Attitude Constraint," 871–90; and Merritt, "Public Journalism and Public Life," 124. Public journalism researchers interested in adapting a hierarchical model might consider a broad, overreaching measure of individuals' core democratic values for this most abstract, "superordinate" belief, or possibly a measure of attitudes toward democratic institutions or First Amendment ideals. Although Converse's initial discussion of ideological constraint frames the theory in terms of the individual, he moves on to discuss belief systems of groups, so it will be appropriate to use ideological constraint to explain the belief systems of journalists. Also, the theory can be used to study different types of beliefs, as demonstrated by Rohrschneider's application of constraint theory to a study of environmental beliefs. Finally, Luttbeg measured attitude constraint among "community leaders" in two small towns in Oregon, so there is precedent for applying constraint theory to special populations.

22. Weaver and Wilhoit, "Daily Newspaper Journalists in the 1990s," 2–21. The findings produced by Johnstone, Slawski, and Bowman regarding staff members' belief systems largely mirrored those that Weaver and Wilhoit would later publish—based on the same survey items—though Weaver and Wilhoit improved the process by offering more meaningful labels and explanations of press functions. The items Johnstone, Slawski, and Bowman used to construct what they called the "neutral" press function were later adopted by Weaver and Wilhoit and used to represent the "information dissemination" press function. Weaver and Wilhoit, renaming it the "investigative/interpretive" function of the press, also adopted the items used by Johnstone, Slawski, and Bowman to represent the "participant" function of the press.

A NEW STRATEGY

The fact that Weaver and Wilhoit recognized these values as well-developed belief systems is an important precedent. The research is particularly important in that it uncovered one belief system (adversarial) that Johnstone, Slawski, and Bowman had not detected. This demonstrates that new investigations may yield evidence of previously unknown journalistic belief systems. The field, it turns out, is not static.

Managing editors, like the reporters they direct, hold fast to the belief in the investigative function of the press, and journalists as a group generally prefer all things traditional. Among other things, the structure of news organizations perpetuates these traditions. The body of research shows that traditional beliefs, in general, and investigative/interpretive beliefs, in particular, have long been "central" to journalists. This study, while it has limitations, builds on previous studies.[23]

Creating a greater variety of attitude measures, particularly public journalism items, raises the possibility of uncovering additional belief systems. The old saw about absence of evidence not translating into evidence of absence applies here; one reason public journalism beliefs have not been documented in previous research is that journalists were not queried on public journalism ideals. Also, it is important to measure journalists' attitudes toward community on a variety of levels—regarding their own particular jobs, the newspapers where they work, and the journalism industry in general.

THREE PAPERS AND THREE COMMUNITIES

The *Wichita Eagle* is one of twenty-eight Knight-Ridder papers. It has been involved in public journalism since the paper's editor, Merritt, began to move away from traditional, detached public affairs coverage in late 1988. Wichita is not the state capital of Kansas (that's Topeka),

---

23. For relevant studies of news organization structures, see Janet Bridges, "Daily Newspaper Managing Editors' Perceptions of News Media Functions"; Keith Stamm and Doug Underwood, "The Relationship of Job Satisfaction to Newsroom Policy Changes"; and Sharon H. Polansky and Douglas Hughes, "Managerial Innovation in Newspaper Organization," *Newspaper Research Journal* 8 (fall 1986): 1–12. The study is limited in that it involves only three newspapers. Results cannot be generalized to the entire newspaper industry, though the findings may be considered important and relevant to the entire industry because the newspapers examined in this study share common attributes and experiences with many other U.S. dailies. Also, the study may be replicated and expanded using a representative sample of U.S. journalists. But the study's greatest limitation is that it employs only a single method—a one-shot survey—to measure the complex concept of public journalism. Longitudinal research would help document change in newsrooms as well as change in social indicators in the community.

but it is the largest city in the state, and its county, Sedgwick, is the largest county in the state. The *Eagle's* home-county penetration dropped from 56.2 percent in March 1988 to 50.3 percent in March 1994.

In Omaha, the *World-Herald* is an employee-owned newspaper. Its editor is Michael Finney, who has kept the newspaper close to the traditional model of objective journalism. The city of Omaha is located in eastern Nebraska, across the Missouri River from Council Bluffs, Iowa,[24] about three hundred miles north of Wichita. Omaha is not the state capital (that's Lincoln), but it is Nebraska's largest city, and its county, Douglas, is the largest in the state. The *World-Herald,* with morning and evening circulation, has sustained a remarkably high home-county penetration level. From March 1988 through March 1994, home-county penetration held at 68 percent.

In Raleigh, the *News and Observer* was owned by the Daniels family for 101 years, until it was sold in 1995 to the McClatchy chain. At the time of data collection, the editor was Frank Daniels III, a member of the family ownership group who steered the newspaper toward new technologies. The newspaper offers its own online service and Internet content, as well as audio text features. Raleigh is the state capital and the second-largest city in North Carolina (trailing Charlotte), and its county, Wake, also is the state's second-largest. Raleigh is located near the Research Triangle Park. The *News and Observer* enjoyed a home-county penetration level of 71 percent in March 1988, when it offered a morning and evening newspaper. By March 1994, three years after evening circulation ended, the paper's home-county penetration had fallen to 48.2 percent.

The newspapers were selected, in part, as a convenience sample, but also because the three papers allow for meaningful comparisons. Analysis of staff attitudes at these three mid-size U.S. dailies is relevant to peer newspapers, and the study will serve as a first step toward a second, national study. Content analysis of a constructed week of the newspapers revealed key similarities regarding news hole size and the percentage of news articles attributed to staff writers.[25]

24. The Omaha metro area, as defined by the Census, includes one Iowa county—Pottawattamie, population 82,628.

25. For a detailed comparison of the markets, see John Bowman Bare, "Toward a Definition of Public Journalism" (Ph.D. diss., University of North Carolina at Chapel Hill, 1995), 83–95. University of North Carolina journalism professor Philip Meyer has undertaken a national public journalism survey of a larger sample of newspaper staffs.

BY THE NUMBERS

To determine whether staff members at the *Eagle, World-Herald,* and *News and Observer* hold attitudes toward public journalism that are consistent enough and organized in such a way that they rise to the level of a fully formed belief system, this study employed Cronbach's alpha as a test. Cronbach's alpha, a gauge of the internal consistency of a group of related items, stands as evidence that a set of attitude measures make up a consistent, well-developed belief system. This parallels Converse's definition of a highly constrained belief system. Also, Spector explains that valid scales "are assumed to reflect a single underlying construct,"[26] thus multiple items that cluster together may represent a single belief system. The analysis followed the rules of scale construction, as described by Spector, and borrows from the Converse and Weaver and Wilhoit methods.

The analysis constructed scales for three types of public journalism beliefs: Personal Public Journalism (journalists' attitudes regarding their personal duty to solve community problems); Community Trust (journalists' faith in community leaders to solve local problems); and Institutional Public Journalism (journalists' attitudes regarding their newspaper's duty to help solve community problems).[27]

Replicating prior research, the analysis constructed scales for two traditional journalism beliefs: Investigative/Interpretive and Information Dissemination. A single survey question was used to represent Adversarial beliefs. Finally, the analysis constructed original scales for two additional traditional beliefs: Community Cynicism (journalists' cynicism regarding the merits of citizens' problem-solving efforts) and

---

Ongoing research carried out by April Simon, under the direction of Philip Meyer, University of North Carolina at Chapel Hill, 1995. The constructed week included newspaper editions from September 5, 1994, July 19, 1994, July 27, 1994, August 4, 1994, August 12, 1994, August 20, 1994, and August 28, 1994. For the seven-day sample, the following space amounts were devoted to editorial content: *World-Herald,* 50.1 percent; *Eagle,* 50.6 percent; *News and Observer,* 47.4 percent. Of all articles published in *World-Herald* editions included in the analysis, 35.3 percent were produced by staff writers; the figure was 40.7 percent for the *Eagle* and 38 percent for the *News and Observer.*

26. Paul E. Spector, *Summated Rating Scale Construction* (Newbury Park, Calif.: Sage Publications, 1992), 31.

27. For a detailed explanation of the scale items and analysis of alpha values and constraint levels, see Bare, "Toward a Definition of Public Journalism," 191.

Non-Consequentialism (journalists' attitudes regarding detached, non-involved news practices).[28]

The study compared the three news staffs' standings on the scale measures, in terms of both alpha values and the absolute score on the measure. Higher alpha values indicate a greater overall consistency and a higher level of organization in the belief systems. Higher staff scores on the scale measures indicate a greater overall agreement with the tenets of the belief system. The ANOVA analyses were repeated for each newspaper, controlling for gender and whether the respondents attended high school within their newspaper's primary circulation area.[29]

Also, for each of the three news staffs, the study ranked the seven belief systems in order of overall agreement, using the Weaver and Wilhoit method to compare belief systems according to each one's relative importance. Weaver and Wilhoit defined the "importance" of each belief according to the percentage of respondents scoring in the "high" category of each measure.[30] To keep things simple, this study converted the range of scores on the scales to a 1-to-100 metric, then designated the "high" category to be 76 and above—the top quarter

28. Community Cynicism is a somewhat self-explanatory concept and should not be unfamiliar to the notion of traditional journalism. Cynicism among journalists may even be considered a romantic quality, and a healthy degree of cynicism is often described as a necessary trait for journalists. See Paul Starobin, "A Generation of Vipers: Journalists and the New Cynicism." Non-Consequentialism as a belief system would be related to the "detached" requirement of traditional journalism beliefs. Journalists remain detached if they refuse to place themselves inside the story, meaning inside the relationship between the reader and the news event. Detached journalists bear no responsibility for what happens after the information is delivered; they stand back from the community and report on what happens. A classic Non-Consequentialism value is found in the item, "My job is to get information into peoples' hands, and what they do with it is no concern of mine."

29. The survey involved whole populations, not samples, so the ANOVA procedures also are primarily illustrative. Differences observed are, by definition, differences between the entire populations, not samples. The comparisons of the alpha values and the results of the ANOVA analyses may help readers judge how "big" differences are, as a practical matter, and may hint at the likelihood that differences observed between these three news staffs also exist in the journalism industry in general. Twenty-eight percent of the *World-Herald* respondents are female, 26 percent of the *News and Observer* respondents are female, and 43 percent of the *Eagle* respondents are female. Also, 53 percent of the *World-Herald* respondents attended high school within their newspaper's primary circulation area. For the *News and Observer* staff, the figure was 13 percent; for the *Eagle*, 43 percent.

30. The "high" category was operationalized as the top quarter of the range of possible scores. For instance, on a scale ranging from 1 to 16, the "high" category would be represented by scores of 13 and above—the top quarter of the possible range.

of the range. For each news staff, the scale with the greatest share of respondents in the "high" category was labeled the dominant belief. According to Converse, the dominant belief is the most central and controls the overall ideology.

Following the Dillman method, the self-administered mail survey ran from July 14, 1994, to October 31, 1994, when data collection ended. The overall response rate was 75.1 percent—74.3 percent for *World-Herald* respondents, 70 percent for *News and Observer* respondents, and 82 percent for *Eagle* respondents.[31]

CONSISTENCY OF BELIEF SYSTEMS

The alpha coefficients revealed that Personal Public Journalism beliefs are well formed at all three news staffs, and are exceptionally consistent and well developed at the *Eagle,* where the alpha value topped .84.[32] On the Community Trust scale, attitudes are not well developed at any of the newspapers.

The *Eagle* and *World-Herald* staffs produced alphas of .70 or above— the threshold for a well-formed belief system—on the measure of Institutional Public Journalism beliefs, with the *Eagle* staff producing the highest alpha. Thus, *Eagle* staff members hold well-developed, consistent belief systems in two of the three innovative areas in question: Personal Public Journalism and Institutional Public Journalism.

Of the traditional belief systems prior research has documented so thoroughly, the Investigative/Interpretive belief is the most developed. Only the *Eagle* staff failed to produce an alpha value of .70, which could hint that, as public journalism constraint has increased at the *Eagle,* the traditionally strong Investigative/Interpretive belief system has weakened in its internal consistency.

31. Don A. Dillman, *Mail and Telephone Surveys* (New York: Wiley, 1978). Surveys were sent to all news staff members at the three newspapers who worked as general assignment or beat reporters, copy editors, sports writers, columnists, feature writers, business reporters, photographers, supervising editors, or government/public affairs reporters. Editors at the three newspapers cooperated by providing the home addresses of all employees eligible to take part in the survey. At each newspaper, editors posted a notice and circulated a memo that staff members would be receiving a survey from researchers at the University of North Carolina at Chapel Hill; the memo also explained that participation was voluntary and not a condition of employment. In all, there were 148 eligible respondents at the *World-Herald,* 150 at the *News and Observer,* and 128 at the *Eagle.*

32. For a discussion on the use of Cohen's test, calculations of constraint levels, and a list of all the alpha values, see Bare, "Toward a Definition of Public Journalism," 90–113.

On the Community Cynicism scale, *Eagle* staff members produced the highest alpha, one that approached the .70 threshold. The *Eagle* staff produced the only alpha value above .70 on the Non-Consequentialism belief measure, at .77. On these two belief systems, evidence of internally consistent attitudes at the *Eagle* indicates that as the paper has adopted public journalism it has become increasingly aware of and sensitive to potentially competing forces—Community Cynicism and Non-Consequentialism.

STAFF ATTITUDES TOWARD JOURNALISM AND COMMUNITY

The three news staffs differed greatly on two of the three public journalism scores.[33] Members of the *Eagle* staff scored significantly higher than staff members from the other newspapers on the measure of the importance of Personal Public Journalism tenets, which means *Eagle* staff members placed greater importance than their colleagues on their opportunities to help people in their community and to solve local problems. Also, the *Eagle* staff scored highest on the measure of Institutional Public Journalism beliefs. Thus, the *Eagle* staff was in strongest agreement with ideals such as, "My newspaper has an obligation to help the community find ways to solve problems."

There were no significant differences between the three news staffs on measures of two traditional journalism beliefs: Investigative/Interpretive and Information Dissemination. But *News and Observer* staff members scored significantly higher than *Eagle* staff members on the measures of the Adversarial belief.

On the Community Cynicism belief system measure, staff members from both the *News and Observer* and the *Eagle* scored significantly lower than staff members from the *World-Herald*, so Community Cynicism scores were highest at the most traditional newspaper. Each news staff differed significantly from the others on the Non-Consequentialism

33. All of the observed differences generally held for all control groups. However, for the measures of Personal Public Journalism and Institutional Public Journalism, differences that existed between the news staffs grew even larger among women staff members, primarily because women at the *Eagle* scored particularly high on the two public journalism scales. So there appears to be nothing unique to women in general that is relevant to public journalism, but there may be something about being a woman *and* working for the *Eagle* that is important to the adoption of public journalism and the rejection of adversarial beliefs.

scale, with the *Eagle* staff, the only group to hold highly constrained attitudes on the measure, scoring lowest.

As Table 1 shows, the dominant belief system for the *World-Herald* and *News and Observer* staffs remains the Investigative/Interpretive belief, which fits with the findings of Weaver and Wilhoit and matches the industry's conventional wisdom.[34] But contrary to previous findings concerning the newspaper industry, Institutional Public Journalism emerges as the dominant belief system at the *Eagle*. It is not so much a case of *Eagle* staff ranking low on Investigative/Interpretive beliefs; the staff simply ranked especially high on the Institutional Public Journalism belief measure. *Eagle* staff members strongly agree that their newspaper, and news professionals elsewhere, have a responsibility to care about and help solve local problems. This stands out as the core ideal in Merritt's public journalism work and is likely the key belief driving the public journalism movement throughout the U.S. newspaper industry.

CONCLUSIONS

Public Journalism as a Belief System

Based on the reliability analysis, there is strong evidence that Personal Public Journalism exists as a well-formed, consistent belief system at the *World-Herald*, the *News and Observer* and, particularly, at the *Eagle*, but the belief is not especially important to any of the news staffs.[35] There was no evidence of a well-developed Community Trust belief system at any of the papers.

The reliability analysis also produced strong evidence that Institutional Public Journalism exists as a well-formed and highly consistent belief system at the *Eagle*, and the *Eagle* staff scored highest on measures of Institutional Public Journalism ideals. In fact, Institutional Public Journalism ranked as the dominant belief system only at the *Eagle*.

---

34. The values presented in Table 1 represent the percentage of respondents scoring in the "high" category—76 to 100 on the new metric—on the eight belief system measures in this study.

35. The alpha produced by *Eagle* staff members for the Personal Public Journalism measure (alpha = .8410) was the highest alpha coefficient for any news staff on any of the belief systems measured in the study.

Table 1. The percentage of respondents scoring in the "high" category on each belief system measure.

Weaver and Wilhoit National Data 1982–83		World-Herald staff 1994		News & Observer staff 1994		Eagle staff 1994	
Investigative / Interpretive	62	Investigative / Interpretive	69	Investigative / Interpretive	71	Institutional Public Journalism	77
Information Dissemination	51	Information Dissemination	66	Institutional Public Journalism	60	Investigative / Interpretive	60
Adversarial	17	Institutional Public Journalism	46	Information Dissemination	51	Information Dissemination	60
		Community Trust	40	Community Trust	43	Community Trust	46
		Adversarial	14	Personal Public Journalism	18	Personal Public Journalism	29
		Personal Public Journalism	13	Adversarial	17	Adversarial	09
		Non-Consequentialism	10	Non-Consequentialism	02	Non-Consequentialism	05
		Community Cynicism	—	Community Cynicism	—	Community Cynicism	—

A NEW STRATEGY

The relative prominence of Institutional Public Journalism at all three papers indicates that the underlying values of public journalism are not necessarily new. Traditional news staffs most likely have always held variations of public journalism beliefs, though the attitudes likely were not as intense, organized, or important as revered investigative/interpretive journalism ideals. It is reasonable to suppose that these values existed in the past but earlier research simply failed to uncover the evidence of them. Nevertheless, if Institutional Public Journalism beliefs have long been a part of news staff ideologies, there is still something new happening in Wichita.

The evidence points to three findings. First, public journalism manifests itself primarily in the form of Institutional Public Journalism (not Personal Public Journalism or Community Trust). Second, while Institutional Public Journalism beliefs are not new to news staffs, public journalism ideals probably rank lower in importance at traditional papers. At the *Eagle,* Institutional Public Journalism stands as the dominant belief system; the belief is less intense and less important elsewhere. With no prior attitude measures from the *Eagle,* it is impossible to know whether the *Eagle* has adopted a new belief system or has always been radically different from the industry norm. However, all available information supports the former conclusion over the latter.

Third, the presence of a new dominant belief system at the *Eagle* likely altered the paper's overall ideology. Because conflicts between belief systems are expected to be resolved in favor of the core belief, Institutional Public Journalism attitudes would be expected to force change at the *Eagle.* Thus, the factor that sets the *Eagle* apart is that its newsroom value decisions appear to be driven by Institutional Public Journalism.

The results support the argument to study public journalism as a belief system, instead of focusing only on editorial content examples and journalistic practices. In fact, the results not only confirm that a public journalism belief system exists today but also, when taken in combination with arguments about traditional journalism, tend to support the notion that a version of public journalism has always been a part of the newsroom culture.

Traditional Journalism Belief Systems

The Investigative/Interpretive belief system is well developed at the *World-Herald* and *News and Observer,* as predicted by prior research findings. However, the results differ from past research in two ways. First, the Investigative/Interpretive belief is not universally dominant; for the *Eagle,* the Institutional Public Journalism belief system is strongest. Second, for *Eagle* staff members, the Investigative/Interpretive belief—the foundation of newspaper ideology—is moderately consistent and well developed, at best.

Thus, for *Eagle* staff members, Investigative/Interpretive attitudes are substantially weaker than public journalism beliefs. It may be that when a news staff adopts a new highly organized belief system as its dominant ideal, old attitudes are diluted in consistency and importance.[36]

The Information Dissemination scale ranked second most dominant for *World-Herald* staff members, and third for the *News and Observer* and *Eagle,* but Information Dissemination attitudes were inconsistent and poorly organized. A relatively small share of journalists at all three papers ranked high on the measure of Adversarial beliefs, just as Weaver and Wilhoit found.

Community Cynicism and Non-Consequentialism

The *World-Herald* staff scored significantly higher than the two other staffs on the Community Cynicism measure. Each newspaper differed significantly from the others on the Non-Consequentialism measure, with the *World-Herald* scoring highest, the *News and Observer* second highest, and the *Eagle* staff lowest. This is the reverse of the rank order of the staffs on the Institutional Public Journalism measure.

Both beliefs are incongruent with public journalism ideals, and the *Eagle's* low scores on the measures tend to indicate that adopting public journalism pushes staff members away from the traditional model of detached, cynical, let-the-chips-fall-where-they-may journalism. *Eagle* staff members strongly favor a model in which journalists care about using the paper's position in the community to help solve local problems.

All this is not negative news for the *World-Herald;* the findings represent observed differences, not judgments. A news staff that pursues

36. In a one-shot survey such as this, it is impossible to know whether Investigative/Interpretive beliefs ever were highly constrained at the *Eagle,* but it is appropriate to conclude that today's *Eagle* staff members hold attitudes toward the Investigative/Interpretive press function that are less constrained than the two peer newspapers measured here and less constrained than can be predicted by known industry norms.

traditional journalism would be disappointed with results that placed it anywhere but lowest on Institutional Public Journalism and highest on Non-Consequentialism. The results do confirm, however, that belief systems other than those noted in prior research are important.

Further, Community Cynicism and Non-Consequentialism are likely to be primary points of conflict when public journalism beliefs are introduced to a news staff. At all three papers, the Community Cynicism scores and the Non-Consequentialism scores were negatively correlated with the Institutional Public Journalism and Personal Public Journalism scores. The negative relationships between the public journalism scales and Non-Consequentialism were particularly strong.[37]

When public journalism is introduced, or when dormant public journalism values are declared important by management, Converse's theory holds that there will be conflict between opposing belief systems. Most likely, the conflict will pit Institutional Public Journalism attitudes against Community Cynicism and Non-Consequentialism. In other instances, Institutional Public Journalism may conflict with Investigative/Interpretive ideals.

When Institutional Public Journalism becomes most central to the news staff's ideology, as with the *Eagle* staff, it will force changes to occur with the incongruent elements of Community Cynicism, Non-Consequentialism, and Investigative/Interpretive beliefs. The process involves softening opposition to involved, solution-oriented journalism that aims to improve public life.

If the experience of the *Eagle* serves as a guide, adopting Institutional Public Journalism as a dominant belief system requires a news staff to reject Community Cynicism and Non-Consequentialism. While not wholly rejecting other traditional objectives, staffs will be forced to deemphasize the relative importance of Investigative/Interpretive beliefs and Adversarial beliefs. Those in the newspaper industry interested in adopting and implementing public journalism must be prepared for these conflicts and trade-offs.

37. For example, for the *Eagle*, the correlation between the Institutional Public Journalism scale and Community Cynicism was –.21; the correlation between the Institutional Public Journalism scale and Non-Consequentialism was –.60; the correlation between the Personal Public Journalism scale and Community Cynicism was –.23, and the correlation between the Personal Public Journalism scale and Non-Consequentialism was –.36.

Links to Content and Practices

Now that a measure of public journalism beliefs has been established, the professional and scientific community should move forward with a second-generation research agenda that aims to determine how public journalism beliefs affect news content and journalistic practices. The issues have been a primary point of contention among public journalism advocates and opponents, and rightfully so, because belief changes that have no perceptible impact are of little value.

Changes in attitudes should precede changes in the kind of practices used by the staff and in the type of content produced. Thus, researchers should develop measures for the relationship between staff beliefs and editorial content, and between staff beliefs and professional practices.

For example, when asked how important it is to them personally, in their daily work, to explain "to readers why it's important they vote," *Eagle* staff members scored significantly higher than *News and Observer* staff members and higher than *World-Herald* staff members.[38] Thus, there may be an association between staff attitudes toward public journalism and the amount of news content published that explains to readers why it is important for them to vote.

Another example: When asked to agree or disagree with the statement, "When my newspaper does a story on complicated problems such as drug abuse, crime or education, it should include information on how readers can find help in these areas," *Eagle* staff members, along with *News and Observer* staff members, scored significantly higher than *World-Herald* staff members. Overall, the *Eagle* staff scored highest. So there may also be a link between staff attitudes toward public journalism and the amount of news content published that explains how readers may obtain assistance with complex problems.

New or Not New?

The nastiest arguments are those in which combatants on both sides of the fight can stake reasonable claims to being right, which is the case with the public journalism debate. It is the primary reason the arguing persists. Critics are right, in part, when they say there is nothing new

---

38. On a 1 to 4 scale, with 1 being Not Really Important, and 4 being Extremely Important, the *Eagle* staff had an average score of 2.62; the *World-Herald,* 2.29; the *News and Observer,* 2.26.

about journalism intended to ignite community-based efforts to help solve local problems. Even at a tradition-bound newspaper such as the *World-Herald,* public journalism belief systems are in place.

However—and this is the big however—public journalism advocates such as Merritt are also correct when they claim they are doing something novel. It is not the *discovery* of public journalism techniques that is new; it is how intensely the beliefs are developed and *how far up the priority ladder* public journalism beliefs are pushed that is innovative.

In most situations, the sets of belief systems that make up a newspaper's overall ideology coexist peacefully. But on occasion, a situation in the newsroom or the community highlights conflict between opposing beliefs. Because the problem must be resolved in favor of the belief system that ranks highest on the priority ladder, newsroom conflict traditionally has been resolved in favor of the dominant investigative reporting ideals. By contrast, the *Eagle* staff would resolve conflict in favor of public journalism ideals. So newspapers that differ just slightly in the way the staffs prioritize beliefs may differ dramatically in mission.

Contribution to Knowledge

The study succeeds in defining Institutional Public Journalism as a well-organized belief system that is dominant at the *Eagle.* Personal Public Journalism was also defined as a highly consistent belief system, but it ranked lower in relative importance.

Despite the obvious limitations of a one-shot survey, there are three factors that tend to support the idea that what has happened at the *Eagle* represents change. First, *Eagle* staff members hold beliefs that differ from known industry standards. Second, *Eagle* staff members hold beliefs that differ from the staffs of two peer news organizations— and those peer staffs hold beliefs that, in large part, do match industry standards. Third, the findings meet the standards of face validity in that they match what would be expected based on the mission statements, journalistic philosophies, and publicly stated objectives of the three newspapers.

The lasting conclusion is not that public journalism beliefs are entirely new, only that the measure is new, and that the *Eagle* has emphasized, intensified, and organized public journalism in an innovative way. This finding is important considering that the future of public journalism may turn on whether traditionalists recognize that the aims of public journalism fit beautifully with old-fashioned values. "In a time of information overload," Meyer explains, the media watchdog can serve society best if it understands that "the new scarce good is public attention. Focusing the light of public attention on any one problem long enough to spark discourse leading to a solution is the object of public journalism."[39]

39. Philip Meyer, "Defining Public Journalism: Discourse Leading to Solutions," 3.

II

TAKING THE
MEASURE OF
PUBLIC
JOURNALISM

5

PUBLIC JOURNALISM AND THE 1992 ELECTIONS

RICK THAMES

No one had coined the phrase "public journalism" when we began rethinking our ways at the *Charlotte Observer* in 1991. There was no debate yet over whether this was more about journalism or more about business. It would be years before people began talking in terms of a trend or a movement. We were simply trying to commit better journalism. We still are. For us, the idea grew out of our frustration over the sorry state of the political debate, dating back to the 1988 presidential election. For months, George Bush and Michael Dukakis hacked at one another over manufactured "issues" such as flag-burning and the furlough of convicted murderer Willie Horton. And the media? We dutifully followed them to the flag factories and prison gates, reporting these and other pseudo-matters as if they had something to do with the future of the country.

Of course, they had virtually nothing to do with it. Not surprisingly, voters stayed away from the polls in droves. Had we journalists been duped? We couldn't guarantee that candidates would speak to the issues that mattered to the public. But didn't we have a responsibility to pursue the information voters needed, anyway? The final blow for my editor, Rich Oppel, came in North Carolina's bitterly divisive race for the U.S. Senate in 1990—incumbent Jesse Helms versus former Charlotte Mayor Harvey Gantt. We capped our traditional coverage of that campaign with front-page play of some ill-fated horse race polls.

"We'd covered the election very well, in a conventional way," said Oppel, now editor of the *Austin American-Statesman*. "Our polls consistently showed that Harvey Gantt was going to win and, of course, he didn't. Readers were very angry with us." In fact, citizens were angry about the whole political process. What we journalists initially reported as voter apathy was actually a growing sense of alienation. Millions of people had tuned us out and dismissed elections as irrelevant to their lives.

Obviously, conventional ways of covering politics didn't cut it anymore. What might? In St. Petersburg, Florida, some folks at a journalism think tank, the Poynter Institute for Media Studies, were asking the same question. Their worry was twofold. Obviously, the country was in trouble if a significant number of citizens remained disconnected from politics. But newspapers were in trouble, too. After all, newspapers exist in large part to provide people with the information they need to participate in civic life. Could it be that declining readership of newspapers was tied to the decline of civic life in America? By 1991, Poynter's staff was seeking solutions. Two events, in particular, inspired them.

One was the work of the *Wichita Eagle,* which had begun focusing election coverage on the concerns of voters, starting with its coverage of the 1990 race for Kansas governor. Readers responded enthusiastically, and indicated they read more political news. The other event was a speech in which *Washington Post* political columnist David Broder, a widely respected journalist, upbraided the press for neglecting voters. "We have to try to distance ourselves from the people we write about, the politicians and political consultants," Broder said, "and move ourselves closer to the people we write for, the voters and potential voters."

The Poynter Institute decided to experiment with new approaches to political coverage. It began looking for a newspaper and TV station to be partners. "We didn't want to find ourselves planning another seminar in 1992 in which journalists sat around, asking yet again, How did we let them do this to us?" said Edward Miller, an associate of the institute and a driving force behind a newsroom experiment. The *Observer* heard about Poynter's plans and volunteered. Charlotte's ABC affiliate, WSOC-TV, signed on as the *Observer*'s partner. That's where I entered the picture. I had been the *Observer*'s government editor in the 1990 elections. Oppel said he wanted me to lead an effort, with Poynter's help, to change our approach to covering politics. How? I asked. "We're looking for coverage that's driven not by the candidates," he said, "but by the voters."

Wait a minute, I thought. Aren't elections about the candidates and their agenda? At least, that defined political coverage as I'd always known it. If we stop doing that, what exactly do we cover? What's our compass? Miller already had that much figured out. Find out what the election should be about, according to average citizens, he said. That's your compass. I've since imagined it as like looking through opposite ends of a pipe. Most journalists peer at the electorate from a distance, through the same end as the candidates and their handlers. No wonder that we write so much that best suits a newsletter for political insiders. The *Observer* would look through the other end for a change, operating from the perspective of voters.

This approach just might reduce our unwitting role as messengers of the candidates' distortions and distractions. Even better, if we managed to draw the candidates out on these "real people" issues, voters had a shot at getting the information they needed to make sound decisions.

A key to this change and everything we've done since in the name of public journalism is this belief: Our nation is only as strong as its civic life, and journalists have a responsibility to inform in ways that allow citizens to get involved in solving society's problems. Somehow, many journalists have drifted from this vital role. We've tended to align ourselves, instead, with this nation's power brokers, government insiders, and political theorists. Some of us go so far as to dismiss average citizens as a naive bunch who need to be saved from themselves. That view is very wrong. The collective wisdom of citizens built this nation—and has kept it on course for more than two hundred years. Why should journalists of the late twentieth century assume any differently?

I'm not suggesting that journalists stop thinking for themselves or give up their role as the community's conscience. We still poke and prod at the powers that be as necessary. We still take unpopular stands. But the public's point of view is a key piece in the puzzle that makes up reality in a democracy. Journalists who have that piece know more. The more they know, the better they can serve the public. "Public journalism is mostly about putting a wide-angle lens on our camera," said Jennie Buckner, who succeeded Oppel as *Observer* editor in 1993. "Searching for the fuller picture. Seeking out the whole story. Helping citizens see how they might fit into the picture." In that spirit, we designed our 1992 campaign coverage in a radically different way, relying largely on four components: issues polling, in-depth issues coverage, citizen involvement (in our coverage as well as the campaigns), and relentless pursuit of the candidates' issue positions.

ISSUES POLLING

Here is how we began to learn what the election was really about. Editors and reporters crafted a questionnaire solely about issues. KPC Research, a Charlotte-based subsidiary of Knight Publishing Co., then conducted telephone interviews in a fourteen-county region surrounding Charlotte (our partnership's readership/viewer area) in late December 1991 and early January 1992. The interviews with roughly one thousand residents helped us to identify a list of broadly based concerns that we came to call the Citizens' Agenda. We intentionally took the poll very early in the election year—still more than five months before the North Carolina primary. We wanted to discover citizens' concerns and publicize them before the spin doctors got in their licks. Average people would get a chance to contribute to the tone of the campaigns for a change. Topping citizens' concerns: the economy, taxes, health care, education, crime, the environment, and values. Now we had a road map for the real political landscape. We would build our coverage based largely on these findings, taking care to recheck at points for any shifts in concerns.

Polling, which can be expensive, isn't the only way to learn about real issues. Some media organizations get the job done with dozens of in-depth interviews with a cross section of the community. They organize representative panels of citizens willing to offer wisdom and advice throughout the campaign. They invite the general public to agree or disagree with their conclusions about election priorities. The important lesson for us was that you must listen closely, and then be prepared to hear some surprises along with those issues you would have expected. In January of 1992, for instance, we didn't expect Carolinians to be as anxious as they were about the economy. One out of four people we surveyed said they were worried they or someone in their family was about to lose their job. This was two months before the New Hampshire primary, and long before anyone said, "It's the economy, stupid."

We also kept picking up references to values: a sense of a nation adrift ethically, morally; staggering support for school prayer. No amount of newsroom brainstorming would have led us independently to prioritize values as a campaign issue. In fact, we doubted its significance even as voters kept bringing it up. Apparently, the Republicans also detected it in their polling. They attempted to connect with that concern through their "family values" campaign theme. In the end, most journalists chased after Gennifer Flowers but dismissed the values theme as a red herring. What could the president do to restore so-called "family values," whatever they were? Yet, concern over values was stronger than ever in 1996. By then, both parties were targeting Hollywood. There was a rush to own the issue of school prayer. Values were, and are, politically relevant, because the public said so. We just weren't listening.

REPORTING ON ISSUES THAT MATTER

Once we knew the concerns of voters, we wanted to do all we could to help them understand these complex issues and the potential solutions. We launched a six-week series of explanatory articles and graphics exploring the Citizens' Agenda—a piece at a time. To produce the best stories possible, we tapped into the expertise of reporters and editors who don't normally get involved in politics. Our medical reporter, for example, wrote about options in health care and assessed the candidates' plans. A business reporter and editor handled our stories about the deficit. A features reporter who writes about family issues explored questions of values. Our police and courts reporters wrote about crime. These reporters wrote with the authority essential for good explanatory journalism. Being political outsiders, they also offered a perspective more like that of most voters.

Their packages appeared on the front pages of six consecutive Sunday papers. Each package also directed readers to the front of our Perspective section, where we published a full-page graphic outlining candidates' positions on the issues in races for president, U.S. Senate, and governor. We hoped readers would become better informed about each issue on 1A, then move to the Perspective front to size up the candidates' stands for themselves. We published hundreds more issue-oriented stories in the coming months, often focusing on individual races and new campaign developments ("Candidate A proposed a flat tax Thursday. How does that affect you?"). For the general election, we produced another issues series, this time tied directly with a series of voter/issue forums broadcast on WSOC. We also revamped our coverage of the campaign trail so that it centered more on issues. We'd spend time, for example, talking to people who had heard the candidate's pitch. Did it connect? Did it have anything to do with their own concerns this election? What more would they like to know? Other times, we'd explore an issue the candidate alluded to in the speech, rather than just report the speech straight up. If it was a previously announced idea, we'd prepare in advance. If it was a new development, we'd double-team the story to get it in the next day's paper.

At the same time we raised the profile of our issues coverage, we placed less emphasis on the predictably empty campaign trail events, the dog-and-pony shows and the made-up issues. It would have been wrong to simply ignore these events. We weren't censors. But our deeper understanding of the public's actual information needs demanded that we rethink news values. The fact is, much of the clatter of the campaign was irrelevant. Anyone who filled 1A with that exercised poor news judgment. So, we designated an inside page—2A—to briefly report the twists and turns of the campaign. Here, horse race polls became news briefs. One candidate's insult of another might merit a mention. Photo opportunities found a hole only if there was space. Changes in campaign staffs might get a line of type. Even a good deal of the speculation about Gennifer Flowers and Bill Clinton's draft history appeared here, rather than on 1A.

Were we at serious risk of burying the news? We didn't think so. Substantial stories built on solid reporting still made their way to 1A. Readers easily found the rest on the second page. We did, however, send the public a signal about news judgment. I believe that readers who turned to 2A understood its insider nature. Here, on any given day, lurked both fact and fiction. And in most cases, they could count on 1A headlines being about real issues central to their concerns.

CITIZEN INVOLVEMENT

Newspapers invite political insiders to the election party all the time. Our pages are filled with their strategic objectives, assessments, and predictions. But we neglect the most influential guest of all—the American voter. Our issues poll was the first step toward returning citizens to their proper place in our coverage of the political process. Now we worked to keep them there throughout the campaign. We peppered our issues stories and campaign trail reports with citizen perspectives. We collected readers' questions in advance of candidates' visits and asked those questions, along with our own. When Pat Buchanan visited our newsroom, we put him before a group of voters instead of our editorial board. We sponsored a debate among candidates for governor and invited citizens to ask some of the questions. We regularly published readers' telephoned comments about campaign developments.

As reporters well know, thoughtful citizen input adds a time-consuming step to every story. We had to improve on the superficial "interviews-at-the-mall" routine if we were to weave quality perspective throughout our coverage. We found the innovation we needed in our Citizens' Panel. The panel consisted of every poll respondent who had agreed at the conclusion of the interview to continue advising the newspaper and TV station throughout the campaign. We had never asked respondents to stay with us this way. I assumed we'd be lucky if a third of them signed on. After all, these were folks selected at random. Many of them didn't read our newspaper and weren't even registered to vote.

To my surprise, more than five hundred of the one thousand respondents in our issues poll said they'd participate. Our pollster checked their demographics and found them to be remarkably similar to the actual sample. We now had people from all walks of life ready to talk to us about the issues. And we had more than names. We had a database that could provide us a list of citizens identified by age, job, income, education, marital status, and—most important—by the issues that mattered most and least to them.

Suddenly, reporters could turn to citizens nearly as easily as they could check with political insiders. Not surprisingly, the highly relevant viewpoints of average people began to crowd sterile political analysis out of their stories. Of course, involving citizens in our coverage meant little in the long run if they still sat out the election. So, we also encouraged them to take part in the political process. Mostly, this took the form of informational stories and graphics about voter registration: how to register in three easy steps; the deadline to register; how to get an absentee ballot; how to decipher the ballot. Again, we saw this as a public service. We provided useful information. On occasion, we became advocates. The *Observer* and WSOC sponsored voter registration booths for a day in their lobbies. As one registration deadline neared, we even published a how-to graphic that included a joint letter from *Observer* Editor Oppel and the county elections supervisor urging people to register. Perhaps the letter belonged on the editorial page (it and the graphic ran inside the local news section). On the other hand, if ever there was an appropriate activity to support on news pages, it probably is voting.

CHALLENGING CANDIDATES TO RESPOND

Candidates were free to raise any issue they chose. But citizens were telling us which issues they needed to know about, at minimum, to make a good decision on Election Day. We saw it as our responsibility to insist that candidates explain themselves on those matters. Each of more than three hundred candidates on the ballot—in races from president to school board—faced issues-oriented questions from *Observer* reporters. (In low-profile races, this amounted to filling out a questionnaire and submitting to a short follow-up interview by phone. In prominent contests, reporters often interviewed and reinterviewed at length.) We edited candidates' positions for clarity and presented them to readers in easy-to-follow graphics that accompanied issue stories and candidate profiles. Some candidates loved this consumer-friendly approach. Some fought it. Then U.S. Senator Terry Sanford was among the first to object. A Democrat who faced no opposition in the spring primary, Sanford said he saw no reason to reveal his positions until voters chose his Republican opponent. We included him in the graphic on Senate candidates anyway. Beneath his photo, an editor's note explained why he said he would not respond. That note and the considerable chunk of white space beneath it led Sanford to reverse his decision two weeks later.

Republican senatorial candidate Sue Myrick (now a U.S. House member) was among those candidates who complained that their positions on an issue could not be summed up in twenty-five or thirty words. She, too, changed her mind after a few weeks of white space—and her position statement for the graphic, interestingly enough, needed no editing to fit nicely in the allotted hole, with room to spare. The more we challenged candidates in this way, the more we understood the raw power of voter-driven coverage. It's easy for candidates to dismiss the questions of journalists, even to turn the situation to their advantage. But candidates dodge the issues and questions of voters at great peril.

Even the campaign staff of the president recognized this. George Bush dropped in on Faith, North Carolina, on July 4, 1992. The small town's patriotic celebration provided the perfect backdrop for photos of the president eating barbecue and sliding into home plate during a softball game. It quickly became apparent to us that a photo opportunity was pretty much all it was intended to be—even though his visit lasted several hours. Bush's campaign turned down our request for an interview and rejected our invitation to meet with a group of voters to answer questions. No time, they said. We replied that we planned to ask readers for questions, anyway, and would publish what they asked. Bush's people were stunned. "You can't just publish unanswered questions like that," said the second or third person who got on the phone with me. Yes we can, I said. If the president can find time to fly into our state and play softball, readers would think it reasonable for him to spend a few minutes clearing up issues important to voters. It was, in fact, exactly how we had handled every other presidential candidate who had campaigned in the Carolinas. And most—including Bob Kerry, Pat Buchanan, Tom Harkin, Ross Perot, and Bill Clinton—had taken time to answer readers' questions. In the end, Bush's folks faxed answers to three questions "cleared by the White House" in advance of the Faith visit. Our coverage of the event included those answers, along with twenty or so unanswered questions. In a note to readers, we explained: "We have forwarded your unanswered questions to the Bush campaign and will publish any answers we receive." This was not exactly the coverage his campaign had worked to choreograph. But it was a lot more enlightening for voters. And later, Bush's campaign did send more answers.

These experiences taught us that it's also news when candidates don't address voter concerns. After all, this wasn't the media's agenda. These were matters that voters said they needed cleared up if they were to make a good decision. Candidates who refused to do so were, in effect, trying to deceive their way into office.

We warn people when elected officials conceal matters that are the public's business. Why shouldn't we treat this form of public deception the same way? As you might expect, little of this or anything else we did that election year came naturally. Many times, we'd look quizzically at one another in the newsroom and marvel aloud that we were about to zig when every other respectable news organization in the country had just zagged. Managing Editor Frank Barrows (then deputy managing editor) often joined me and others by the national desk as we debated how to handle the latest manufactured issue to pop up on the wire services. "We said we would do politics differently this year," Barrows said after we made one especially tough call bucking conventional wisdom. "I'd rather stay true to that and risk making an occasional mistake than to look back a year from now and kick ourselves for what we didn't have the courage to do."

Criticism came from all corners. Competing reporters ridiculed our own for asking voters' questions at press conferences. Many folks inside our newsroom questioned the absence of stories about the horse race and political strategies. One reporter not involved in the coverage—referred to internally as the Poynter Project—derisively termed it the "Pointless Project." But the twenty or so reporters, editors, and artists who worked closely on the effort (known almost everywhere else as the Charlotte Project) quickly became convinced that this, indeed, was better journalism. "It gave us a focus by giving us a new way of looking at things," said veteran *Observer* political reporter Jim Morrill. "It was liberating to realize that candidates were no longer the ones who controlled the agenda and pulled our strings."

EVALUATING THE EFFORT

Was there anything to suggest that citizens felt the same way? It certainly appears so, considering the number who got involved in our coverage and later went to the polls. However, attempts to measure the project's impact through empirical data produced decidedly mixed results. First, the promising anecdotes. More than twenty-four hundred citizens contacted the newspaper with questions for candidates, comments on political developments, and solutions to the various problems we explored through our issues stories. Roughly one thousand more agreed to advise us through our Citizens Panel (we began with the five hundred volunteers in our first poll and kept adding names with each subsequent poll). In sheer numbers, voters who turned out for the general election in Charlotte's home county (Mecklenburg) exceeded the all-time high by 27 percent. Adjusted for population growth, Mecklenburg's turnout (56.9 percent of the voting-age population) represented an increase of 8.1 percentage points over 1988. It also exceeded turnout at the state (50.4 percent) and national (55.2 percent) levels.[1]

Any number of factors unrelated to the newspaper could have contributed. But Bill Culp, the county's elections director for twenty-seven years, was convinced that the changed coverage was a significant factor. "The coverage was also responsible for a 20 percent increase in phone calls to our office for more information," he said. "Callers would say, 'I read such and such in the *Observer.*'" On the other hand, large-population counties in North Carolina whose media generally stuck

1. Previous published references to the Charlotte Project (e.g., Miller, *The Charlotte Project*) give the Mecklenburg turnout as 60 percent of the voting-age population. Election officials released the smaller figure after discovering an error in their tabulation.

to traditional coverage methods also saw increases in turnout. Wake County, home of Raleigh, the state capital, gained 12.5 percentage points. Guilford County gained 8.7, Forsyth County 7.9, and Cumberland County 4.9. Overall, Mecklenburg's percentage-point gain ranked twenty-ninth highest among the state's one hundred counties. There were other attempts to scientifically measure impact. Poynter's series of tracking surveys turned up both positives and negatives. Pollsters looked for changes in the use of the local media, as well as any change in attitude toward the media. On the positive side they found that *Observer* readers, compared to readers of other area newspapers:

• Experienced a disproportionate increase in interest in politics during the campaign.

• Were more positive about the newspaper's helpfulness in making them feel a part of the political process.

• Felt more of a connection between coverage of the candidates and the issues affecting them personally.

On the negative side:

• *Observer* readers still were more likely to sense bias in politics stories than readers of other area newspapers.

• *Observer* readers' perceived understanding of state and local politics actually went down. Researchers think the newspaper's heightened coverage of the presidential race played a role. It could be that our focus on that race overshadowed our work on the state and local races.

Poynter also met three times with live focus groups—one male and one female to talk about the newspaper's coverage. "The focus groups reinforced the belief that readers were noticing many of the innovations in the *Observer,*" Ed Miller wrote in a report on the project. "What's more, there were indications that readers were using these new features to get more involved in the campaign." For example:

• The groups liked the straightforward issues graphics, praising them repeatedly. "It's not biased; it gives you the facts," said one. "I clipped them all," said another.

• Readers, especially women, appreciated the use of average people in the coverage. "I can identify with these people," one said. "These are our neighbors." Said another: "It made me more aware of what I should be thinking about . . . It made me want to be more informed and involved."

• They appreciated the coverage of potential solutions and agreed that newspapers should do more than just highlight problems.

All told, the evaluation's contradictory signals didn't discourage us. We assumed all along that it would be foolhardy to expect dramatic changes in readers' attitudes after only a year's worth of change. After all, we've spent decades alienating the public with our traditional approaches. We've got a lot of mending to do. I think it's safe to say that we're at least moving in the right direction. A lot of other journalists feel the same way. In 1994, dozens of newspapers built on what we had learned, tying their coverage more firmly to the needs and concerns of voters. Many more did so in 1996. At the *Observer,* we've expanded our public journalism to include other topics, including education and crime. Our most extensive effort, "Taking Back Our Neighborhoods," inspired more than eight hundred individuals and groups to get involved in solving the problems of ten inner-city neighborhoods plagued with crime. Some still fret that we are treading a slippery slope. They are right. But the same can be said for almost any form of journalism we practice. Think of what would become of the investigative reporter who decided that anything goes. For that matter, imagine the outcome for any reporter who strayed from basic principles on even the most routine daily story. Our slope is a bit slicker at the moment because we're still learning. That makes many of us uneasy, as well it should. What saves us is the same thing that insulates us from disaster every day we practice journalism of any form: our judgment, grounded in our unwavering values: truth, fairness, accuracy, objectivity, public service. In fact, we believe that public journalism, done well, serves only to enhance those values. "Journalism that arises from the needs of the public and is of true relevance and service to the community has been, historically, a bedrock of the best newspapering," said *Observer* Managing Editor Barrows. "Public journalism is a concerted effort to refocus on that mission."

6

PUBLIC JOURNALISM AND NEWSROOM STRUCTURE

The Columbia, S.C., Model

SCOTT JOHNSON

Evangelists of the public journalism movement, notably Kansas journalist Davis "Buzz" Merritt, Jr. and New York University professor Jay Rosen, warn that newspapers and democracy are in big trouble. These institutions may die unless citizens and journalists work together in the search for solutions to the issues facing communities, they say. It is critical, therefore, that news organizations reconnect with their alienated communities first by listening to what the people think, and then by helping them come to judgment on the best way to solve the problems.

Opponents contend that public journalism crosses the line between objective reporting and advocacy, further imperiling the profession's credibility. Public journalism threatens traditional values in the field and embraces boosterism, they argue.

While the debate rages, newspapers from Florida to Washington State are embracing the principles of public journalism and practicing, in different ways, what Rosen and Merritt preach.

This chapter explores the ability of one such newspaper, the *State* in Columbia, South Carolina, to achieve many of the goals of public journalism through a fundamental restructuring of its newsroom and reporting processes. This restructuring of traditional departments into quality teams or "circles" flattens the management hierarchy. It groups reporters and editors around issues rather than beats based on institutions or government buildings. These "circles" follow the agendas of communities rather than bureaucracies, a major tenet of public journalism. The stories and projects cited in this essay will demonstrate how newsroom restructuring has changed the culture of news coverage at the *State,* moving it away from reporting that relies on the "clash of extremes" to that which also seeks common ground and the core values at issue in community decision-making.

For that reason and others, newsrooms interested in doing public journalism on a daily basis would be well served to consider a similar model of newsroom governance. "Nonhierarchical newsrooms are almost mandatory for good public journalism," said Gil Thelen, executive editor of the *State.*

PUBLIC JOURNALISM AND NEWSROOM RESTRUCTURING

Newsroom restructuring has made the *State* more responsive to the citizenry that public journalism seeks to reinvigorate, the newspaper's leaders say, for two main reasons: common goals and empowerment.

Common goals

One of the core principles behind the internal reorganization was the desire to refocus coverage away from beats based on faceless institutions to issues about which citizens care deeply. Newsroom beat structures typically deploy reporters to buildings where traditional sources of news and information can be found—city hall, the courthouse, the State House. As a result, the coverage may reflect the agendas of bureaucrats and government insiders rather than the public at large. The only contact many reporters have with regular citizens is at a public hearing, when conflict and extremes dominate debate.

The "circle" system challenges reporters at the *State* to cover issues first and the politicians and bureaucrats only as they affect the concerns of everyday citizens.

"You can cover the State House by covering committees and focusing on the processes inside, or you can cover it without ever going to the building and focusing on the people outside," said Steve Brook, a news editor at the *State.* "We are making more of an effort to start outside.

It's not top down, where we say here's what the legislature wants to do, but bottom up, where we say here's what the community says it wants the legislature to do."

Before restructuring, the newspaper determined its list of key issues facing the General Assembly each year based primarily on a survey of lawmakers and information provided by lobbyists and agency administrators. Today, that same survey is published in the newspaper and generates thousands of responses. Reporters conduct follow-up interviews with respondents whose lives are affected by a particular issue. A citizens' agenda is then crafted for the General Assembly and monitored throughout the six-month legislative session.

This renewed focus on how citizens, rather than political careers and government processes, are affected helps the *State* see news differently and makes public journalism a daily undertaking.

"In theory, we are talking more to people and removing the focus from buildings. We are putting more emphasis on how people are affected by the decisions enacted for them. That should make the newsroom more responsive," Brook said.

Empowerment

Newsroom restructuring has embraced empowerment and bottom-up management.

A recent survey showed one in five journalists expects to leave the field within a few years. The trend raises serious questions about the newsroom working environment. Also, traditional, hierarchical newsroom structures may not provide the resourcefulness required to succeed in today's marketplace.

Newsrooms have changed little over the past century. Their command-and-control organizational structures were designed for production efficiency and operate much like Henry Ford–era assembly lines. The typical newsroom consists of a news desk, copy desk, city desk, business desk, sports desk, features desk, photo department, and graphics or art department. The organization clearly reflects how news is assembled and processed, thus clarifying and defining the tasks and responsibilities of each employee on each desk. Authority flows down the supervisory chain in a classic line-authority model. Information that flows up and down this chain of command reflects a high centralization of power and authority. While decisions can be made rapidly at the top levels, the level of group satisfaction and group commitment can be low. The standard way of doing things in newsrooms "goes against creativity and innovation," Thelen said.

Restructuring the newsroom into an organization based on teams or "circles" replaces the traditional command-and-control system with one based on participatory management. Meetings are open and input is not only sought, but expected, on everything from story ideas to budget and hiring decisions. A circular pattern of communication exists similar to that which can be found in task forces or committees. While committees often are slower to make decisions and demand greater communication and people skills, they produce higher levels of group satisfaction and commitment.

Developing a willingness to collaborate internally is necessary if journalists are going to understand collaboration within the broader community they serve, Thelen said. "We have tried to create a deliberative newsroom where we model democratic behavior. There is collaboration, problem solving, and negotiation. That is a mirror of the process outside in the community. It gets to the heart of what community deliberation is," he said. "We have tried to practice the democratic arts. Unless we know how to do that within the newsroom, it is hard to explore that within the community."

THE "CIRCLE" SYSTEM: CREATION AND IMPLEMENTATION

Newsroom restructuring and the circle system began at the *State* in 1991 with a simple truth: Too many good stories were falling through the cracks of a beat structure that looked comprehensive on paper but didn't work very well. There was little collaboration. Each staff and department focused primarily on getting its pages or sections completed on time. Reporting responsibilities had never been redrafted to account for recent downsizing and attrition.

The structure, crafted following the merger in 1988 with the *Columbia Record,* was traditional. The metro editor supervised reporters who covered city hall, county council, and cops and courts in the Columbia area. The government staff focused on the General Assembly, politics, and state agencies. The state editor ran the bureaus. The features, business, Neighbors, and sports staffs focused on putting out their own sections, occasionally contributing to the front page.

In some areas, however, the structure impeded news coverage. Education was divided among several reporters and three editors, each with his or her own priorities and agenda. State House and local government reporters rarely discussed the impact of legislation on cities and counties. The walls between departments were not easily scaled.

The groundwork for change was laid during a series of team-building exercises in early 1991 involving newsroom leaders. Senior editors and department heads wrestled with the *State*'s mission and personality—issues that had gone unresolved since the merger. Working together for the first time as a management team, they crafted a statement of newsroom values that laid to rest past sins while charting a path for the future.

The document acknowledged that the *State* had been held back by the perception or reality that it was a place where:

• Promises were not kept.
• Professional advancement was hindered by favoritism, and where longevity counted for more than merit.
• Some jobs and positions were regarded as more important than others.
• Ideas were limited by who you are and what you do.
• Politeness and conformity were placed above helpful and creative confrontation.
• Change was feared and avoided.
• Moving up and on in journalism was not encouraged.

In contrast, the editors agreed, the *State* of the future would be a place where:

• High standards for excellence in journalism prevail.
• Talent, energy, creativity, and innovation are valued and rewarded.
• Honesty is central to communication and relationships.
• Expectations are clear and responsibilities are shared.
• Respect for each person's abilities and contributions is the norm.
• Open discussion of ideas and operations is encouraged.
• A flexible newsroom structure and work hours are designed to best benefit the newspaper and the individual.
• People are rewarded for remaining and excelling at the *State* and are supported in pursuing other opportunities if they choose.
• People have fun.

Beyond these core newsroom values, the newsroom leadership developed a set of guiding principles that would underpin restructuring.

Many of the principles reflect the goals of public journalism. These fundamental principles are:

• The newspaper's coverage needs to better reflect the community and be more useful to readers. "We should pay attention to what readers are telling us. We should become a model capital city newspaper, increasing our emphasis on six key issues: education, race relations, environment, poverty, effective governance and economic development."

• The traditional newsroom organization, built on institutions, generally takes the newspaper away from the interests of readers. "We should explore the culture of Columbia as an anthropologist would, then broaden our interests to the state, region, and nation. But begin always with people, not institutions."

• News does not develop along territorial boundaries established within the newspaper's organization. "We should work as teams and be flexible, beginning with the notion that each reporter is a general assignments reporter first, a specialist second. Each team should contribute to the success of the entire newsroom. Interests and responsibilities often will be shared. We should have no foregone conclusions about what the story will end up saying or where it will appear in the newspaper."

Work on newsroom restructuring began in earnest in June 1991. Department editors started discussing the idea with their staffs. Over the next several weeks, a number of goals were identified. It was agreed that through restructuring, the newsroom would:

• Broaden the definition of news. Figure out what is missing from the daily news report and include it in the new structure.

• Zero-base all beats and coverage. Determine what we are covering that we should drop, and what we are neglecting that should be added.

• Knock down the walls between departments and staffs. Build a newsroom that's driven by ideas rather than production deadlines.

• Become more flexible and responsive. Create teams with expertise in a topic and build in "structural redundancy," so that coverage does not evaporate just because one person is out.

• Establish clear lines of responsibility and accountability.

• Create a new editing structure that improves stories at every step in their evolution. Ideas should gain momentum, not lose it, as publication approaches. This means heightened coordination between editors and photography, graphics, design, and the copy desk.

• Use restructuring as a springboard for morale. Staffers would have a chance to participate in tough decisions brought on by the reality of downsizing.

The newsroom was divided into brainstorming groups that cut across department lines in an effort to stimulate creative suggestions rather than turf protection. Each group was asked to discuss what its members would like to be reading in the *State*. Every staff member was involved, from news clerks to the executive editor. No idea was considered too off the wall. The list of suggestions filled more than a dozen pages.

A small group of editors shaped the values, goals, and list of suggestions into a working structure. Paula Ellis, managing editor at the time, refined the structure further to incorporate the concept of quality teams. "The *State* would not have become a fertile field for public journalism had we not been actually creating a more democratic process in the newsroom," said Ellis, who is now assistant to the publisher. "The only reason we looked for a different way of structuring the newsroom was our desire to create different relationships that would cause us to see more stories and see stories differently. We needed to change the way we see."

The effort, she said, was always grounded in the "every day—what's the story we're putting in the paper. The stories we were writing, I believed, helped create a sense of hopelessness, a sense of helplessness. . . . I wanted to do something about that."

Beats were clustered into "circles" based on broad themes that reflected the newspaper's core coverage franchise. Each was given a new name to symbolize the intended departure from traditional coverage and operations. The circles included: Quality of Life, which covered such areas as crime, housing, food/nutrition, health, and the environment; City Life and Governance, which explored issues affecting citizens from town council to Capitol Hill; Community Roots, which explored issues firmly rooted in the Columbia community, such as religion; Leisure, which covered entertainment and related recreational activities; Transactions, which focused on business news; and Passages/Learning, which explored "cradle to grave" issues including parenting, child care, education, and aging.

The original timetable called for reorganization to be implemented in mid-October, but it took longer than planned to inventory all existing beats, build new beats, and decide staffing. The restructuring was implemented in January 1992. Desks were rearranged so that circle leaders could sit with their teams. Editors responsible for the news hole also were grouped to improve communications, as were the photography, graphics, and design desks.

Lori Roberts, who covers youth issues as a member of the Passages circle, said changing the newsroom physically helped reinforce the idea that staffers were being encouraged to approach stories and their jobs in new ways.

"One of the biggest roadblocks I hear from reporters is that this is so different from what journalists have been told and taught," said Roberts, whose own background is less traditional, with formal training in English and speech communication rather than journalism. "A lot of this has to do with the comfort zones of reporters and what they are used to, what people are used to reading. Not wanting to push ourselves into people's personal lives and feeling uncomfortable with that in general. Public journalism and restructuring challenge traditional objectivity. You have to put yourself into it, you really do."

LESSONS LEARNED

In the system's five years of operations, there have been successes, failures, surprises, and changes.

Reporters whose stories automatically were slotted for features pages are winding up on 1-A, while other reporters are contributing to the weekly Neighbors section for the first time. The health reporter is writing business stories while the consumer writer is tracking bills in the State House. The quality of photographs and graphics has improved. There are fewer battles over turf, and more collaborations between reporters when issues overlap.

The newspaper is more planned than reactive. Every six months, each reporter identifies the top five issues on his or her beat in collaboration with the circle editor. This "contract" helps the newspaper's leadership set priorities and map coverage on major topics. Once these priorities are determined, reporters are expected to look beyond process and meetings to tell stories that start with the people affected by an action or issue.

The system isn't perfect, however. There have been a number of missteps along the way.

PUBLIC JOURNALISM AND NEWSROOM STRUCTURE

It quickly became apparent that the newspaper's crime and court coverage, which had been assigned to metro reporters based on community beats, was lacking. The changes had overloaded some reporters with the result that they lost contact with beat cops. As a result, the circles were reworked. A smaller team was created within City Life and given responsibility for spot crime and court coverage, and some public safety issues. The Quality of Life circle continued to explore broader criminal justice and public safety concerns.

Over time, there were other changes. Governance and City Life initially met as one large group, with twenty or so reporters, but later split into separate circles. City Life further restructured internally, moving away from the initial "East Metro–West Metro" design but still concentrating on community coverage. Local school beats were moved from City Life to Passages. Community Roots developed into a self-directed unit with no circle leader. Quality of Life later was broken up, with reporters assigned to Governance, Roots, and the investigative team. Two reporters were assigned to the assistant advance news editor.

Designers and copy editors restructured around the concept of the "presentation desk." Sports was considered a circle for some purposes, but continued to operate relatively independently with its own copy and design desk.

Throughout, there remained ongoing tension between circle leaders responsible for assigning stories and news editors responsible for producing a quality daily and enterprise report. Initially, there was more competition than collaboration among news editors as they struggled to fill the daily and advance sections without directly supervising reporters. Often, a reporter would receive competing assignments from the news desk. And a news editor would find out at the last minute that a story planned as a centerpiece for an advance section had been dropped to chase a breaking story.

Both examples point to the increased level of communication demanded by the new system. Circle editors spend much of the day keeping news editors and others updated on the status of stories. The democratic aspect of the circle system, meanwhile, increased the number of meetings significantly as staff input was sought on decisions previously made exclusively by upper management.

Senior editors, meanwhile, were troubled that some staffers saw the new structure as providing freedom from responsibility, when the opposite should have been true. Also, the heightened degree of inter-dependency created a need for communication and interpersonal skills that hadn't been anticipated.

These issues and others were addressed during a reevaluation of the circle system undertaken by the newsroom's leadership in 1995. Among the issues on the table:

• How well did the current structure serve the newspaper in covering the six "bread and butter" issues: Education, environment, effective governance, economic development, poverty, and race relations? The last two were especially problematic, since the newspaper no longer had a reporter assigned to those specific topics.

• Was the newsroom flexible and responsive? Was there collaboration? Did news editors collaborate sufficiently? Were stories evaluated properly, or did editors commit to and position the stories too early, before they were adequately assessed?

• Was the concept of stories as "contracts" valid?

• How well did the system serve the desire to report community news?

• Were there clear lines of accountability between reporter and circle editor, circle editor and news editor, news editor and the office of the managing editor?

• How had the idea that reporters are general assignments reporters first affected beat coverage? Had the newspaper's expertise slipped because such extra demands were placed on reporters?

In June 1995, staffers divided into thirteen groups of ten members each to begin discussions on these and other points. Each group represented a cross section of the entire newsroom. An extensive inventory of beats was conducted to compare what existed with the original concepts.

The bottom line? "Most newsroom staffers seem satisfied with the circle system of newsroom organization," according to a report based on the groups' discussions. "The four-month effort to revisit the system and find its cracks uncovered no widespread dissatisfaction with the system itself. While not unanimous, many newsroom staffers feel they have more control over their work lives. The system seems to be a good method for delivering the information our readers want and need.

"The newsroom is concerned, however, about some elements of the system's evolution. Some of the original tenets are either dead or comatose. The shuffling of editors and reporters has disorganized or distorted coverage of some topics. And a few coverage areas that were correctly emphasized in the original restructuring were never developed."

What emerged from the discussion was a restatement of the goals underlying the circle system and suggestions for improvements. The goals, as restated, were:

• We want all reporters writing across the newspaper.
• We remain committed to covering community news and being a capital city newspaper.
• Our five pillars of coverage continue to be economic development, education, governance, environment, and race/poverty/gender.

To better achieve these goals, the newsroom decided to eliminate a full-time beat covering issues affecting the elderly, a school reporter position, and one other slot to gain a race/poverty/gender reporter, a food reporter, and a health reporter. The job of assistant business editor also was eliminated to re-create the Quality of Life Circle with a full-time editor. The City Life group was split into two new circles—Community Life and Public Safety—each with an assigning editor, thus decreasing the overall reporter-to-editor ratio.

RESULTS: CASE STUDIES

The connections between public journalism and restructuring at the *State* can also be seen in how the newspaper has approached daily and enterprise reporting on major issues facing the community.

Setting the Agenda

One of the *State*'s pioneering efforts in helping the community effect change has been the annual "Setting the Agenda" package. It began in 1988 under the direction of Government Editor Brad Warthen, who came to the newspaper after working for Buzz Merritt in Wichita. The idea behind the package, based on polling data and interviews with experts and citizens, was to tell the General Assembly what it should focus on during the coming legislative session.

In 1992, as newsroom restructuring and public journalism concepts began to take hold, the *State* decided to add a public comment component to "Setting the Agenda." A questionnaire was designed and published in the Sunday Impact section, asking readers to respond to the same questions that were being asked legislators and included on the poll. Some editors inside the newsroom wondered whether anyone would bother clipping out the form and mailing or faxing it back. The result was staggering: more than four thousand responses were received. The public comment feature continues today with similar results.

Power Failure

The *State*'s "Power Failure" project in 1991 took "Setting the Agenda" a step further, building on the concerns of citizens to examine why state government wasn't working and to seek solutions. A catalyst for the series was "Operation Lost Trust," an FBI sting that resulted in the arrest of more than two dozen state legislators and lobbyists for vote-selling and drug crimes.

South Carolina's political system at the time was more or less a formalized version of the "Old Boy Network," designed to serve the antebellum landed gentry. All power derived from the legislature. The governor had no direct control over the executive branch of state government. Judges were elected by the legislature, so they tended to be former lawmakers. All of these things were known to insiders but not the public at large.

The first of seventeen installments told South Carolinians that the legacy of the "Legislative State" was a $7 billion mess that answered to no one. Until things changed, the series said, the state would continue to be last where it wants to be first, and first where it wants to be last. Subsequent installments presented examples of how these problems affected the lives of ordinary citizens. The topics ranged from legislative corruption to highway department incompetence, from the disorganized welfare system to the free-for-all state budget process. The project documented the lack of effective leadership in the state, and the understandable disconnection of the electorate.

While Thelen considers "Power Failure" more akin to an old-fashioned newspaper crusade than public journalism, many in the community saw it as aimless government bashing. The newspaper began a series of meetings with groups of state workers, lawmakers, and lobbyists to explain that the purpose was not to condemn them, but to explain that they worked in a system that undermined their best efforts. Many left the meetings persuaded of the need for systemic change.

To leverage its reporting, the *State* formed partnerships with other news organizations in South Carolina in an effort called "We the People." The newspaper built a coalition of other daily newspapers and television stations in Charleston, Spartanburg, Myrtle Beach, and elsewhere, to present a series of public forums to address the issues raised in "Power Failure." Colleges and universities in those markets provided the venues for the five forums, which assembled people from all walks of life to confront the need for reform. "The forums were where certain deliberations occurred," said Thelen. "Before, there had not been that vehicle for conversation." The solution suggested by the series— a sweeping reorganization of state government—became law in 1993. "Power Failure" was praised as a catalyst for positive change and seen by some as the newspaper's "declaration of independence" from a power structure with which it had been historically aligned.

An Economy Adrift

In the early 1990s, restructuring of state government threatened to erode one of Columbia's economic pillars. Higher education, another economic mainstay, also was under pressure. A series of tight state budgets had resulted in almost one thousand "frozen" jobs at the University of South Carolina, the area's largest institution. Corporate headquarters, primarily in banking, also were becoming an endangered species. And the military faced an uncertain future given the prospect of federal government downsizing.

All of this led the *State* to one conclusion: Columbia's economy was stagnant and, even worse, showed signs of retreating. The newspaper decided to examine the problem and explore solutions. Readers were surveyed; about three hundred wrote back to say they perceived the local economy as too dependent on government and the military.

In a six-day series titled "An Economy Adrift," the *State* let readers tell how they had been affected by the economy. The newspaper also told success stories and offered possible solutions, two dozen of which came from readers.

"The project worked through the community's concerns about the economic base," Brook said. "Traditionally, it had been very stable . . . Our theory was that, because of the changing economy, the traditional base was not the best model for the future. We asked people if they bought into this thesis. The response was that people were concerned and thought there was a danger."

Brook said the newspaper then went back to readers who responded to its survey to ask for possible solutions. "They said the community needed to get its act together, that local governments needed to cooperate and reach out for economic areas that had not been aggressively pursued—light industry, distribution. That's what has happened," he said.

After the series was published, Midlands leaders rededicated themselves to building a more diverse economy. County and city governments united to successfully sell the area to new businesses. In 1994, the Columbia economy attracted almost one thousand new jobs from relocating companies.

Brook said the community leaders' quick response to the series eliminated the need for the newspaper to take a more active role, as with "We the People." Columbia's mayor called an economic summit within months of the series to address the issues raised. The *State* was able to retain its traditional journalistic distance as a result, Brook said. That proved advantageous, he added, since there remained in the government community lingering resentment over "Power Failure" and what some readers saw as an effort by outsiders (i.e., Knight-Ridder Inc., which bought the *State* in 1986) to tell them what to do.

Confederate Battle Flag Debate

From its "Power Failure" and "Economy Adrift" series, the *State* learned it could identify community concerns and foster a discussion of those issues. Before the 1994 General Assembly convened, the newspaper decided to apply that knowledge and change its method of covering the ongoing dispute about the Confederate battle flag.

The flag was put on top of the State House in 1962 by lawmakers without notice until the creation of single-member House districts in the early 1970s. The new districts resulted in the election of the first black lawmakers to the South Carolina House since Reconstruction. It took a decade for a Legislative Black Caucus to organize and force a vote on the battle flag. That vote, to remove the banner, failed in 1983. In the following decade, factions in the flag debate moved squarely into their corners, never to meet in anything close to consensus.

In late 1993, however, black lawmakers began to offer compromise proposals. One plan would have replaced the battle flag with the less divisive Confederate national flag, the Stars and Bars. The idea failed, but got people talking. While politicians were dismissing the flag as "just a symbol," the *State* decided to explore the values and beliefs underlying the symbol that caused South Carolinians to feel so strongly.

"We discovered that one of the most important things to citizens who follow this issue is respect for heritage and the contributions of those who have gone before," said Nina Brook, a former legislative reporter who covered the flag story.

"Black citizens wanted to talk about the contributions of black lawmakers during Reconstruction, a period many white people dismiss as horrible. White descendants of Confederate soldiers wanted to talk about the hardships their ancestors endured in an undersupplied army, a blockaded nation," she said.

Two stories were particularly noted as contributing to the dialogue: the first examined the unresolved feelings Southerners have about their history and the institution of slavery; the second let South Carolinians tell in their own words why they felt so strongly about the flag.

The newspaper also opened new channels with groups such as the Sons of Confederate Veterans and the Columbia Interdenominational Ministerial Alliance, which previously had been ignored because they were perceived as not having a role in the outcome of the issue. "You wind up getting more people to talk with you because you're viewed as less cynical," Brook said. "You are seen as someone who understands that there is more going on here than meets the eye. Your story is not going to read like the AP account."

By the end of the session, legislators passed a law directing that the battle flag remain over the State House. The measure removed the legal uncertainty over the flag's status that had prompted Columbia's mayor and other community leaders to file a lawsuit seeking the banner's removal. The lawsuit was dropped.

Despite the fact that the *State*'s editorial page had called for removal of the Confederate battle flag, Brook said the newspaper accomplished its goal of helping the community understand and work through a difficult issue. "You can help expand the debate and involve people who typically are not given credibility. You can't dictate what the results are going to be. That's an important lesson we learned. You can't always predict how it's going to come out," she said.

Election Coverage

The 1994 elections provided the *State* yet another opportunity to test public journalism principles. Before the newspaper began its coverage of the Columbia mayoral race, it asked readers via a questionnaire to list the concerns they wanted addressed. The answers? A redeveloped downtown and redeveloped riverfront. Lower crime. A better economy. The *State* then shaped its coverage so that it became a discussion of the issues that citizens wanted addressed, rather than a reflection of the agendas of would-be mayors.

Subsequent polling for the upcoming gubernatorial race showed citizens wanted candidates to focus their discussions on the issues of crime, education, taxes, health care, and jobs. Following the Wichita and Charlotte election project models, the newspaper devoted a Sunday Impact section to each of the issues. The reporting focused on people's concerns and fears. For each issue, the *State* published a set of questions and verbatim responses from the candidates. When only one of the seven contenders could explain how he would pay for his crime package, that was laid out for the voters to see.

The *State* also convened a voters advisory group that met monthly with political writer Lee Bandy. The group reacted to the candidates' positions and performance in televised debates. Members' observations were published as stories in the newspaper.

To Raise a Child

During 1993, reporters and editors at the *State* had been meeting to discuss ways to write about children and their issues. The Passages circle hosted a luncheon with community members to ask for ideas and feedback.

Then, in January 1994, a student was fatally shot in a public high school. That tragedy got the newspaper and Passages group moving faster. Concerned reporters and editors brainstormed on how to write about the difficulties of making it alive through adolescence. Staffers participated in a values clarification exercise, an effort to determine some of the basic truths the community might believe about children. Within this process, the newspaper also decided it wanted to move people toward healing action, not depress them with more bad news. Three overriding values were identified:

• It takes an entire village to raise a child.

• Our community should have safe, sacred places for children and adults.

• Conflict arises, and when it does, it should be resolved without violence.

As reporters and editors brainstormed story ideas, they began to see a pattern. To express the value of safe, sacred places, the *State* could write stories about people, programs, and institutions helping kids. To express the value about conflict, the newspaper could write stories about heroic children and teens, kids who had survived horrors with grace and who could be role models for hope.

The final plan called for a series that contained three stories in every installment: a story about a "kid hero," a youth who has solved/survived a serious problem, like alcoholism, teen pregnancy, abusive parents; a story of an adult who helped that child or others solve the particular problem; and a basic graphic stating the problem.

The series was tagged with the saying, "It takes an entire village to raise a child." The goals with each installment were to show the strength of children, reveal helper role models in the community, educate readers about the social issue, and inspire others to help. Writers were instructed to keep in mind the desire to move people to action. Each installment would include a "how to help" box.

The first part dealt with a teen pregnancy. Education reporter Lezlie Patterson found a young woman who became pregnant in middle school, but who had a fierce desire to succeed. She kept her child, remained in school, and earned college scholarships. The teen was frank about the incredible barriers her early motherhood erected and her wishes to break the cycle with her son. The "kid hero" participated in a "teen awareness" program in which teens talk to other students about sexuality, contraception, pregnancy, and marriage. The director of that program became the "adult hero."

Roberts said the series likely would have been done without newsroom restructuring, but not in the same way. "It would have been different, more formulaic. There would have been less of the child's point of view, and more from adults and 'experts.' The child would have been secondary. The way we did it, we did get the child first."

Killing Our Future

News stories in 1994 made children and violence a compelling issue in Columbia and the rest of South Carolina. In response, the *State* began an extended project, "Killing Our Future," to look behind the image. The Passages and City Life teams were the primary collaborators.

In the first installment, Lezlie Patterson explored the roots, impact, and aftermath of the fatal shooting of a student at a local high school. A month later, reporter Chris Crumbo explored the perception and realities of violence among and by children and young people.

The March installment explored how guns impact on violence among the state's young people. Reporter Margaret O'Shea's story focused on the ease with which young people can obtain these deadly weapons. April's installment by Crumbo tackled the many faces of violence toward children—from corporal punishment to being carried in the womb by drug-addled mothers.

In May, reporter John Allard explored the lethal mixture of teens and cars. His articles noted why teens seem to make bad decisions behind the wheel and what remedies might be offered to slow down the pace of teen highway deaths. Roberts explored in June the issue of teen suicides. The main story dealt with the overall issue of teen suicide while sidebars tackled personal stories of those who lost children to suicide.

July's package by Crumbo and staff writer Lisa Greene tied into the Susan Smith murder trial, which was in progress. Their topic was sexual abuse of girls, specifically incest.

Starting in August, the *State* explored the connection of sexual abuse and death row convicts. O'Shea found that the common thread of the men on South Carolina's death row was that all were abused sexually. Sidebars tackled the dilemmas of a day in the life of a family court judge.

September's package by Greene looked at South Carolina's over-crowded juvenile court system. A consensus emerged that the system was badly broken and needed a massive infusion of cash, judges, prose-cutors, and public defenders. Greene spent a day in court, and recorded the nature and severity of the cases and the time that the judge spent on them. The story showed that children move through the system at warp speed with little consideration given to the merits of rehabilitation versus punishment.

Over the year, more than one hundred letters were received from readers worried about the future generation. The project ended with a package of stories calling for children's issues to be put at the top of the 1996 legislature's agenda.

CONCLUSIONS

Restructuring the *State*'s newsroom into teams has generated significant changes in the planning and execution of news coverage. Reporters are encouraged to outline problems and point to solutions, including providing notes at the bottom of stories that direct readers how to get involved.

"In my mind, it's about getting out and knowing the community, how the community defines news," Roberts said. Restructuring allows "more freedom to get to the good stories."

Former State House reporter Nina Brook said the greatest benefit of restructuring is the encouragement to approach work differently than in a traditional newsroom.

"As a political reporter, it's safe now for me to write things not just about politicians. . . . I can go talk to people outside the confines of the capital. While that's not new to journalism, it is more emphasized and pushed here."

Since restructuring, groups of citizens have met regularly with teams of reporters and editors to discuss concerns. That communication, wherein citizens voice their concerns in a collegial setting before conflict drives the participants into polarized camps, has kept the newspaper more attuned to the values of its community.

"Newspapers traditionally have had a patriarchal contract with their communities," Ellis said. "News and information was handed down from on high, along with advice on how the community ought to behave. This has been institutionalized on the editorial pages. In a way, it was command-and-control behavior. . . . Communities were more willing to be led and gave us their trust. It's more pluralized now and that is not as clear."

In the newsroom, there is more collaboration among reporters and staffs on daily and enterprise stories, Brook and other editors said.

"Previously, if you needed to do a project, it would be done within one staff. Now, many others are involved—one from this group, another from that group. Broadening the groups involved in the product results in a far broader context," news editor Brook said.

Thelen said he believes public journalism has found fertile ground at the *State* and has grown in no small part because of the new newsroom governance. "Our restructuring began without a conscious linking to public journalism. Once we started down the road, we realized it was consistent with, supportive of, and at the root of public journalism. Both involve moving away from the extremes to get where reality is. They involve breaking down walls and creating dialogue where it wasn't before. . . . So many of the principles are exactly the same."

7

EFFECTS OF A MULTIMEDIA PUBLIC JOURNALISM PROJECT ON POLITICAL KNOWLEDGE AND ATTITUDES

FRANK DENTON AND ESTHER THORSON

The practice of journalism is frequently seen as a romantic enterprise. During the 1970s, the occupational image even bordered on the heroic, with the likes of Woodward and Bernstein of Watergate fame and with Seymour Hersh exposing the tragic My Lai massacre in Vietnam. But of arguably more consequence to American democracy is the daily and weekly romantic behavior of editors and reporters as they push ideas and information into the public sphere. They use their own values, instincts, and judgments to decide which topics, information, and news should be given priority and which can be safely omitted or deferred. Yet largely unremarked in the huge body of literature on the American press and politics is the romantic assumption journalists too often make about this process: that the bread they cast on the waters will, if all goes well, enrich the democratic body politic.

However, when journalists do make time to reflect on what they do, most of the critical focus is on the art or craft of reporting and editing, and very little is in the way of a social science assessment of whether their journalism "works."

What does "works" mean? Journalism, reasonably enough, has been considered successful if something happens, changes, as a result of its

The research discussed in this chapter was supported by the Pew Center for Civic Journalism.

coverage. That is, newspapers and magazines and, especially, television took the reality of the Vietnam War into the nation's living rooms, and public support for the war and its Washington champions crumbled, ultimately ending the conflict. The *Washington Post* and other news organizations exposed Watergate, and the government changed.

Such clear outcomes, as ideal as they might be, are uncommon, even exceptional. Day in and day out, at the national, state, and local levels, re-porters and editors decide what is important and put it in print or on the air, and public policy changes or does not, sometimes as a result of the journalism to some degree, sometimes not. But the occasional heroic outcome, national or local, has encouraged many journalists, probably most of them, to measure their effectiveness by their impact on public policy makers, a focus which can make story sources and subjects the goal of the journalism. In many ways, that is not necessarily a poor stan-dard, even when it disregards the important middle step, the people.

However, that direct relationship between the journalist and the policy maker, the cause and the effect, can become a dance, an elaborate ballet, with each trying to influence the other, often interactively and even collaboratively. The extreme situation is, of course, in Washington. For one example, Marvin Kalb analyzed the famous Nixon memo of 1992, when the former president choreographed the "leaking" of his analysis of the emerging Russia to ensure maximum direct impact on the Bush administration. With meticulous timing, Nixon placed copies of the memo with carefully selected journalists at the *New York Times, Washington Post,* and other media powers. "Nixon knows the memo will leak, but he doesn't know how it will leak," Kalb wrote.[1] "It's different each time . . . Nixon not only understands the power of the print and electronic press, but he enjoys the manipulation of the press as a way of advancing his own agenda. He is fully familiar with the inter-relationship of press, politics and public policy."

While the Washington "press corps" is widely—outside the capital—thought of as elitist, incestuous, isolated, and myopic, the same sort of thing happens constantly at every level of government and politics. Lo-cal beat reporters compare notes on "source management" or "source

1. Marvin Kalb, "The Nixon Memo," Discussion Paper D-13, Joan Shorenstein Barone Center, John F. Kennedy School of Government, Harvard University, 1992. This paper was later developed into a book: Marvin Kalb, *The Nixon Memo: Political Respectability, Russia and the Press* (Chicago: University of Chicago Press, 1994).

discipline," implying a quid pro quo, often unspoken, with contacts on their beats: Keep me supplied with insider news tips, and you'll come across better in my stories. On some beats, notably police and politics, a sort of professional Stockholm Syndrome can seduce a reporter into sympathizing and identifying with his or her sources.

Despite the prevalence of such dynamics at every level of government and politics, the American democracy seems to function. In his important book *The Paradox of Mass Politics,* W. Russell Neuman says the fact that the system appears to work even without the involvement of very much of the citizenry is "the paradox of mass politics." He explains that while only "a very small, attentive top stratum of the mass public," political or single-issue activists, is paying attention and getting involved at any given time, policy makers tend to respond because they never know when the activists will succeed in pushing an issue into the public eye.[2]

But the democratic ideal says that public policy begins and ends with the people, and that journalism and the government play only supporting roles: journalists inform and public officials implement. When the journalists and the officials become too cozy, or even seem to collaborate, where does that leave the people? Frustrated, alienated and, too often, tuned out. After a series of focus groups across the country, Richard C. Harwood concluded that Americans are not apathetic but feel ignored, powerless, and disenfranchised, left out of the choreography among politicians, bureaucrats, special interests, and big institutions—including the press. People do care and want to be involved, Harwood found, but only if they feel they can make a difference.[3]

In something of a quiet revolt, the people are voting with their feet. The mainstream news media are suffering record low levels of credibility, and perhaps partly as a result, newspapers and network TV news programs are losing their audiences. Who is gaining? The populist gadflies, like Ross Perot and Rush Limbaugh, who at least speak the language of the people rather than of the power elites.

PUBLIC JOURNALISM

That vulnerability of the current oligarchic system and, especially, the vision of a new, more involving democracy, is what led to the development

2. W. Russell Neuman, *The Paradox of Mass Politics: Knowledge and Opinion in the American Electorate.*
3. "Citizens and Politics: A View from Main Street America."

of public journalism, a philosophy of journalists' actively working to engage and involve the public in public affairs. For the sake of discussion, the two kinds of relationships among the people, their government, and their news media are presented in Figure 1.

Part of the allure of the traditional relationships, with the heroic style of journalism, is the obviousness of outcomes; for example, a bill passes or fails, the president resigns or not, the alleged miscreant is indicted or no-billed. On the other hand, the more important word in "public journalism" is the first one, with the second being the means to an end, instrumentality for democratic processes. Thus, the first true test of public journalism is whether it succeeds in involving the public, without much regard to whether the people actually choose to be moved or whether there is a visible outcome. The simple spirit of public journalism calls for a straightforward way of measuring its effects among the public.

Because public journalism is still in an experimental, developmental phase, it is easy to lose the way and fall back on traditional standards of assessing success. For example, in an effort to evaluate a public journalism project, one study measured the success of a Texas newspaper's campaign to make children's issues a higher priority on the community agenda. Saying the newspaper's project "exemplifies the spirit of public journalism," the study's authors used as their method a content analysis of the newspaper's coverage and a comparison of city funding for children's programs before and after the coverage. Since funding increased, the study concluded that the newspaper's effort succeeded.[4]

The authors' misdirection was primordial. They defined public journalism as "an emerging perspective that emphasizes prosocial initiatives by newspapers to bring community concerns and issues to the attention of the general public and, especially, public officials." For at least fifty years, throughout the social-responsibility era of the press, journalists have seen prosocial initiatives as part of their role, and it has been a quarter century since McCombs and Shaw explicated public agenda-setting as an important function of the press.[5]

What is arguably new about public journalism is the active *involvement* of the public. Even increased public awareness of an issue, a traditional measurement of mass communication effects, is not enough. The mass

4. Marcus Brewer and Maxwell McCombs, "Setting the Community Agenda," 7–16.
5. Maxwell E. McCombs and Donald L. Shaw, "The Agenda-Setting Function of the Press," 176–87.

Two Models of Journalism

Traditional Model

Public Journalism Model

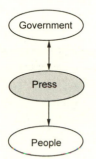

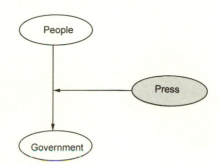

of people can be quite aware of community or national affairs and still be so alienated or simply uninterested that they neither engage in public discussion nor express their will, even by voting. Democracy is no more served by informed but uninvolved citizens than it is by ignorant uninvolved citizens. Public journalism, as Figure 1 shows, means to place responsibility for public affairs squarely on the public, by informing, involving, and empowering them with information. Its champions likely would admit to idealism, even utopianism.

Again using the Texas case as an example, there are very plausible alternative explanations for the relationship between news coverage and increased funding for children's programs. City council members may have increased funding for children's programs because they personally learned from, and were swayed by, the newspaper coverage. Or, they may have responded because they anticipated or even feared a public expression, through the process of the "paradox of mass politics." Or, in the absence of any showing of a cause-and-effect relationship, the increases in news coverage and funding of children's needs could well have been coincidental. There was simply no evidence that the increased emphasis on children's programs, however worthy, had any relationship to public deliberation and will.

FRANK DENTON AND ESTHER THORSON

INVOLVING THE PEOPLE

If public journalism, at its core, is involving the public in public affairs, then the assessment of the success or failure of such journalism should turn on the measurement of that public involvement, with the clearest possible relationship to the journalism.

In the fall of 1994, the citizens of Wisconsin in and around Madison unwittingly participated in an elaborate, multimedia field experiment to determine whether, and how, a concentrated, coordinated public journalism project, called "We the People/Wisconsin," could involve the public in important election campaigns. The experiment sought to address specific weaknesses in the relationship between the news media and the public.

Contrary to the ideal of the knowledgeable, interested, involved, and active citizen, the electorate has been characterized as largely apathetic and ignorant about public affairs. Most people pay close attention to politics and government only during times of crisis or when government actions directly and personally affect them. For example, Neuman reported that only a slight majority (on average, 56 percent) can identify any congressional candidate in their district during campaigns. Most citizens are not actively studying public affairs, attending meetings, helping candidates, or otherwise participating in public affairs. "A more realistic model of the typical citizen acknowledges that most political learning is fragmentary, haphazard and incidental," Neuman wrote. "The citizen does not 'study' the candidates but rather picks up bits and pieces of information over time, gradually accumulating a composite picture of the prominent issues and candidates. This is a process of low-salience learning. The key distinction is between information seeking and information acceptance."[6]

For their part of the relationship, the news media do not seem to be engaging their audiences in public affairs. McGuire pointed out that many published studies do not report significant media effects, and those that do account for no more than 2 to 3 percent of variance in the effects measures. Neuman said the power of the media has been "exaggerated," because of not only the uninterested public but also competition from entertainment media and inherent constraints and limitations of the media to inform and persuade. He particularly points

6. Neuman, *The Paradox of Mass Politics*, 8–29, 148.

to the shallowness of much journalism, such as horse race campaign coverage.[7]

Public journalism would have a news organization purposefully organize its resources and activities to educate and interest people in the public sphere. Such planned, focused initiatives are seen as necessary because one of the reasons journalism has failed to teach citizens about public affairs may be what Denis McQuail called the news media's "lack of purposefulness." That is, very diverse content is selected and presented serendipitously in response to a perceived public interest in general news about their world. James Carey pointed out that news itself is fragmentary, incomplete, and episodic, making it difficult to keep up with and comprehend. John P. Robinson and Mark R. Levy give some blame to "the way news media tell the story, particularly when so few news stories take into account the public's limited skills and interests in processing news content." While some people, notably those with low cognitive skills, may learn better from television and magazines, Neuman, Marion R. Just, and Ann N. Crigler suggest that the structure and style of newspapers make it more difficult for average people to learn about political issues. News could be truly comprehensible, Gerald M. Kosicki and Jack M. McLeod say, but it would require an idealized citizen to view it over time and across media, an impossibility in real life.[8]

The public journalism approach to comprehensibility might be to reach people through various and perhaps innovative techniques (such as town hall meetings and interactive features) and show them how public affairs affect them and how they can have an impact in public affairs. The key may be ensuring that the project is concentrated, in deference to the voter's attention span, and concerted, among media.

Overall, people seem to learn, or retain, very little directly from the news media, particularly specific information from news stories. Television news viewers cannot recall much of newscasts they have seen before. Taking out other factors, particularly education, the same seems

7. W. J. McGuire, "The Myth of Massive Media Impact: Savagings and Salvagings," in *Public Communication and Behavior,* vol. 1, edited by W. Comstock (New York: Academic Press, 1986). Neuman, *The Paradox of Mass Politics,* 156, 148.

8. Denis McQuail, *Mass Communication Theory,* 2d ed. (Newbury Park, Calif.: Sage, 1987), 292. James Carey, "The Dark Continent of American Journalism," 292. Robinson and Levy, *The Main Source,* 15. Neuman et al., *Common Knowledge,* 106. Gerald M. Kosicki and Jack M. McLeod, "Learning from Political News: Effects of Media Images and Information-Processing Strategies," 72.

to be true of the print media. Neuman cites an "inverse law:" Generally, "the higher the level of abstract, issue-oriented, political content, the smaller the audience it is likely to attract."[9]

On the other hand, people are receptive to information that helps them gain personal power in dealing with public issues. Neuman, Just, and Crigler found that their subjects were particularly enthusiastic about media content that told them what they could do about something. This is consistent with the findings of the Harwood focus groups, which concluded that Americans have a "reservoir of civic duty" and want to be involved. Harwood called for "somehow" reconnecting people and politics.[10] A central goal of public journalism is to address issues and candidates in a powerful, focused way that shows people how they can make a difference.

Public journalism is rooted in journalists' concerns about disconnections, not only between citizens and their government but also between people and their news media, particularly newspapers. Public journalism is self-interested in that it seeks to make the participating media more valuable to consumers by connecting them to their community.

TESTING THE THEORY

The field experiment reported here sought to involve citizens in the political process by a planned, coordinated information and news campaign across three media and four media outlets. As part of a public journalism effort, the project attempted to structure media reports to be comprehensible, coordinate different media, direct media content, and provide information specifically to empower citizens.

Typically, media effects research is performed in a laboratory or by post hoc audience measurement of routine, uncoordinated media coverage. For example, media knowledge effects usually are measured by selecting a few apparently important items that have appeared in the news, then demonstrating how few survey respondents are familiar with the information.[11]

For this project, the participating media were involved from the conception and cooperated throughout. They were the media partners

9. W. Russell Neuman, "Patterns of Recall among Television News Viewers," 115–23. Robinson and Levy, *The Main Source*, 87–105. Neuman, *The Paradox of Mass Politics*, 137.
10. Neuman, Just, and Crigler, *Common Knowledge*, 111. "Citizens and Politics," 62.
11. Neuman, Just, and Crigler, *Common Knowledge*, 2.

in "We the People/Wisconsin": the *Wisconsin State Journal,* the morning and Sunday newspaper in the state capital; Wisconsin Public Television; Wisconsin Public Radio; and WISC-TV, the CBS affiliate that is dominant in the Madison market. Editors and news directors agreed in advance to coordinate extraordinary treatment of two statewide election campaigns as part of their public journalism partnership to improve democratic participation. Most of these partners had been working together for more than two years, beginning with town hall meetings and a presidential campaign debate in 1992 and continuing through a series of projects, ranging from health-care reform and the federal budget deficit to statewide issues and elections. In the fall of 1994 the partners, working with the researchers, targeted the gubernatorial and U.S. senatorial campaigns for an intense public journalism initiative. The project was particularly difficult because both campaigns were lackluster, with the incumbents heavily favored to win, as they ultimately did.

In addition to their traditional campaign coverage, the four media partners agreed to cooperate on, and coordinate presentation of, an intense effort that began in late September and concluded on Sunday, November 6, before the Tuesday election. The project had two parallel tracks: town halls and debates, and civics training.

Town Halls and Debates

Continuing an effort that had begun in the 1992 presidential primaries, the partners sought to pull ordinary citizens into issue identification and discussion and to have them question the candidates at debates. In the gubernatorial campaign, the project held well-attended town hall meetings in three cities around the state, then a debate with questions from the town hall participants. The Friday night debate was simulcast live on public TV and public radio, followed by a listener call-in discussion program on public radio. In addition, the debate was taped; public TV broadcast the tape twice the following Sunday, and the commercial station broadcast it once that day. The newspaper made the debate the centerpiece of its Saturday front page. Later, transcripts were made available through the newspaper, and approximately two hundred were disseminated by request. The debate, especially with such intense exposure, generated substantial news coverage and interest in the community because a citizen wearing an American-flag shirt successfully demanded from the candidates specific commitments on a particularly salient issue.

The Senate discussion was less elaborate. One town hall meeting was held just before a scheduled debate. The incumbent declined to take part, so the town hall participants questioned the challenger on live, statewide public television. The rest of the hour-long program was devoted to discussion of media coverage and campaign practices, with experts answering questions from the citizens in the studio and from statewide call-ins. This program also was taped and rebroadcast on public and commercial TV. It drew some news coverage, though not as much as the gubernatorial campaign.

Civics Training

Because of the alienation/empowerment issue, the project also sought to provide readers, viewers, and listeners with specific information about political tactics to allow them to gain some feeling of control over the campaign activities swirling around them. The *Wisconsin State Journal* researched and presented a series, "Armed and Dangerous," that sought to educate readers about how candidates and their keepers try to manipulate debates and how political advertisements are used to create attitudes and beliefs. One part of the series pointed out that many candidates promise to solve problems beyond the powers of the office and taught readers exactly "what politicians can and can't do for you." The last part, which explained the reasons for and implications of negative campaigning and helped readers cut through it, was published the Sunday before the Tuesday election. The packages featured a "voter's bill of rights" so citizens would understand what they deserve out of candidates and campaigns. The helpful advice parts of the series were reprinted in later newspapers, particularly on the editorial page.

Because this sort of detailed information and help is more suited to print than electronic media, the radio and TV partners were less involved here. However, some of the "Armed and Dangerous" information was worked into their programs: On the Friday night before the election, statewide public TV had a segment on negative campaigning, and the newspaper package the following Sunday promoted two related programs that day on the commercial TV station. Statewide public radio devoted a popular call-in program to the subject. Just before the election, the public journalism project compiled much of the newspaper's campaign coverage and Armed and Dangerous material into a booklet named "Voter's Self Defense Manual." Approximately three hundred copies were made available to the public. They were quickly claimed.

Throughout all these experimental treatments in all the media, the name and logo of We the People/Wisconsin were used repeatedly and prominently.

WHAT WE FOUND

It was important that citizens' knowledge and attitudes were measured both before and after the campaign. In September, before any of the We the People activities on these two campaigns, interviewers used random-digit dialing to select and interview 230 adult residents of Dane County, which includes Madison. Then the day after the election, the interviewers recontacted 141 of the original group and asked them the same questions and more. In addition, the post-election questionnaire was administered to a separate random sample of 516 people in the county. Of course, a problem is that while the follow-up test likely has around a 5 percent margin of error, the margin is much higher for the pretest. Therefore it would take at least a 10 percentage point difference to provide confidence in the significances of the pre- and post-test differences. For now the argument can only be that the consistently higher scores of the post-test provide somewhat more assurance that the observed differences reflect some real ones.

The forty-four-item questionnaire measured respondents' knowledge of the candidates, issues, and campaign activities; the nature of the candidates' ads; the respondents' voting behavior and choices; their media use; their familiarity with, reaction to, and attitude toward the public journalism project; their sources of political information; attitudes toward the campaigns; and self-perceptions of political efficacy and cynicism.

The public journalism program had been active and visible in the community for more than two years, so it was to be expected that public awareness would be high. In fact, most respondents (54 percent of males and 49 percent of females) had heard of the program. The highest awareness, 60 percent, was among middle-income people (annual income in the $30,000–$50,000 range). Whites were more familiar with the project (52 percent) than minorities (39 percent for all minorities, 46 percent for blacks), though there were few minorities in the sample of this largely homogenous county. Among higher-educated respondents, 55 percent were aware, compared to 38 percent of those whose education did not go beyond high school.

Those surveyed were asked how they heard about We the People, and those crediting each news medium increased after the fall campaign. Of those who knew about the project, the largest group, 51 percent before the campaign, said they learned about it from the *State Journal;* 56 percent was observed after the campaign. It may be, then, that even though awareness through the newspaper already was high, it increased through the experimental campaign. The percentage of those who credited WISC-TV was 37 percent before the campaign and 49 percent afterward. Public TV was cited by 34 percent before and 50 percent after, and public radio's 24 percent increased to 30 percent after the election. (The percentages total more than 100 because respondents were allowed to cite all the sources in which they remembered learning about We the People. The numbers should be tempered by the fact that roughly 20 percent credited another, nonparticipating newspaper or a nonparticipating TV station, indicating confusion or invention.)

Hierarchical regression analysis allowed further exploration of awareness. Education and whether one actually voted accounted for 1 percent of the variance in awareness of the public journalism project, but after that variance was removed, readership of the newspaper and viewership of public television accounted for an additional 5 percent of the variance in the awareness variable.

"We the People" also may have succeeded in pulling people into the political process. Asked whether the program "encouraged your interest in politics," 26 percent of those aware of "We the People" answered yes before the campaign, indicating the general success of the two-and-a-half-year-old program; the figure increased to 32 percent after the town hall meetings, debates, "Armed and Dangerous" stories, and other parts of the experimental project.

Those surveyed also were asked whether "We the People" "informed you about what issues are important to Wisconsinites." Before the election, 51 percent said yes; the number was 55 percent afterward. "We the People" was related to what people felt they "knew" about their own knowledge. In another hierarchical regression, after the effects of education, likelihood to vote, and source of news were removed, people who were aware of the project were significantly more likely to feel they knew enough to decide between the candidates in both elections. We asked the same people before and after the campaign whether they felt they "can meaningfully participate in the political process," and their responses were significantly more positive afterward.

To see whether the "Armed and Dangerous" series actually succeeded in arming citizens to make them more "dangerous" in the political process, we asked six specific questions to test knowledge offered in the journalism (e.g., whether "The We the People project made available a free voters' self-defense manual for anyone who asks for it," "People learn the most from debates in which real citizens ask questions," and "One thing a U.S. senator cannot do is lower your property taxes"). A hierarchical regression analysis showed that people who had higher incomes and those who voted were most likely to know the correct answers to those questions; these two demographic variables accounted for 5 percent of the variance in knowledge about "Armed and Dangerous." That was to be expected, but after the effects of these variables were removed, awareness of the public journalism program was a strong predictor of the "Armed and Dangerous" knowledge, accounting for an additional 2 percent of the variance.

As for the nature of the media content, yet another regression analysis showed that knowledge of material known to have been widely and frequently available in both news and advertising was predicted primarily by demographic variables and by advertising exposure (accounting for 11 percent of the variance). However, 5 percent of the variance in knowledge of material known to have been less widely available was accounted for by exposure to We the People, even after education, age, income, and having voted accounted for an initial 12 percent of the variance.

The real test of public journalism, however, may be whether it motivates people to actually become involved in the political process. Before the election, 19 percent of our respondents said We the People made them more likely to vote—a striking number to anyone who has tried to motivate people to actually get to the ballot box. Interestingly, that number fell to 11 percent after the campaign, perhaps indicating disillusionment with either the specific candidates or with the campaign tactics revealed in the media coverage. Inconsistent with this notion, however, were four questions designed to assess political cynicism, which showed no measurable increase related to We the People.

Journalists concerned about the acceptance, credibility, and future of their media may see a ray of hope in the answers to this question:

"Has hearing about the We the People program . . . made you feel more positive toward the organizations that are sponsoring We the People?" Before the election, 29 percent responded positively; after the experiment, the figure increased to 42 percent, strongly indicating that such public journalism efforts may be one way that newspapers can build a new relationship with readers and potential readers.

WHAT OUR FINDINGS MEAN

This research was one of the first measurements of whether a planned, coordinated, focused multimedia public journalism effort can affect the citizenry's knowledge and attitudes. The results are very encouraging to those who want to improve the democratic processes and to those who believe the news media can take a more active role in facilitating those processes. Our results indicate that the public recognizes this contribution to their democracy and appreciates it.

At the same time, we believe this project makes important contributions to news media research. Unlike laboratory experiments and post hoc audience measurements, this field experiment involved collaboration with, and responsible orchestration of, four leading news organizations across three media as an experimental treatment. The focused treatment and measurement occurred within a tight and controlled time frame, during and after the political campaign. We think this unique experimental design greatly increases the external, as well as internal, validity of this project.

We found that the public journalism effort achieved widespread public awareness, and most important, the people who knew of the project said that, as a result, they were more interested in and knowledgeable about the election and more likely to vote. More specifically, the public journalism project succeeded in providing some citizens with specific information and tools to become more "armed and dangerous" in dealing with political campaigns. While demographic differences account for knowledge of political information that is widely available, the newspaper and public TV coverage succeeded in communicating specific, known media content. The public journalism effort to uncover political manipulations did not appear to feed cynicism.

As news organizations across the country experiment with public journalism, using their considerable resources to motivate a reluctant citizenry to become involved in an atrophying public sphere, there is much more to be learned. If journalists and researchers can continue to collaborate as we have here, methodological improvements can sharpen experimental treatments and measurements and, therefore, knowledge. Longer-term longitudinal experiments could show how learning and attitudes change as a result of public journalism.

However, given the nature of public journalism, perhaps assessment mechanisms should be a natural and necessary component of such efforts. The experience of "We the People/Wisconsin," as well as other civic journalism projects at the *Wisconsin State Journal,* shows that public interests and outcomes vary greatly among issues. Constantly monitoring the involvement of the people can help keep this type of journalism appropriately focused. Reliance on an assumption of effectiveness among the fickle and complex public could be as misleading as merely measuring changes in official policies.

8

AUDIENCE IMPACT OF A MULTIMEDIA CIVIC JOURNALISM PROJECT IN A SMALL MIDWESTERN COMMUNITY

ESTHER THORSON, EKATERINA OGNIANOVA, JAMES COYLE, AND EDMUND B. LAMBETH

This chapter reports how the learning, attention, and evaluative attitudes of news consumers were affected by a month-long civic journalism project carried via radio, television, and newspaper. The study looks descriptively at effects indicators such as what percentage of people became aware of the project, learned factual information from it, and reported various degrees of liking and trust for the content of the stories and for the participating news media themselves.

The most important question asked here, however, concerns what happens when people encounter civic journalism projects via more than one news medium. Previous studies have suggested that people who get their news from more than one medium show enhanced learning and attitudinal responses *to each medium* in comparison to those who only use one medium.[1] This effect can be called "news media synergy." In

1. Esther Thorson and Edmund B. Lambeth, "An Evaluation of the Cognitive, Attitudinal and Synergistic Effects of a Multimedia Civic Journalism Project." In the summer of 1993, Lambeth originated the Community Knowledge Project, which, with the support of Associate Dean Thorson and the three teaching newsrooms of the School of Journalism at the University of Missouri, carried out three civic journalism projects in Columbia, Missouri. The Thorson/Lambeth paper and the chapter in this book are outgrowths of that project.

the study described here, researchers asked whether a specific four-week civic journalism project that focused on aspects of local jobs and employment deemed critical to the healthy development of the region would benefit from news synergy. They also wanted to know how the strengths of newspaper, television, and radio coverage would combine to affect the impact on the news audience.

Since the fall of 1993, researchers and editors at the University of Missouri School of Journalism have been working together on civic journalism projects that coordinate news across three media: a commercial television station, a city newspaper, and a National Public Radio station. One of the projects of this collaboration centered on jobs and employment in the mid-Missouri county where the university resides. After completion of a four-week series on jobs and employment, a random-digit dialed phone sample of citizens in the county was carried out to evaluate the level of awareness that had been created, or what was learned from the stories; what was liked; and how the impact on learning and attitudes varied as a function of whether people had encountered the series in all three media, two of them, one of them, or had not been exposed at all. Given the emphasis that has been placed on the role of media partnerships in the doing of civic journalism,[2] distinguishing between the individual and combined effects of media partnerships is highly relevant to a thorough-going evaluation of civic journalism in its various forms and formats.

PREVIOUS RESEARCH

Because civic journalism is so young, there have been few studies that looked specifically at its news audiences. Edward D. Miller, working with the Poynter Institute for Media Studies, reported around 25 percent of *Charlotte Observer* readers noticed changes in how politics was covered after civic journalism efforts. *Observer* readers were also reported to have been more positive about being a part of the political process, and more likely to feel the issues affected them directly. Davis Merritt reported that in Wichita, the percentage of people who evaluated their newspaper positively increased significantly after it had engaged in civic journalism projects. Sherie Dill reported that the percentage of readers

2. Ed Fouhy and Jan Schaffer, "Civic Journalism—Growing and Evolving," *Nieman Reports* 49, no. 1 (spring 1995).

ESTHER THORSON, EKATERINA OGNIANOVA, JAMES COYLE, AND EDMUND B. LAMBETH

of the *Wichita Eagle* who said they were more likely to vote because of the coverage increased, and more people rated the political coverage as being fair.[3]

In a study of the audience for a public journalism series in Madison, Wisconsin (see chapter 7), more than 50 percent of those interviewed were aware of the series. Those aware of the project reported a 6 percent increase in interest in politics over those unaware of it. Although those who were aware of the series were no more cynical than those reporting no exposure, they were significantly more knowledgeable about general information concerning the election and specifically about the material in the civic journalism series.

One previous study reported not only respectable levels of awareness, knowledge, and positive attitudes in response to a multimedia civic journalism series on health care but also the phenomenon of news media synergy,[4] which is the central focus of the present study.

The research reported here builds on the studies that have been done to date. One question is whether there is evidence that effects are greater on people when they are exposed to news stories via a variety of media than when they are exposed to a single medium. A second question is whether the effects of coordinated coverage are greater than one would expect from adding the collective effects of the individual media consumed singly.

MEDIA SYNERGY

The concept of news media synergy began appearing in the mass communication literature only recently. The word "synergy" denotes coordinated, cooperative action, but it is also used to describe the optimal combination of processes and parts resulting in the creation of something that exceeds their sum. Synergy has been extensively used as a word to define co-occurring and mutually enhancing processes in biology, physics, and chemistry, but also in philosophy of science, the study of social systems, and psychological phenomena.[5]

3. Edward D. Miller, *The Charlotte Project: Helping Citizens Take Back Democracy.* Davis Merritt, Jr., *Public Journalism and Public Life: Why Telling the News Is Not Enough.* Sherie Dill, "Wichita Reverses a Trend."
4. Thorson and Lambeth, "An Evaluation."
5. S. Casswell, "The Nature and Effectiveness of Media Advocacy, Counteradvertising, and Health Promotion Messages," in *The Effects of the Mass Media on the Use and Abuse of*

Media synergy can be defined in terms of the attentional, cognitive, and attitudinal impact of communication delivered by a diversity of media. It is assumed that the media mix itself leads to synergy. When a person receives messages from a variety of media, he or she integrates them in the psychological processes of encoding, storage/categorization, and retrieval. In this respect, the media mix addressed in the present chapter is different from the idea of mixing media to reach diverse audience/market segments.[6]

> Moriarty described synergy in the communication domain as linkages in a receiver's mind as a result of messages that connect. Synergy suggests that an entire structure of messages—with its links and repetition—creates impact beyond the power of any one message on its own. . . . Synergy exists through the function of memory—messages that are conceptually integrated and that repeat essential units of meaning over time through different channels and from different sources come together to create coherent knowledge and attitude structures in the receiver.[7]

In mass communication, concepts close to media synergy have been examined mostly in the framework of persuasion theory, diffusion of innovations, and public communication campaigns where the media are among the instruments of information dissemination. For example, public communication campaigns for many years have relied on the concept of media supplementation, or the enhancement of message

---

Alcohol, edited by S. E. Martin (Bethesda, Md.: U.S. Department of Health and Human Services), 269–76. S. Moriarty, "The Circle of Synergy: Theoretical Perspectives and an Evolving IMC Research Agenda," 333–53. Esther Thorson and Jeri Moore, eds., *Integrated Communications: Synergy of Persuasive Voices.* C. Schooler, J. Flora, and J. W. Farquhar, "Moving toward Synergy." D. A. Borchardt, "Confronting the Concrete and the Abstract in Critical Thinking," paper presented at the meeting of the International Society for Exploring Teaching Alternatives, Chicago, October 1988. C. K. Smorada, "The Personal Development Seminar: Probing Disciplinary Perspectives." W. Thomas, ed., *Synergy Access: A Global Newsletter on Futuristic Communications, Media, and Networking.* W. C. Meierhenry, "Instructional Theory: From Behaviorism to Humanism to Synergism," *Instructional Innovator* 25 (1980): 16–18. J. Marmor, "Cultural Factors in the Darker Passions," *Journal of the American Academy of Psychoanalysis* 20 (1992): 325–34. C. Weingartner, "Synergistic Manipulation," *ETC.: A Review of General Semantics* 36 (1979): 371–77. J. L. Wise, "Sonocollage: A Multi-Media Process to Reorganize Experience" (Ph.D. diss., University of Massachusetts, 1981).

6. S. H. Chaffee and M. J. Petrick, *Using the Mass Media: Communication Problems in American Society* (New York: McGraw-Hill, 1975).

7. Moriarty, "Circle of Synergy," 333.

ESTHER THORSON, EKATERINA OGNIANOVA, JAMES COYLE, AND EDMUND B. LAMBETH

persuasiveness in one medium by a similar message in another. The recent Stanford Five-City Multifactor Risk Reduction Project included media supplementation, viewed as a way to achieve communication synergy.[8] Schooler et al. proposed a synergy model in which the different messages coming from the media and the environment form several stages of cognitive and attitudinal responses, with a change in behavior as a final result.

In reviewing the literature on media synergy it is important to distinguish between the effects of simple repetition and the idea that the processing of a message from one medium is somehow transformed by the fact that messages from other media have been or will be processed. We look first at simple repetition effects. We then examine the "transformational" or Gestalt notion of how messages interact with each other.

SIMPLE REPETITION SYNERGY

The first and most straightforward aspect of media synergy is the notion that *encountering a message via two media creates a greater impact than simply encountering the same message twice in the same medium.* The attitudinal and cognitive explanations for such an outcome differ.

Classic research on memory shows that repetition is a key to learning and memory. Generally, the more repetitions of information, the greater the likelihood that an individual will be able to recognize or recall that information. Exposure to television and its "packaging" of the message is likely to provide slightly different information than exposure to newspaper packaging of the message. The resultant cognitive impact may be a richer, more elaborated, more organized perception of the information. Thus, learning from two messages from two media may carry more impact than learning from two messages repeated in a single medium.

On the other hand, impact on liking, being persuaded, and other attitudinal responses seem to increase quickly with repetitions, but then may become more negative with still further repetitions. In the domain

8. C. I. Hovland, I. L. Janis, and H. H. Kelley, *Communication and Persuasion.* W. J. McGuire, "Theoretical Foundations of Campaigns." E. M. Rogers, *Diffusion of Innovations,* 3d ed. (New York: Free Press, 1983). Schooler et al., "Moving toward Synergy."

of mass media, the impact of repetition on attitudes and cognition has been most extensively examined for advertising—where repetition is considered crucial to creating effects.[9]

GESTALT SYNERGY

A second important notion of media synergy can be characterized as "the whole is greater than the sum of its parts," and is therefore called "gestalt synergy." The term *Gestalt* comes from the German psychologists Kohler and Koffka, who developed a theory usually applied to the human perceptual process.[10] Koffka defined "gestalt" as referring to "which parts of nature belong as parts to functional wholes, to discover their position in these wholes, their degree of relative independence, and the articulation of larger wholes into sub-wholes." Applying this concept to learning from various media, we suggest that people who encounter a message from a particular medium may show a certain amount of enhanced response. For example, they may remember 50 percent of what they hear. But those who encounter messages from that medium and also related messages from another medium may remember more than 50 percent of the message in the first medium. For both individuals, there was a single encounter with the message from the first medium. But the input from the second medium enhances the processing of the input from the first medium. That is, what an individual derives from a particular medium is actually enhanced by the fact that a second medium was also used.

The strongest empirical evidence that this kind of process occurs also comes from advertising research. Studies on advertising campaigns show that cognitive and attitudinal responses to ads improve when people are exposed to a conjunction of media rather than a single medium. Other studies have shown that television plus print (in most cases, magazine) promotional plans were more effective than television-only plans. Clancey obtained similar results in comparing the effects of television alone and television plus radio, with the media mix yielding

9. C. Pechman and D. W. Stewart, "Advertising Repetition: A Critical Review of Wearin and Wearout," in *Current Issues and Research in Advertising,* vol. 12, edited by J. H. Leigh and C. R. Martin, Jr. (Ann Arbor: University of Michigan, 1989), 285–330.

10. K. Koffka, *Principles of Gestalt Psychology* (New York: Harcourt, Brace and World, Inc., 1935). Wolfgang Kohler, *Gestalt Psychology* (New York: London, 1929).

twice as high awareness and recall of advertising. Lodish also recommended that product promotion plans include a variety of media and be scheduled for diverse times of the day.[11]

Although some of the reasons behind such campaign strategies are to reach different demographic segments, for example nonviewers, or to introduce products to markets not heavily targeted by competitors, this literature also clearly contains the idea of gestalt synergy. Confer suggested that the addition of a medium in a campaign deepens and broadens the communication. Similarly, Ennis argued that "multiple media deliver stronger communication versus one medium" and "media tests involving a second medium often provide a more positive market response than heavier spending in the same medium." Specifically, this literature emphasizes that a second medium reinforces the key points in the persuasive message received through the medium of first exposure. In a laboratory study, Keller demonstrated that when packaging of a brand did not match content of ads by repeating an illustration or headline, people remembered the ad claims at a fairly low level. But when the package provided cueing with the ad's illustration or headline, there was a 33 percent increase in memory for ad claims. In addition to the enhancement of memory for the ad claims, there was a concomitant increase in favorable brand evaluations. A reasonable interpretation of this result is that synergy between advertising and another promotional element, such as packaging, is possible and more likely to occur when there are common features that packaging and ads share.[12]

11. L. Weinblatt, "Norms/Advertising Hurdles/Media Synergy," speech delivered to the Advertising Research Foundation, New York, September 1991. G. M. Fulgoni and G. Garrick, "The Relationship between Ad Exposure and Sales," speech delivered to the Advertising Research Foundation, New York, March 1988. M. Confer, "The Media Multiplier," speech delivered to the Advertising Research Board Foundation, New York, May 1991. M. Confer, *The Research Study: The Advertising Impact of Magazines in Conjunction with Television, Waves I and II,* Report no. 65, Magazine Publishers of America, 1992. E. Papazian, ed., *TV Dimensions '94* (New York: Media Dynamics, 1993). B. Warrens, "The Road to Accountability," speech delivered to the Advertising Research Foundation, New York, May 1993. Press Research Council, *The Media Multiplier* (London, 1990). M. Clancey, "Imagery Transfer," speech delivered to the Advertising Research Foundation, New York, December 1990. L. M. Lodish et al., "Key Findings from the 'How Advertising Works' Study," speech delivered to the Advertising Research Foundation, New York, November 1991.

12. A. A. Achenbaum, "Effective Exposure," 11–13. F. B. Ennis, *Marketing Norms for Product Managers* (New York: Association for National Advertisers, 1985). Papazian, ed., *TV Dimensions '94.* Warrens, "Road to Accountability." J. P. Jones, *How Much Is Enough?*

One explanation for such cross-promotional effects is that the message encountered second promotes cognitive rehearsal or playback of the first message. Maibach and Flora showed that cognitive rehearsal of a persuasive message enhances attitudinal and behavioral responses. Edell and Keller found that people mentally replay a television commercial's content when they hear its audio track on the radio.[13] They also found no differences in brand name and brand claims recall, attitude toward the brand, and purchase intentions in two conditions: when people were subjected more than once to the same television commercial versus when they were exposed to a combination of a television and a radio ad that was basically a replay of the audio track of the television commercial. The authors concluded that television-radio campaigns, which can cost less than television alone, are therefore likely to be more efficient than the latter. They further suggested that radio and television are a good pairing because of their sharing of audio characteristics and cues.

Overall, then, there is clear evidence in the area of advertising and marketing that the impact of a message in one medium can enhance the processing of a related message in another medium. What is not clear is whether and to what extent this can happen when multiple media undertake the coordination of a series of news stories. That is the question to be pursued here.

THE STUDY AND ITS HYPOTHESES

A classic question in mass media research is the extent to which media messages have "effects." In attempts to answer this most basic of questions, media "effects" have been defined in a number of different

(New York: Lexington Books, 1992). Confer, *The Research Study.* C. Atkin and E. Atkin, "Issues and Initiatives in Communicating Health Information," in *Mass Communication and Public Health: Complexities and Conflicts,* edited by C. Atkin and L. Wallack (Newbury Park, Calif.: Sage, 1990), 13–40. J. A. Edell and K. L. Keller, "Analyzing Media Interactions: Print Reinforcement of Television Advertising Campaigns," working paper (Durham, N.C.: Fiqua School of Business, Duke University, 1993). K. L. Keller, "Memory and Evaluation Effects in Competitive Advertising Environments," *Journal of Consumer Research* 17 (1990): 463–76. K. L. Keller, "Brand Equity and Integrated Communication," in *Integrated Communication,* edited by Thorson and Moore, 103–32. D. Poltrack, *Television Marketing* (New York: McGraw-Hill, 1993).

13. E. Maibach and J. Flora, "Symbolic Modeling and Cognitive Rehearsal: Using Video to Promote AIDS Prevention Self-Efficacy," *Communication Research* 20 (1993): 517–45. Edell and Keller, "Analyzing Media Interactions."

ESTHER THORSON, EKATERINA OGNIANOVA, JAMES COYLE, AND EDMUND B. LAMBETH

ways. One measure is the *awareness* of messages, for example, awareness of political ads or awareness of health campaigns. A second way is in terms of *learning* from messages, as for example, learning what lifestyle changes are appropriate for gaining good health.[14] A third way of defining media effects is in terms of *persuasion*—for example, changing an attitude or a behavior. The present study looks at all three potential effects of media synergy.

A civic journalism project on jobs, employment, and underemployment was designed as a test for the hypotheses. In the study, we examined whether each of the three participating news media—newspaper, television, and radio—produced a measurable impact on awareness, recall of each project's stories, learning from the content of the stories, evaluation of the stories, and a more positive attitude toward the media in response to their innovative efforts. We hypothesized first that people exposed to any of the media participating in the projects would show awareness of the stories and promotional cues, recall of the stories, and learning from their content, and would report positive attitudes toward the media themselves in comparison to those not exposed.

Determining exactly *how* news coverage in different media may synergize via their various functions requires a level of detail in coordination of writing, illustration, filming, and sound usage that fell well beyond the scope of how the media coverage was coordinated in the study. But the coverage was sufficiently orchestrated to allow a search for the *occurrence* of synergy. Thus we hypothesized that learning and attitudinal responses to a single medium will be affected by whether other media were also encountered.

To explore the idea that news coverage might lead to synergistic attentional, cognitive, and attitudinal effects on the audience, the Columbia civic journalism projects brought together the daily and Sunday *Columbia Missourian,* the NBC-affiliated KOMU-TV, and public radio station KBIA. The study was designed as a quasi-experiment, in which the civic journalism projects carried out in the community provided the treatment condition. There was no a priori identified control group,

14. S. A. Lowery and M. L. DeFleur, *Milestones in Mass Communication Research* (New York: Longman, 1988). L. L. Kaid, "Measures of Political Advertising," *Journal of Advertising Research* 16 (1976): 49–53. R. D. McClure and T. E. Patterson, "Television News and Political Advertising," *Communication Research* 1 (1974): 3–31. K. E. Bauman et al., "Three Mass Media Campaigns to Prevent Adolescent Cigarette Smoking," *Preventive Medicine* 17 (1988): 510–30.

although those people who were not exposed to the media coverage, identified by a series of gate questions in the phone survey, provided the baseline "controls."

The media coverage about jobs was carefully coordinated among the three participating media. Each medium mentioned and promoted the other media's coverage. The reporters and editors from all three media discussed in detail what the stories would look like, how they would be linked, and which medium would contain what information. The series ran for four weeks during February and early March 1994. The television station kicked the series off with a Friday (10 P.M.) story on the job market in Columbia, emphasizing that the low 3 percent unemployment rate still meant that some people in the community did not have jobs. The next day, the radio station did a story on how the homeless in Columbia live and what they do to search for jobs. The next day, the newspaper had a short introductory story on the front page. There was also a full-page grouping of stories on the front page of an inside section. (This pattern of a brief front-page story and then a longer story in a section ["Showcase"] inside the Sunday paper was continued throughout the four weeks.) The newspaper's first story focused on how few blue-collar jobs there were in the city, leaving semiskilled workers stuck in minimum-wage jobs. Each story carried an "Our Community" logo. This logo was also employed in all of the television stories. For the next three weeks, the general pattern was a single ten o'clock TV news story on Thursday or Friday, radio stories on Thursday and Friday at six o'clock, and an in-depth story in the newspaper on the following Sunday. During the second week of the series, the radio and newspaper examined the work of a center that helps people find jobs. The TV story looked at people who have set up home businesses. The third week focused on entrepreneurship, with all three of the media looking at small businesses, the source of most new jobs in the North American economy. The stories examined how such businesses operated, and how one could create and run one successfully. During week four, the three media returned to the issue of unemployment. The newspaper looked at how unemployed people in Columbia attempted to find jobs and meanwhile make ends meet. Radio and television again looked at how the local job services attempted to match people with jobs.

After the series ran, effects of the news stories were tested with a random-dialed phone survey of 310 individuals in Boone County, Missouri. The phone calls were made during the week after the series

ESTHER THORSON, EKATERINA OGNIANOVA, JAMES COYLE, AND EDMUND B. LAMBETH

was completed. All interviews took place within the subsequent two weeks. Each phone interview took approximately twenty minutes. The response rate was approximately 50 percent, after eliminating nonworking numbers, business numbers, and answering machines.

To identify those who were exposed to the jobs stories, a series of "gate" questions was used in each of the two surveys. In the first one, respondents were asked whether, in the last month, they read the participating newspaper at least a couple of times a week. If they answered affirmatively, they were asked whether they had noticed a series of stories on jobs in the newspaper and whether they had seen any references to jobs coverage in the other media of the community. They then heard some descriptions of specific stories and were asked whether they remembered reading anything about them. They were then asked multiple-choice knowledge questions based on the content of the stories.

After the newspaper section, respondents were asked whether, in the last couple of weeks, they had watched the targeted television station's noon or ten o'clock news programs. Again, if they answered affirmatively, they were asked the same questions as for the newspaper, but revised to fit with the television coverage. Third, they were asked whether they had listened to the targeted radio station's news in the last couple of weeks. The same set of radio questions then was asked. Only respondents who indicated they had been exposed to the medium were asked the questions relevant to it.

The recognition questions were worded in the following way for each medium: "Do you remember any stories about . . . ?" There were five such questions for newspaper, four for television, and four for radio. For newspaper, the responses were yes, read it; read some but not all of it (considered a positive response); noticed it, but didn't read it; don't know; and no answer. For television, the responses were yes, watched it (considered a positive response); noticed it but didn't pay attention; no, don't know; and no answer. For radio, the answers were yes; heard some but not all of it (considered a positive response); noticed it but didn't pay attention; and no. Next, respondents were asked multiple-choice "fact" questions (five in the newspaper section, four for television, and four for radio). Examples of these questions include: (a) The unemployment rate in Columbia is: 1 percent; 3 percent (correct); 7 percent; 9 percent. (b) Job hunting is hardest for: those in the health professions; those who are homeless (correct); women. (c) The best place to find a job is through: city hall; one of the local high school counselors; Columbia Job Center (correct); the university's job placement program.

Respondents were then asked to evaluate the stories (in each medium they reported consuming) as excellent, good, fair, or poor. They were then asked whether the medium's recent emphasis on jobs improved a lot or somewhat, worsened a lot or somewhat, or had not changed their opinions of their medium. The last within-gate question was whether they had seen any reference to the jobs stories in the other two participating media.

After the questions in the radio section of the questionnaire, all respondents were asked to rate the local media on several seven-point scales. The local media were rated in terms of how accurate, relevant, caring, and competent respondents thought they were. A series of demographic questions concluded the questionnaire. It should be noted that the sample quite accurately reflected the population of the county in terms of gender and race statistics, but showed a somewhat higher income distribution than that of the county.

TESTS OF THE MEDIA CONSUMPTION HYPOTHESIS

The first hypothesis suggested that respondents who consumed the individual targeted media would report noticing the special coverage, would recognize particular stories, would accurately answer factual questions, would show a positive attitude toward the media, and would be aware of promotional cues to the media partners. Of those who reported exposure to each of the three media, more than half noticed the newspaper series, one-third noticed the television series, and one-quarter noticed the radio series. When asked about the individual stories that had run in the series, newspaper readers recognized 22 percent of them on average; television and radio consumers recognized fewer than 10 percent of the stories on average. The percentage was higher for those who indicated they had seen the media cross-promotions. Nearly 60 percent of the newspaper readers, 30 percent of the television viewers, and 43 percent of the radio listeners said they had seen the series advertised as appearing in one of the other media. Newspaper reading also produced the greatest percentage of correct answers to the factual questions (newspapers, 19 percent correct; television, 8 percent correct; radio, 17 percent correct on average). It is, of course, not appropriate to conclude that the newspaper was the best teacher because the coverage in the three media varied so much and the factual questions were not the same across the three media. Interestingly, 75 percent or more of everyone who encountered the series, regardless of the medium, rated the stories as excellent or good.

The second hypothesis suggested that the learning and attitudinal responses to the project in a single medium would be affected by whether people also encountered the project in one or both of the other media. To test this hypothesis, we examined the response patterns of people who reported encountering the job stories in either one, two, or three of the participating media. The results are shown in Tables 1, 2, and 3. The three tables represent answers to the newspaper (Table 1), the television (Table 2), and the radio questions (Table 3) specifically. The newspaper results in Table 1 can be used as an example. The table shows responses by the people who read the newspaper alone, those who read the newspaper but also consumed one of the other two media, and those who read the newspaper as well as encountering the jobs stories in both of the other two media. It should be emphasized that the data presented in the columns of the table were based on identical questions. Only the people who answered the questions varied, and they did so in terms of the number of media in which they reported being exposed to the jobs stories.

We look first at the newspaper results (Table 1). As can be seen, those who read the newspaper in conjunction with one other medium always did better in terms of awareness of the newspaper series, percent of stories they correctly recognized, percent of correct knowledge answers, percent calling the stories excellent or good, and those indicating they saw other media promoted. There was also an increase for those encountering two other media, except for the percent of correct knowledge answers.

The synergy results were not so strong for evaluative attitudes toward the media. Ratings of accuracy, relevance, and competence went up from newspaper alone to newspaper with one other medium. But there was not a consistent increase for those encountering newspaper plus two other media.

Table 2 shows the results for television's impact. Again, there was a fairly clear increase from television alone to television with one other medium, although the pattern was not as consistent as for the newspaper questions. Again, media ratings on accuracy, relevance, caring, and competence went up for television with one other medium, but went

TABLE 1

Responses to the Newspaper Questions as a Function of the
Number of Media in Which Civic Project Was Encountered

Newspaper

	Single medium	With one other medium	With two other media	Significance of number of media after demographics removed
Noticed the series	37%	59%	71%	p < .05
Mean % of stories recognized	14%	24%	33%	p < .05
Mean % correct factual answers	10%	23%	20%	p < .05
Percent calling stories excellent or good	67%	82%	93%	n.s.
Mean ratings of media (7 = high; 1 = low)				
Accurate	4.2	5.1	4.6	
Relevant	4.8	5.3	4.9	
Caring	5.3	4.1	4.6	
Competent	4.9	5.2	5.4	
Percent seeing another medium promoted	33%	58%	83%	p < .10
	n = 27	n = 71	n = 24	

ESTHER THORSON, EKATERINA OGNIANOVA, JAMES COYLE, AND EDMUND B. LAMBETH

TABLE 2
Responses to the Television Questions as a Function of the Number of Media in Which Civic Project Was Encountered Newspaper

	Single medium	With one other medium	With two other media	Significance of number of media after demographics removed
Noticed the series	27%	31%	47%	p < .10
Mean % of stories recognized	8%	7%	14%	p < .05
Mean % correct factual answers	6%	8%	13%	p < .10
Percent calling stories excellent or good	83%	86%	43%	n.s.
Mean ratings of media (7 = high; 1 = low)				
Accurate	4.5	5.1	4.6	
Relevant	4.7	5.2	4.9	
Caring	5.0	5.1	4.6	
Competent	4.3	5.1	5.4	
Percent seeing another medium promoted	13%	44%	25%	n.s.
	n = 39	n = 72	n = 24	

TABLE 3
Responses to the Radio Questions as a Function of the
Number of Media in Which Civic Project Was Encountered
Newspaper

	Single medium	With one other medium	With two other media	Significance of number of media after demographics removed
Noticed the series	20%	30%	14%	n.s.
Mean % of stories recognized	7%	6%	8%	n.s.
Mean % correct factual answers	12%	20%	13%	n.s.
Percent calling stories excellent or good	40%	52%	0%	n.s.
Mean ratings of media (7 = high; 1 = low)				
Accurate	4.7	5.1	4.6	
Relevant	5.0	5.2	4.9	
Caring	4.8	4.6	4.6	
Competent	4.9	4.9	5.4	
Percent seeing another medium promoted	40%	52%	0%	n.s.
	n = 57	n = 87	n = 24	

ESTHER THORSON, EKATERINA OGNIANOVA, JAMES COYLE, AND EDMUND B. LAMBETH

down when television was encountered with two other media. The same kind of mixed results occurred in the patterns for radio (Table 3).

These results in general support the idea of gestalt synergy, and are strongest for newspapers. Answers to exactly the same questions varied as a function of whether people had encountered the job stories in one medium, two, or three. In general, there was a boost with one other medium. There was generally not a boost with two other media, and the attitudinal responses fairly consistently decreased with two other media in comparison with one other medium.

Because people in each of the media groups responded to the same questions, it is probable that the differences in their performance resulted from the differences in their media exposure. But of course, it is also possible that people who consume a single news medium are different in important other ways from multiple media consumers. That is, people who only listen to the radio news or only read newspaper news are probably different from those who consume various combinations of media news, and it might be these differences that account for the "synergy" findings, rather than the encountering of multiple media. The most obvious candidates for differences in people in the three media groups are demographics, that is, individual characteristics such as income, party affiliation, gender, education, or how long people have lived in the region.

To examine the occurrence of media synergy in a way less confounded with these demographic variables, a series of hierarchical regressions was used to control for the effects of the demographic variables, and then examine the effects of the number of media used.[15] When the dependent variable of interest was dichotomous, it was necessary to use logistic regressions. When the dependent variable was continuous, multiple regression was used.

The results of this additional analysis are shown in the fourth column of Tables 1–3. Where it is indicated that the number of media encountered was significant, this means that responses to exactly the same questions improved when people had consumed two or three media rather than one, and that this was true *even after all of the demographic differences in people had been statistically removed*. As can be seen in comparing Tables 1–3, for both newspaper and television questions, the synergy pattern was strong even after the effects of demographic differences in respondents

15. J. Cohen and P. Cohen, *Applied Multiple Regression/Correlation Analysis for the Behavioral Sciences*, 2d ed. (Hillsdale, N.J.: Lawrence Erlbaum Associates, 1983).

were removed. Synergy clearly occurs for attention to the stories and knowledge about them. Synergy in noticing the cross-promotions was marginally significant for newspapers and nonsignificant for the other two media. Positive evaluations of the stories did not significantly increase, however, for any of the three media. There were no significant synergy effects for radio.

Synergy effects for ratings of the quality of the media after controlling for demographic differences was examined in more detail than the other dependent variables. Instead, the effects of specific combinations of media were examined after controlling for demographics. For all four evaluative dimensions (accuracy, relevance, caring, and competence), the people who consumed both television and newspaper were more positive. None of the pairings with radio produced synergy in the positiveness with which the media were perceived.

CONCLUSIONS

The main goal of this study was to determine the attentional, cognitive, and attitudinal effects on people exposed to a multimedia civic journalism series on local jobs and employment. The editors and producers of news at a newspaper, a network television affiliate, and an NPR station worked together to produce a coordinated series of stories that looked at how the structure of employment in the region affected the lives of its citizens. Each medium promoted the stories being run by its partners, and there was an attempt both to repeat main ideas across the media, and also to let each medium tell the story in a way best suited to its own communicative strengths.

A random-digit dialed survey of county residents immediately following the month during which the series ran showed first that the series was noticed by half of those who read the local paper, a third of those who watched the television station's news, and a fourth of those who listened to the radio station's news. These results are best characterized as a half-full, half-empty finding. The stories ran for four weeks, and it seems surprising that more people did not report being aware of them. The awareness levels remind us again of the low levels of involvement with which people apparently process news, and how hard it is for news to cross into awareness.[16] On the other hand, half of the newspaper

16. For example, Richard McKelvey and Peter C. Ordeshook, "Rational Expectations in Elections," *Public Choice* (1984): 44, 61–102. Markle Commission on the Media and the Electorate, 1989, "Summary Report" (New York: Markle Foundation).

readers and a third of the television viewers did pick up on the fact that the media were engaged in some "special" news coverage.

Looking further at the purely descriptive aspects of the impact of the civic journalism project, newspaper readers recognized more of the specific stories that had appeared, answered more factual questions correctly, and saw more promotions for the other two media. More newspaper readers rated the stories as good or excellent than did television watchers or radio listeners. Interestingly, there were no differences in how readers, watchers, and listeners rated the overall accuracy, relevance, caring, and competence of their news media. Looking broadly at these results, it can be said that at least for the civic journalism series examined here, newspaper coverage was a clear winner.

On the other hand, it was clear in this study that gestalt synergy operated for the multimedia civic journalism project, but that it resulted because of the combination of newspaper reading and television watching. As is typical in studies where the sample is fairly representative of the population as a whole, the number of radio listeners was so small that the power to find effects was probably too low.

Importantly, the synergistic relationship between television and newspaper was apparent even after controls were used to mitigate possible effects of demographic differences in people who only read or who only watched versus those who did both. Those who experienced the stories in the newspaper and on television were more likely to notice the newspaper stories, correctly recognize particular stories, answer knowledge questions, call the stories excellent or good, and say they saw another medium promoted. They also rated the media in general as more accurate, relevant, and competent. Those who experienced the jobs stories in the newspaper and on television were more likely to notice the television stories, call the stories excellent or good, and say they saw another medium promoted. They also rated the media in general as more accurate, relevant, caring, and competent.

These findings of television-newspaper synergy should encourage those who argue that public journalism projects have a greater effect with coordinated, cross-media coverage of issues that are determined to be critically important to their communities, like the jobs and employment series was here. The present findings offer concrete means to create citizen awareness of, and learning from, news of public affairs, as well as credible hope that the democratic process can be improved as a result of their use.

Nonetheless, this study concludes with the recommendation that replication studies be conducted to refine and elaborate the findings presented here. Specifically, there is a need for additional tests of coordinated news coverage to identify the particular content and structural elements that create gestalt synergy. Replication studies of media synergy also should assess the impact of repetition of information within news stories and in follow-up stories on different days, in addition to repetition across different media.[17] Finally, because news consumers have busy schedules and must often make time to spend with news media, it is critical that each medium in a synergy project include a vigorous program of cross-media promotion. The marketing value of such cross-promotion may also encourage future cooperation of various, usually competing, media in synergy projects. If that happens, media consumers should be informed about the multiple functions of the new communication directed to them, so readers, viewers, and listeners could keep a critical eye on its development and effects.

17. Robinson and Levy, *The Main Source.*

9

PUBLIC JOURNALISM

What Difference Does It Make to Editorial Content?

SALLY J. MCMILLAN, MACY GUPPY,
WILLIAM KUNZ, AND RAUL REIS

Civic journalism has been called a "movement toward a basic cultural change," one that could rekindle the democratic process in the United States. Proponents of civic journalism see it as a revived relationship between news organizations and the public. Critics, however, dismiss it as one of the usual tasks of newspaper promotion departments, "only with a different kind of name and a fancy, evangelistic fervor."[1] Little actual measurement has been done to determine whether civic journalism makes a significant difference in the way that news is gathered and reported. Assessing whether civic journalism makes a difference is the goal of this chapter.

The relationship between journalists and the public is prominent in the literature on civic journalism. Civic journalism is often represented as a shift from the traditional journalistic practice of detachment (or objectivity) to one of engagement with the public on public issues. Jay Rosen suggests objectivity is no longer a viable contract between journalists and the public. He proposes that in place of the ritual of objectivity, both the media and the public are recognizing the need for a new kind of journalism: "Traditionally, journalists worry about

---

1. Davis Merritt, Jr., "Civic Journalism: A Movement toward a Basic Cultural Change," *Wichita Eagle*, October 30, 1994. Tony Case, "Civic Journalism Denounced."

getting the separations right. . . . Getting the connections right is our problem now."[2]

In addition to raising questions about the viability of objectivity, civic journalism also challenges other practices of the media profession. Among the reported changes to journalistic practice are greater reliance on locally generated (as opposed to wire service or syndicate) stories; use of graphic devices to call attention to content that relates to public life; and greater focus on issues rather than processes, particularly in political campaigns where traditional coverage has focused on the horse race and/or the character of candidates.[3]

Daniel Hallin argues that journalists should rethink their place in the political debate: "Journalists need to move from conceiving their role in terms of mediating between political authorities and the mass public, to thinking of it also as a task of opening up political discussions in civil society. . . . If the candidates in an election campaign, for instance, don't seem to have much to say, why not look for someone else who does?"[4] His argument would suggest that a fundamental change in political coverage would be to extend the range of voices that are heard so that average citizens can become engaged in the political process.

The presidential campaign of 1988 is often identified as a low-water mark for the political process, media coverage, and citizen engagement with public issues. Some journalists began to search for a new kind of journalism that could eschew horse race coverage and revive citizen involvement in issues of public life. That search was inspired by not only democratic ideals but also financial concerns. For example, a 1989 Knight-Ridder symposium noted that voter participation in the 1988 election was the lowest for any presidential election since 1924. The report juxtaposes this fact with the observation that nationwide newspaper readership had declined from 73 percent of adults in 1967 to 51 percent in 1988 and suggests that changes in the ways newspapers

2. Rosen, "Beyond Objectivity," 51. Rosen, "Getting the Connections Right," 11.

3. See for example Steven Smith, "War in the Gulf, Trouble in the Street: Lessons from the 1991 News Year," transcript of the Robert W. Chandler Lecture, Eugene, Oreg., November 1, 1991; Andrea Yeager, "Putting Children First," *APME Readership Committee*, August 1994, 10–14; Michael Bales, "Tuning In to Public Concerns," *APME Readership Committee*, August 1994, 22–24.

4. Daniel Hallin, "The Passing of the 'High Modernism' of American Journalism," *Journal of Communication* 42 (summer 1992): 20.

cover the political process might reinvigorate both voter participation and circulation.[5]

Much of the literature describes the *Wichita Eagle* as the first newspaper to engage in this new kind of journalism.[6] Davis Merritt, the editor of the *Eagle,* writes that the paper revised its approach to the 1990 Kansas gubernatorial campaign because the 1988 campaign had left people frustrated and discouraged. These factors make the *Eagle* an appropriate focus for an analysis of civic journalism, one which attempts to answer a fundamental question: Have the changes undertaken in the name of civic journalism, including the development of focus groups and public forums and the creation of a citizen agenda, had a significant impact on the construction of news?

Civic journalism has not focused on political campaigns alone. The roots of the movement, though, have been traced to state and local elections. Therefore, this study was limited to analysis of election-related stories. Such campaigns allow one to compare the content of one newspaper over time and with other outlets because they provide regular and fixed sample periods.

A content analysis was conducted on the *Wichita Eagle*'s coverage of the Kansas gubernatorial campaigns of 1986, 1990, and 1994. Because the *Eagle* introduced civic journalism in the 1990 gubernatorial campaign, these dates provided the opportunity to examine content before, during, and after the implementation of a civic journalism program.

To provide a comparison with a newspaper that had not employed civic journalism, an identical analysis was conducted on the *Topeka Capital Journal* in the same years. The *Capital Journal* was selected for two reasons. First, because the selected sample focuses primarily on statewide election coverage, it was necessary to study a newspaper in the same state that would presumably be covering the same issues. Second, the control paper's circulation needs to be as similar as possible to the *Wichita Eagle*'s. The newspapers in Topeka and Kansas City come closest to matching the circulation of the Wichita paper. However, since the Kansas City metropolitan area straddles the Kansas-Missouri border, the *Kansas City Star* provides election coverage for two states, which makes it less suitable for comparison with Wichita.

---

5. See for example Shepard, "The Gospel of Civic Journalism," 28–35. "Newspapers, Community and Leadership: A Symposium on Editorial Pages," 1.

6. See for example Peter Bhatia, "Behind Civic Journalism," *APME Readership Committee,* August 1994, 4–9; Rosen, "Community Connectedness."

The time period for the study was defined as between Labor Day and the general election in each of the three years. A stratified sample was drawn without replacement to construct a composite two-week period for each year. Because the sampled period included part of September, all of October, and part of November, the pool from which days were drawn was adjusted to ensure the number of days selected for each month was proportional to the number available for that month.

The unit of analysis was all news stories that addressed state or local elections, including Kansas gubernatorial races, U.S. Congressional races in Kansas, and all other state or local races. Editorials, columns, and letters to the editor were not coded because the focus of this study was on shifts in news coverage rather than changes in the opinion sections of the newspapers.

Four coders used a standard coding form for recording information about the content of the newspapers. In each of the sampled papers, coders looked for stories related to the state or local elections and then coded details including story origin, sources cited, and story topics. Intercoder reliability was checked for 10 percent of the sampled dates to ensure that coders were in general agreement about how sites should be coded. A simple formula, Holsti's coefficient, was used to measure how frequently coders made the same decisions for coding. Using this formula, the overall agreement was 87.9 percent. However, Holsti's formula does not adjust for agreements that could have occurred due to chance. Another formula, Scott's pi, was used to adjust for such chance agreement. This test must be run separately for each item coded. Results of the pi test are reported in the upcoming section that provides detail on each of the primary variables.

HYPOTHESES

The literature led us to five hypotheses about news coverage. First, Steven Smith has suggested that locally written stories are often a requirement of civic journalism projects because stories generated by wire services do not adhere to goals that have been established by papers that are seeking to become more "connected" with their communities.[7] Thus in our first hypothesis, we predict that newspapers that have adopted civic journalism will use more locally written stories than will newspapers that have not adopted civic journalism.

7. Smith, "War in the Gulf."

In this study, the newspaper "that ha[s] adopted civic journalism" is the 1990 and 1994 *Wichita Eagle;* newspapers that have not adopted civic journalism are the 1986 *Wichita Eagle* and the *Topeka Capital Journal* in 1986, 1990, and 1994. In testing our first hypothesis, stories were considered locally written if the author was a staff member of the newspaper being analyzed. Coders had 100 percent agreement about all of the variables (date, newspaper, and story origin) examined in this hypothesis.

Both philosophical and practical definitions of civic journalism identify a new, or revived, respect for citizens as sources of news and commentary. Thus we predict that after the implementation of civic journalism, newspapers will change both how often they use citizens as sources and how early in the news stories those citizen sources are cited.

Our second hypothesis is that newspapers that have adopted civic journalism will use more citizen organization and unaffiliated sources than will newspapers that have not adopted civic journalism. Our third is that newspapers that have adopted civic journalism will cite citizen organization and unaffiliated sources earlier in the story than will newspapers that have not adopted civic journalism.

Official sources include: candidates, candidates' staff, political consultants, state or federal representatives, and government employees. Institutional sources are representatives of organizations that represent business, professional, political, or economic interests. Citizen organizations speak on public issues but are not publicly funded and do not represent business, professional, political, or economic interests. Unaffiliated sources are individuals who are not identified in the story as having organizational affiliations. Observed agreement on the source variables was .75 and expected agreement was .52 resulting in Scott's pi of .48. This means agreement between coders was reduced to 48 percent after adjustment for chance agreement.

The literature also suggests that civic journalism changes the newspaper's emphasis in election coverage. Specifically, greater emphasis is placed on issues and the candidates' competence to address those issues while less emphasis is placed on the election as a horse race and on the character of the candidate.

Our fourth hypothesis is that newspapers that have adopted civic journalism will write more stories on issue and candidate record topics, while newspapers that have not adopted civic journalism will write proportionally more stories on horse race and candidate character topics.

Horse race stories focus on the political race, often focusing on who is leading in the polls. Record stories include information about the candidate's past performance in public service and/or business. Character stories report on aspects of the candidate's personal life or on events that might reveal the candidate's character. Issue stories report the candidate's stand on public policy and/or community concerns. The coding system allowed the recording of one or more of the four topics as having been covered. Observed agreement on topic variables was .78 and expected agreement was .60, resulting in a Scott's pi of .45. This means agreement between coders was reduced to 45 percent after adjustment for chance agreement.

The civic journalism movement has also touched on the role of the media as facilitators of public life programs. This mobilizing function of the media has been suggested in earlier research that has defined and tracked the role of newspapers in providing mobilizing information.[8] Thus in our fifth hypothesis, we expect that a higher proportion of election stories will include mobilizing information in newspapers that have adopted civic journalism than in those that have not adopted civic journalism.

Mobilizing information is any detail in an election story that provides the following: locates entity in space and time (e.g., date, time, room number), and/or sufficient information to enable people to identify and contact the entity, and/or explicit or implicit behavior models.[9] Coders had 100 percent agreement on this variable.

To test the hypotheses of this study, statistical tests were used to determine if political coverage changed significantly after the introduction of civic journalism. If a difference in coverage was found, it was considered to be significant if the probability that the differences occurred due to random chance was 5 percent or less.

FINDINGS

The three sampling periods produced a sample set of 84 newspapers, 14 for each of the two newspapers in each of the three sampling periods. Those newspapers produced a data set of 354 stories, with 190 of the

---

8. James B. Lemert, "Effective Public Opinion," in *Public Opinion, the Press, and Public Policy,* edited by J. David Kennamer (Westport, Conn.: Praeger, 1992).

9. See Lemert, "Effective Public Opinion," for a discussion of both operational and conceptual definitions of mobilizing information.

coded stories from the *Wichita Eagle* and the remaining 164 stories from the *Topeka Capital Journal*. The data set for both newspapers increased between 1986 and 1990, and decreased between 1990 and 1994. There were no unusual trends observed that would minimize the reliability of the sample.

Hypothesis 1

Hypothesis 1 predicts that papers that have adopted civic journalism will use more locally generated stories. Table 1 illustrates the relationship between civic journalism and story origin.

These findings support hypothesis 1. In both 1990 and 1994 the *Eagle* used more locally written stories than it did in 1986. However, the difference between local and wire stories is better explained by differences in the two newspapers' use of staff people to cover political news rather than by changes due to adoption of civic journalism. The *Wichita Eagle* used locally written stories 95.4 percent of the time in the 1986 sample period, so there was little room for increase. By contrast, the *Topeka Capital Journal* relied more on wire and syndicated stories in each of the three sample periods than did the *Wichita Eagle*.

TABLE 1
Civic Journalism and Story Origin

	Percent local	Percent wire service	Row total
Eagle			
1986	95.4	4.6	18.4 (n = 65)
1990	96.3	3.7	22.9 (n = 81)
1994	100	0	12.4 (n = 44)
Capital Journal			
1986	64.6	35.4	13.6 (n = 48)
1990	60.9	39.1	19.5 (n = 69)
1994	74.5	25.5	13.3 (n = 47)
Column Total	82.5 (n = 292)	17.5 (n = 62)	100 (n = 354)

$X^2 = 62.58$, df = 5, $p < .001$

Hypothesis 2

Hypothesis 2 predicts that papers that have adopted civic journalism will use more citizen and unaffiliated stories while papers that have not adopted civic journalism will use more official and institutional sources. Table 2 reports use of sources.

This table shows a pattern of significant difference, but that difference is not consistent with hypothesis 2. The first two columns of Table 5 report all stories that use a single source. Contrary to the hypothesis, use of citizen organizations or unaffiliated individuals as the single source dropped after the introduction of civic journalism—and most unsettling is that use of these sources dropped to zero! Furthermore, the use of individuals with official or institutional ties as single sources in a story increased with the introduction of civic journalism. The third column of Table 2 emphasizes this trend as illustrated by the decrease in combined sources. Comparisons with the Topeka paper do not suggest that extenuating circumstances (for example, the presence of a vocal official source in one year of the sample) were responsible for the results.

TABLE 2
Civic Journalism and Citing of Sources

	Citizen or unaffiliated	Official or institutional	Combined	Row total
Eagle				
1986	4.9	72.1	23.0	19.0 (n = 61)
1990	0.0	83.8	16.2	23.1 (n = 74)
1994	0.0	82.9	17.1	10.9 (n = 35)
Capital Journal				
1986	0.0	93.0	7.0	13.4 (n = 43)
1990	7.8	78.1	14.1	19.9 (n = 64)
1994	4.5	88.6	6.8	13.7 (n = 44)
Column Total	3.1 (n = 10)	82.2 (n = 264)	14.6 (n = 47)	100 (n = 321)

$X = 18.66$, df = 10, $p < .05$, numbers in cells are percents

Hypothesis 3

Because the literature suggested that adoption of civic journalism would make a difference in how the newspaper relates to sources, hypothesis 3 extends analysis of sources to examine whether citizen organizations and unaffiliated sources were referenced earlier in political stories by papers that have adopted civic journalism than by those papers that have not. Table 3 reports four separate one-way ANOVA tests in which civic journalism is the independent variable and story placement of each of the four source categories is tested as a dependent variable. Mean scores represent the average first-appearance paragraph of a particular type of source. The terms "civic journalism" and "not civic journalism" in the first column refer respectively to 1) the *Eagle* in 1990 and 1994 and 2) the *Eagle* in 1986 and the *Capital Journal.*

Only the data about official sources support hypothesis 3. After the Wichita paper instituted civic journalism, official sources did, as hypothesized, appear later in stories. However, contrary to expectations, citizen sources also appeared later in the stories.

TABLE 3

Civic Journalism and Prominence of Sources

(Dependent Variable = Mean Paragraph of First Appearance)

	Mean	N	df	F
Official				
Civic journalism	2.61	109	1	6.58**
Not civic journalism	1.97	188		
Institutional				
Civic journalism	6.93	30	1	1.94
Not civic journalism	5.07	56		
Citizen				
Civic journalism	12.55	11	1	7.22**
Not civic journalism	4.64	25		
Unaffiliated				
Civic journalism	5.43	7	1	1.53
Not civic journalism	3.19	16		

$**p < .01$

Official sources have the lowest mean score. They are most often the first-cited source in stories despite the introduction of civic journalism. Additionally, the first citation for all nonofficial sources was later in the stories after the introduction of civic journalism.

Hypothesis 4

Hypothesis 4 predicts that newspapers that have adopted civic journalism will contain more stories on issue and record topics, while newspapers that have not adopted civic journalism will contain more stories on horse race and character topics. Table 4 combines topic categories into three types: stories that report on only issues and/or candidate record, stories that report only on horse race and/or candidate character, and stories that include issues and/or candidate record as well as horse race and/or candidate character topics.

The findings reported in Table 4 support hypothesis 4. Issue and/or record stories dominate the election coverage of the *Eagle* after it adopted civic journalism. Furthermore, a comparison of the *Eagle* and the *Capital Journal* reveals that this pattern is determined by the introduction of the civic journalism program rather than by existing differences in patterns of coverage at the two newspapers. Both the

TABLE 4
Civic Journalism and Topics of Stories

	Issue/ record	Horse race/ character	Combined	Total
Eagle				
1986	34.5	25.5	40.0	18.8 (n = 55)
1990	62.5	9.7	27.8	24.6 (n = 72)
1994	58.8	11.8	29.4	11.6 (n = 34)
Capital Journal				
1986	37.5	37.5	25.0	13.7 (n = 40)
1990	51.9	28.8	19.2	17.7 (n = 52)
1994	55.0	12.5	32.5	13.7 (n = 40)
Total	50.5 (n = 148)	20.5 (n = 60)	29.0 (n = 85)	100 (n = 293)

$X^2 = 25.92$, df = 10, p < .001, numbers in cells are percents

SALLY J. MCMILLAN, MACY GUPPY, WILLIAM KUNZ, AND RAUL REIS

Capital Journal and the pre-1990 *Eagle* were more likely to focus on horse race and/or character stories than was the *Eagle* in the 1990 and 1994 sample. However, in isolating the *Eagle*'s coverage of topics, the trend toward more issue/record coverage seems to have been slightly less dramatic in 1994 than in 1990.

Hypothesis 5

Hypothesis 5 predicts that a higher proportion of election stories will include mobilizing information in newspapers that have adopted civic journalism than in those that have not. Table 5 illustrates the relationship between civic journalism and mobilizing information.

The findings reported in Table 5 show support for hypothesis 5. The 1990 and 1994 *Eagle* does include more mobilizing information in election coverage. It is encouraging to note that the proportion of stories in the *Wichita Eagle* that included mobilizing information increased in each year of the sample.

SUMMARY AND CONCLUSIONS

The cornerstone of civic journalism is the notion that the media must invigorate the public sphere through the dissemination of useful

TABLE 5
Civic Journalism and Mobilizing Information

	Mobilizing information	No mobilizing information	Total
Eagle			
1986	9.2	90.8	18.4 (n = 65)
1990	12.3	87.7	22.9 (n = 81)
1994	27.3	72.7	12.4 (n = 44)
Capital Journal			
1986	12.5	87.5	13.6 (n = 48)
1990	13.0	87.0	19.5 (n = 69)
1994	4.3	95.7	13.3 (n = 47)
Total	12.7 (n = 45)	87.3 (n = 309)	100 (n = 354)

$X^2 = 12.17$, df = 5, $p < .05$, numbers in cells are percents

information that facilitates the discussion of important issues among citizens. The attempt to rethink the relationship between the media and citizens, and the government, is quite important. This study represents an early benchmark in evaluation of civic journalism.

Quantitative analysis of political coverage in the *Wichita Eagle* and *Topeka Capital Journal* provides limited support for the hypotheses set forth in this study. Some differences were found in the *Wichita Eagle*'s 1990 and 1994 election coverage and coverage in the 1986 *Wichita Eagle* and in the *Topeka Capital Journal*. Stories in the *Wichita Eagle* since the adoption of civic journalism focus more on issues and candidates' records than on the horse race or candidates' character, and a higher proportion of stories include mobilizing information. The hypothesized relationship between civic journalism and use of locally generated stories was found, but data are skewed by the fact that the Wichita paper used locally generated stories in a higher proportion than the Topeka paper even before civic journalism programs began.

One finding of this study raises particular concerns about the efficacy of civic journalism. Quantitative measures of the types of sources cited in news stories showed limited support for the hypothesized relationship. In general, the test newspaper relied as much on the "usual suspects" as sources of news as did the control newspapers. Refined measurement tools might show a new respect for citizens as news sources, but it is disturbing that straightforward measures such as those used in this study did not reveal new trends in types of sources used or placement of sources within election news coverage.

Two limitations of this study should be noted. First, the relatively low Scott's pi coefficients of agreement for news sources (.48) and story topics (.45) suggest that future studies should examine ways to operationalize these variables more clearly. Second, this analysis is focused only on the *Wichita Eagle* rather than on a number of newspapers that have been involved in civic journalism. Because the Knight-Ridder chain and the *Eagle*'s Davis Merritt have been central figures in the movement, one can question how representative the *Eagle* is of civic journalism as envisioned outside of the Knight-Ridder chain and even at other newspapers within the chain. Content analysis tools could be refined and applied to other newspapers and broadcast media to gain greater breadth and depth of understanding of how civic journalism alters media content. Moreover, one can question how different the results would be during a presidential election, when it would be more

SALLY J. MCMILLAN, MACY GUPPY, WILLIAM KUNZ, AND RAUL REIS

difficult to localize a portion of the election coverage and there is more polling and pontificating in the national media.

Civic journalism is about more than political campaigns and elections. There are local initiatives that address socially and politically contentious issues such as race relations, crime, education, community planning, and economic development. Before one can draw conclusions about the civic journalism movement, an evaluation of those initiatives is in order. While many Americans would agree that the election process could be enhanced with more discussion and dialogue, there would be far less consensus on the causes of, and/or solutions to, issues such as crime and decline in quality of education. In the coverage of contentious issues such as these, one must most vigorously question the role of the media as a facilitator of debate, or a promoter of the status quo, and its place in the power structure in the United States.

10

PUBLIC JOURNALISM AND SOCIAL CAPITAL

The Case of Madison, Wisconsin

LEWIS FRIEDLAND, MIRA SOTIROVIC, AND KATIE DAILY

Public journalism has a history, if a relatively brief one. It has expanded from a handful of experiments in 1990 to approximately three hundred projects nationwide in 1997,[1] and the number is constantly growing. There is evidence on the face of things—projects and conferences, articles in academic journals and the journalism and trade press, educators' groups and informal networks—that public journalism is moving from an early experimental phase in which the projects that gave rise to public journalism solidified and nurtured a philosophy, ethics, and set of newsroom practices, to a second phase. In this new phase, public journalism practitioners and researchers alike begin to move beyond the questions, "What is public journalism and what should it do?" to "What has public journalism done and how can it be done better?"

Empirical research on public journalism to date has focused heavily on a description and inventory of projects, a literal and figurative process of mapping the growth of public journalism. This has been both necessary and understandable in the charting of its birth. Now, as public journalists in newsrooms across the country move beyond projects, they will simultaneously turn inward—to ask how public journalism can become more firmly established in news routine—and outward toward

1. Lisa Austin, Research Director, Project Public Life and the Press.

the communities with whom they collaborate in the reconstruction of public life.

This outward turn poses a new series of difficult questions for each project and newsroom: What is the community that we serve, and how do we know that community? What are its problems, and how can we best pose them? Underlying all of these questions is another one: What is the "social capital" of a given community, or what are the resources embedded in civic and public life that allow journalists and communities to build and rebuild public life?

FROM RECONSTRUCTING PUBLIC LIFE TO BUILDING SOCIAL CAPITAL

Public journalism began as a reform movement within journalism institutions. Because this early history has been increasingly well documented,[2] our discussion is oriented to establishing some central premises and directions in order to better situate the concepts of public life and social capital for the purposes of empirical analysis at the level of our case.

The concept of "public life" has been at the center of the writings of James W. Carey and Jay Rosen, public journalism's most prominent theorists, and Davis "Buzz" Merritt, its best-known practitioner. Carey makes clear that the category of public life is not a residue of a golden age to be recovered, but a counterfactual normative ideal:

> The "recovery of public life" is not an attempt to recapture a period, historical moment, or condition, but, instead, to invigorate a conception, illusion, or idea that once had the capacity to engage the imagination, motivate action, and serve an ideological purpose. Public life refers to an illusion of the possible rather than to something with a given anterior existence.[3]

Rosen characterizes public journalism as the kind that "invites people to become a public" and that "calls on the press to help revive civic life and improve public dialogue." For Merritt, public life is "the means

2. See for example Miller, *The Charlotte Project;* Rosen, "Getting the Connections Right"; Rosen, "Making Things More Public"; Jay Rosen and Lisa Austin, "Public Life and the Press: A Progress Report" (New York: Project on Public Life and the Press, 1994); Jay Rosen and Davis Merritt, Jr., *Public Journalism: Theory and Practice;* Kramer, "Civic Journalism: Six Case Studies."
   3. James W. Carey, "The Press, Public Opinion, and Public Discourse."

by which democracy is expressed and experienced," including "any activity where people try to address common goals or address common problems."[4]

Public life, then, for Carey is a normative ideal to be counterposed to a cynical concept of democracy in which only power counts. Rosen emphasizes the role of this ideal in the reconstruction of public dialogue. And Merritt stresses activity to meet common goals. In assessing public journalism's impact, we draw on each of these standards, but our goal is to begin to map the *social dimensions* in which the experience of dialogue and the practice of problem solving take place. This mapping situates the spatial dimensions of public life, the "sites" or spaces of public dialogue, in the context of the social networks that comprise communities. Both the space of dialogue and the structure of networks have their own forms. They frequently overlap, but we believe it is an analytical mistake (albeit perhaps a rhetorical strength) to assume a uniform citizenry to whom the initial efforts of reconstructing public dialogue are addressed. In contrast, we assume that the term "citizen" covers a multiplicity of groups and networks that intersect in many ways for differing purposes. This is *not*, we stress, to suggest that the core concept of citizen is unimportant, or that it can or should be reduced to substructures of competing interest or identity groups. Rather, we suggest that the active reconstruction of public life requires a more detailed understanding of social capital—the networks of social trust that communities draw on to solve common problems. Put in the language of public journalism, we need to trace the pattern of "disconnections"— within the newsroom; between citizens and politics; between citizens and the press; and among groups of citizens themselves—in order to see how they might be reconnected.

We will, then, present this series of disconnections in the context of Madison, Wisconsin, and explain how the news organizations that we have evaluated have come together to address them. First, however, we discuss our conception of the relation between public life and social capital-building.

The understanding of public life articulated by public journalism theorists is deeply influenced by theories of deliberative democracy. Briefly, deliberative democracy holds that citizens and their representatives are

4. Rosen, "Getting the Connections Right," 1. Merritt, *Public Journalism and Public Life*, xii.

capable of deliberating about public problems and their solutions under conditions that are conducive to reasoned reflection and refined public judgment, including a mutual willingness to understand the values, perspectives, and interests of others, and the possibility of reframing these in the light of a joint search for common interests and mutually acceptable solutions.[5] Theories of deliberation stand in contradistinction to direct plebiscitary democracy, whether in the form of referenda, polls, talk shows, or other mechanisms compelling conformity to majority opinion. They also challenge pluralist notions of interest group competition and the elitism that substitutes political experts for citizen deliberation.

The emphasis on deliberation that runs throughout much of public or civic journalism is reflected in the fact that virtually every major public journalism project began as an effort to improve deliberation, either through the formation of citizens' agendas, candidate debates with citizen panels, town hall meetings, or deliberative opinion polls. Despite this emphasis on deliberation, however, there is relatively little practical reflection on the *forms* of deliberation. Both deliberative and plebiscitary democratic forms, insofar as they address *audiences,* treat publics as *masses.* For public journalism projects, this is a largely unavoidable consequence of the organizational structure of news. When readers and viewers are addressed as *citizens at large* through public media projects, they are being addressed only indirectly as citizens who are embedded in the multiple contexts of practical problem-solving activity. Deliberation begins in discussion in these contexts. A state- or metro-wide candidates' debate, when all is said and done, still treats citizens as potential consumers of public journalism. They are asked to read, watch, listen, to the products of the public journalism project and then to act on their conclusions in the political marketplace.[6]

This is one of the more difficult organizational ambiguities of public journalism. One of the first "disconnects" that news organizations see is

5. For a more complete explication see Lewis A. Friedland and Carmen J. Sirianni, "Critical Concepts in the New Citizenship."

6. For the origins of public journalism projects see Rosen, "Making Things More Public." For the theory of deliberative polling see Fishkin, *Democracy and Deliberation: New Directions for Democratic Reform.* Rosen has made a strong distinction between "the media" and journalism. While this distinction has some currency, in practice news organizations, including those committed to public journalism, are simultaneously institutions of mass media *and* of journalism. As such, they are subject to the economic imperative of producing a mass audience daily. This requirement is prior to the practice of journalism, even for the best public journalism institutions.

that between citizens and their political leaders. The understanding that citizens are disconnected from the newspaper or television organization usually follows hard on its heels. This leads to attempts to improve deliberation, in order to resolve the disconnect. But the initial form of these attempts is still largely constrained by traditional newsgathering practices and a commercial structure that continues to treat audiences as aggregates, whether citizens or demographic targets. An extended period of experimentation often follows, involving a redefinition of mission and self-reflection, as news organizations attempt to change traditional practices.

We see this pattern repeated, with some variation, in each of three core cases of public journalism: Wichita, Charlotte, and Madison. After initial experiments with deliberation, each of the newspapers in these projects moved forward to address community issues or problems, with different strategies of thematizing issues, presenting them to their communities, and linking problem solving to deliberation. We characterize this second phase as the problem-solving phase of public journalism projects, in which projects move toward addressing social questions within the community with the idea of reconnecting groups of citizens with other groups of citizens.

This move toward problem solving operates at two levels. First, by thematizing community problems, public journalism projects create a framework for deliberation in existing community problem-solving networks. The project links networks of actors that might not have come together, making them aware of each other, and allows them to address each other, at least indirectly. Under traditional newsgathering practices these networks often remain only dimly perceived. Second, as news organizations begin to thematize issues and problems within their communities, they move from a general conception of "the community" or "our readers" or "viewers" to specific groupings of organizations. In short, in addressing community problems through general deliberation, they are moved to map their communities in ways that they generally have not done and are often unprepared to do.

This mapping is one form of tracing of social capital at the community level. Briefly, we can define social capital as those stocks of social trust, norms, and networks that people can draw on to solve common problems. Networks of civic engagement, such as neighborhood associations, sports clubs, and cooperatives, are essential forms of social capital. The more dense these networks, according to social capital theory, the more likely that members of a community will cooperate for mutual benefit.[7]

The writings of Robert Putnam have circulated widely within the public journalism community and have come to dominate the definition of social capital. Putnam claims that civic life in the United States began a long cycle of decline in the 1950s that is coming to fruition now. A recent series of articles argues that this decline is the result of the end of a "civic generation" born in 1910 and its replacement by a generation raised on television. In fact, Putnam claims that television is the clearest culprit behind the civic decline he finds.[8]

There is not the space to thoroughly review Putnam's thesis here. However, we want to note several important pieces of countervailing evidence, as well as some structural similarities between Putnam's argument for the decline of social capital, and the arguments undergirding deliberative democracy. In a massive study of civic participation, *Voice and Equality*, Verba, Schlozman, and Brady interviewed more than fifteen thousand Americans to provide a profile of political and nonpolitical voluntary activity.[9] The authors consider a broad range of political activities: voting, getting involved in campaigns, making political contributions, working informally in the community, and contacting government officials; attending protests, marches, or demonstrations; serving without pay on local elected or appointed boards; and being politically active through voluntary organizations. They develop a civic voluntarism model that considers both the *motivation* and *capacity* to take part in political life, as well as the resources necessary to participate:

7. This is, of course, only the barest definition of social capital. For a more complete explication see James S. Coleman, *Individual Interests and Collective Action;* James S. Coleman, *Foundations of Social Theory;* Friedland and Sirianni, "Critical Concepts"; Lewis A. Friedland, "Public Journalism: Deliberation and Social Capital," *Critical Studies in Mass Communication* (forthcoming); Carmen Sirianni and Lewis A. Friedland, "Social Capital and Participatory Democratic Innovation: Learning and Capacity Building from the 1960s to the 1990s," paper presented to the American Sociological Association (Washington, D.C., August 20, 1995); Carmen J. Sirianni, "Citizen Participation, Social Capital, and Social Learning in the United States 1960–1995," in *Increasing Understanding of Public Problems and Policies* (Farm Foundation, 1995), 21–35; Carmen J. Sirianni and Lewis A. Friedland, *Civic Innovation in America* (forthcoming).

8. Robert D. Putnam, "The Prosperous Community: Social Capital and Public Life"; Robert D. Putnam, "Bowling Alone: America's Declining Social Capital," 65–78; Robert D. Putnam, "The Strange Disappearance of Civic America."

9. Sidney Verba, Kay Lehman Schlozman, and Henry Brady, *Voice and Equality: Civic Voluntarism in American Politics* (Cambridge: Harvard University Press, 1995).

time, money, verbal skills. Finally, they consider the *networks of recruitment* through which political activity is mediated.

Almost half of their respondents reported being affiliated with an organization that takes stands in politics. Strikingly, almost 20 percent reported having worked informally with others in the neighborhood or community on some community issue or problem. Almost 15 percent attended local board meetings, and 3 percent reported sitting on organizational boards. The study demonstrates a relatively high level of civic activity, in contrast to the image of decline. In a major empirical review of the data on civic participation, Everett Ladd of the Roper Center strongly disputes Putnam's finding of decline.[10]

A second objection to Putnam's thesis of decline is historical. Skocpol argues that many of the institutions that Putnam points to as being bulwarks of association in civil society were in fact the result of initiatives of the state, or of federated action at the national level.[11] This national, regional, and state civic infrastructure was the essential support for even the most local of civic efforts. For example, the PTAs, a central theme for Putnam, began as the National Congress of Mothers and worked with other national women's voluntary organizations to establish "mother's pensions" (later AFDC), a federal Children's Bureau, and programs for women's and infants' health. These in turn stimulated action at the local level.

The third criticism is theoretical. Consonant with our understanding of the deliberative model, the decline model takes social capital in the aggregate, and then finds aggregate measures of decline. The data are inconclusive, as we have just seen. But more significant is the failure to distinguish among *forms* of social capital. It is not clear how indices of decline impact on *citizen problem-solving capacities* rather than raw indices of association. For example, membership in the League of Women Voters may have declined by 42 percent since 1969, but local leagues have developed a wide variety of civic innovations to address environmental and child care issues that were not on the agenda a generation ago. Membership in the National Federation of Women's Clubs may be down by half, but newer women's groups have addressed issues such

10. Verba et al., *Voice and Equality*, 51–52. Everett C. Ladd, "The Data Just Don't Show Erosion of America's 'Social Capital,' " *Public Perspective* 7, no. 4 (1996): 1–6.

11. Theda Skocpol, "Unravelling from Above," *American Prospect* 25 (March–April 1996): 20–25.

as domestic violence that were masked and embedded in older forms of social capital that vested patriarchal authority in the family.

Even excluding advocacy organizations, there has been a tremendous growth in civic innovation by locally based environmental organizations since the 1970s. The empirical arguments for an overall decline of social capital must be carefully distinguished from nostalgia for earlier times. This is most obvious for those forms that were illiberal and socially exclusivist (as Putnam acknowledges in his 1996 article). Their decline should be seen as a net gain. The decline of other forms of social capital, like bowling leagues, may not be that significant if they did not lend themselves to being mobilized for new forms of community problem solving.

Our argument is not that social capital may not be declining in some aggregate sense (although we remain skeptical). Rather, wherever one stands on the issue of the overall decline of social capital, civic innovation has been occurring over the past several decades in many arenas and in a variety of forms, and these innovations represent substantial social learning upon which we might continue to build.[12] This is of direct relevance for public journalism and its ongoing projects. Because public journalism projects are challenged to map their communities' social problem-solving capacities when they move from a deliberative to a community problem-solving orientation, the framework that they adopt directly affects the map that they will derive. If a project retains a purely deliberative framework, it will concentrate on those citizens and groups that are most oriented toward public talk. This may, we want to stress, remain positive for both the community and news organizations. But such projects are more likely to draw in those already articulate networks of community leaders who generally participate in community affairs. The predominantly deliberative orientation may even exclude those groups who do not already share it.

Similarly, if a general "problem-solving" orientation is adopted toward social capital development, the relevant map of the community will be divided into "problem groups," or those needing help, and "problem solvers," those professional groups and institutions oriented toward social problems. This can result in the unintended consequence of marginalizing the very groups whose cooperation is necessary to rebuild community life. We argue that a problem-solving orientation that moves

12. See Sirianni and Friedland, *Civic Innovation*.

beyond pure deliberation, or the simple identification of problems, will have to involve citizens in developing their own solutions to community problems. And this is an active role for which news organizations, public journalism–oriented or otherwise, are generally not prepared.

WE THE PEOPLE AND CITY/SCHOOLS OF HOPE

The practice of public journalism in Madison, where two public journalism projects have been operating since 1992, illustrates a stark contrast between projects oriented toward deliberation and community problem solving. We the People (WTP) is a deliberative project whose core partners were originally Wisconsin Public Television, the *Wisconsin State Journal,* and Wood Communications, a local public relations firm. These three were later joined by the CBS affiliate, WISC-TV, and Wisconsin Public Radio. The second project is City of Hope and later Schools of Hope, spearheaded by the *Wisconsin State Journal* and joined later by WISC.

Each project represents an almost pure type. We the People involves only deliberation, consisting of town hall meetings leading to aired deliberative events, split almost evenly between elections and policy issues. City/Schools of Hope (C/SOH), on the other hand, was, from its inception, an attempt to actively intervene in the very heart of the decision-making process in Madison. Taken together, the two projects represent the strengths and limits of pure deliberation and pure intervention, and, through their limits, point to new directions for both.[13]

WE THE PEOPLE

We the People began as a collaborative effort among the aforementioned Madison news organizations and the *St. Paul Pioneer Press* and public station KTCA in Minneapolis–St. Paul to cover the 1992 presidential primaries in the Upper Midwest. The original aim was limited to producing a joint town hall meeting that would have a greater impact on the region than would those conducted in a single city.

13. Our emphasis here is on theory and analysis. We recommend that the interested reader consult several thorough narrative summaries of We the People and City of Hope, including Rosen and Austin, "Public Life"; Frank Denton and Esther Thorson, "Civic Journalism: Does It Work?"; Kramer, "Civic Journalism: Six Case Studies"; Rosen, "Making Things More Public."

The principals in each organization—Dave Iverson, director of news and public affairs of Wisconsin Public Television; Tom Still, associate editor and Frank Denton, managing editor of the *State Journal;* and James Wood of Wood Communications—agreed to continue the experiment with the Wisconsin U.S. Senate race in fall 1992. Still says that in the beginning "what we were doing was giving people a chance to have some sort of access—direct access—to public officials, or elected officials, or would-be elected officials. We viewed it . . . as basically something of a TV production, and an exercise in democracy, or vice-versa; an exercise in democracy that was a TV production."[14]

The project began to shift with the April 1993 statewide race for superintendent of public instruction. According to Still, "Those town halls changed the nature of our coverage. It changed how we viewed the race from a reportorial point of view. Our lead reporter who was covering that election went to all of our forums, and she did that much better a job because of it." The next two projects, property tax relief and the federal deficit, were more directly focused on policy issues, without any direct tie to elections.

This was the beginning of a pivot away from a purely electoral conception of the project to one that embraced a broader range of public policy issues. As Table 1 shows, We the People continued to alternate between electoral and policy themes, and was divided almost evenly between the two as of mid-1995.

Each of the WTP programs has been deliberative in both style and substance. Their primary goal has been to expand citizen discussion of a specific political race or set of policy issues. In this limited sense WTP has remained fairly conservative in its goals, compared with electoral projects in Charlotte, Wichita, or elsewhere that have actively developed "citizen's agendas." Despite some use of issues polling to guide discussion, We the People has stopped short of the broader goal of developing citizens' agendas by both agreement and design. Iverson of Wisconsin Public Television was not influenced by the concept of public journalism in 1992 when early project decisions were made: "I had never heard the phrase 'public' or 'civic' journalism until the Winter of '94 . . . I don't see it, and never have, as a radical departure."[15] Iverson continues to hold the view that We the People is not really anything more than "good

14. Interview, Tom Still, December 6, 1995.
15. Interview, David Iverson, December 6, 1995.

TABLE 1
We the People Projects

Date	Topic	Format	Type
March 1992	Presidential Primary	Debate	Election
October 1992	U.S. Senate Race	Debate	Election
April 1993	Superintendant of Schools	Debate	Election-Policy
June 1993	Property Tax Relief	Town hall/hearing	Policy
July 1993	Federal Deficit	Town hall/hearing	Policy
March 1994	Health Care Reform	Town hall/jury	Policy
June 1994	We the Young People	Town hall	Policy-Election
October 1994	Gubernatorial Debates	Town hall/debates	Election
October 1994	U.S. Senate/Young People	Town hall	Elections
March 1995	Wisconsin Supreme Court	Citizen jury	Election
April 1995	People's State Budget	Town hall/hearing	Policy
July 1995	Land Use	Town hall	Policy

serious journalism" that leads toward the core function of strengthening the citizen's right to know.

Iverson conceives of a continuum of orientations toward public journalism. At one end is a "convening role" in which journalists act to "gather people together to take part in some common enterprise whether to debate an issue or question candidates." Such events would not take place without the active organizing intervention of news institutions. Iverson sees WTP in this framework and does not feel that this kind of action is "crossing over." Second, having helped organize the event, news institutions helped form a "steering committee" consisting of politicians and news organizations, which Iverson identifies with the Hope projects, a step with which Iverson is not comfortable. Third, sitting at the same table with local politicians and citizens, journalists participate, voting on whether or not to take a specific course of action. Fourth, news organizations can openly advocate positions while playing a convening role. Iverson says, "I sort of stop at the first stop, and I can't quite go comfortably beyond that."

We will explore the specific aims and structure of City of Hope in a moment, but, in brief, it started as a strongly activist project that began with major opinion elites in Madison. Because City of Hope has convened politicians, newspaper representatives, business leaders, major voluntary organizations, and others in a top-down manner, it has stimulated controversy among opinion leaders, activists, and journalists alike. This controversy has led some, like Iverson and to a lesser extent Still, to draw clear lines between the deliberation of WTP and C/SOH.

Both Still and Denton say that the two projects have remained separate within the *State Journal*. According to Still, Hope has operated on a separate track "that at times was a civic journalism track and at times wasn't." For Still, the top-down process by which leaders were assembled is the distinguishing difference. "Schools of Hope and City of Hope were up front about saying, 'Here's what we think is wrong, and here's how we're going to set about changing that.' We the People has always asked the question, 'What do you think is wrong and how would you like to change it?'"

At a November 1995 meeting, We the People principals articulated the basic mission of the project: WTP exists to facilitate conversations and to help reestablish the link between people and politics. According to Still, "We're not out there to push for any agenda, to push for any candidate. We view ourselves as a catalyst for stronger community conversation and therefore more vital public life."

We the People, then, is a project wholly oriented toward deliberation. It is a statewide project, which makes assessing its effects on the quality of deliberation in Madison more complex. Because our study is limited to the structure of the project and its effects *within* Madison, we need to be cautious in assessing the effects of a statewide project in a single community. Nonetheless, the principal participating news organizations are headquartered in Madison. The culmination of every WTP event has been a televised town hall meeting either in Madison, or, if involving sites in the rest of the state, anchored there. Because there is a distinct electoral and policy skew to WTP, its strongest effects should be located in Madison, the state center of policy and government. All of the topics, whether electoral or policy, affect Madison. To the extent that WTP has stimulated public conversation, then, it should certainly be as strong or stronger in Madison than elsewhere in the state.

ASSESSING DELIBERATION

The strengths and limits of We the People's deliberative approach are becoming more clear now after four years. We begin with the strengths.

First, the longevity of the project is significant. Among a select group of Madisonians—those in the opinion-leading strata—it has established itself as a local deliberative institution. According to Still, Iverson, and Denton, when a topic comes up in conversation and someone thinks it should be treated by WTP, it is often invoked as a verb: "Why don't you 'we-the-people' this issue?" It is an achievement for three media partners (later joined by two others) to have established and maintained a working collaboration over four years.

Second, longevity lends institutional weight to the process of deliberation itself among those who are aware of the project.[16] Each new venture is taken more seriously. The WTP project of summer 1995, "The Search for Common Ground," focused on land use, and was jointly televised on Wisconsin Public Television and WISC. The project yielded an extraordinary 12 rating and 31 share in Dane County (it reached 12 percent of all homes with television, and 31 percent of all homes watching television at that time), easily winning its time period. According to an aide to Dane County Executive Rick Phelps, interest and awareness in this important issue climbed substantially in the period following the project.

Third, there is some evidence that those who are aware of the project are engaged, at least episodically, in key election or policy issues. A survey by Thorson and Denton taken in fall 1994 following the November election found general project recognition of 51 percent. However, probes of the sample found that only 20 percent could correctly identify the source of the project. Similarly, a survey taken by the Mass Communications Research Center at the University of Wisconsin earlier in fall 1995 found recognition levels of 43 percent. Of those who had heard of the project, 35 percent reported that they were likely to attend a town hall meeting on juvenile crime. However, follow-up depth interviews (conducted by Daily and Sotirovic) with twenty-four of the survey's participants found that of the twelve who had been selected from the group reporting awareness of We the People, recognition was very superficial.

16. Interview, Roberta Gassman, February 22, 1996.

Random sample telephone surveys of Madison residents demonstrate that We the People viewers and readers tend to be more educated than those who have not heard of WTP. The surveys were conducted in fall of 1994 and 1995, and yielded samples of 158 and 261 Madisonians respectively. In 1994, WTP viewers and readers were more likely to be women than men, but in 1995, gender was not a significant correlate of WTP exposure. In 1995, Madisonians exposed to WTP tended to be older and earn higher incomes than residents not familiar with the project.

More interestingly, the forms of participation that WTP viewers and readers report have expanded over time: in 1994, Madisonians exposed to WTP were more likely to have attended a community meeting and were more likely to have voted in a recent election than those unfamiliar with WTP. The following year, WTP viewers and readers also tended to attend community meetings and to vote more than their counterparts; in addition, they were more likely to have contacted a public official about a community issue or problem than those unexposed to the project. In 1995, survey respondents were asked about their willingness to attend a community issue forum in the future. WTP viewers and readers were more likely to express a willingness to engage in community-level meetings than those not familiar with the project. In fact, the likelihood of attending a future community meeting was the strongest participation correlate to WTP exposure.

There may be a link between this increased willingness to participate and our fourth point. Starting in 1995, a movement to formalize citizen deliberation has taken place in Madison. Groups have been formed to continue community dialogue linked both to Study Circles and National Issues Forums. Both national organizations help set up local ongoing deliberative forums, with Study Circles stressing the process of dialogue, and National Issues Forums stressing action oriented toward public problem solving. In Madison, the Study Circles leadership group is fairly distinct from WTP, although aware of the project, while National Issues Forums involves some informal overlap (Still is involved).

We can say, then, that a certain plateau of institutional public deliberation has been reached in Madison, aided and stimulated in no small way by the success of We the People. This conclusion must be qualified, however, by two limitations involving the problem of continuity in the choice of deliberative topics, and the effect of the project on prompting readers and viewers toward community problem-solving activity at some level.

First, there has been a tendency to treat issues episodically with relatively little continuity. Table 1 shows a wide range of topics, but relatively little overlap or repetition. There *have* been some continuities among topics, for example, property tax relief, the people's state budget, and gubernatorial debates that focused on these issues; or between We the Young People and youth voices in the gubernatorial and senate debates. But these thematic links, and in some cases carryovers among participating citizens, are separated by a wide gulf of time, and perhaps more important, a large flow of other information that is only episodically related back to We the People. None of the major partners regularly follow up on issues raised in WTP projects, even though they do refer back to the projects occasionally in stories and editorials. So despite the underlying message *during* a given project that "we are now deliberating seriously about important issues that take time," there is an implicit, countervailing message: "Now we are done with this issue and can move on to the next one." While media sponsors as well as viewers and readers know this is not true, no one has directly communicated to citizens: "We are tackling a difficult issue that will require strong, clear, continuous deliberation. We will keep coming back to it until we have seen some progress emerging toward a consensus on a framework of how we as a state or community might move forward."

There are a number of reasons for this gap. The most important one is the operation of the news routine. A We the People project requires mobilizing a great deal of organizational energy among all of the partners, often using key editing, producing, and reporting personnel that have to be drawn out of the daily reporting pool. There is a legitimate and understandable tendency to breathe a collective sigh of relief when the project is over, and return back to "daily life" in the newsroom until the next project. A second important reason is the philosophy of weak deliberation purposely chosen by at least some of the major partners. The notion that it is the function of WTP to "hold the door open," no more and no less, tends to reinforce a sense that what the community does with the framework offered by each individual project is primarily the business of the community, and not the media partners. If a project strikes a public chord, fine, then the public will proceed to deliberate further. If not, that is unfortunate, but it is not the job of WTP to advance the agenda, even if the agenda is militantly nonpartisan and is restricted to further and deeper deliberation on an agreed topic of public importance.

The second limitation is the reluctance of We the People partners to link the deliberative process to ongoing problem solving. This is in no small part explained by the project's statewide scope. Because sites change for each project, the only constant location is Madison. As we have noted, the process of organizing each program is episodic. Wood Communications personnel identify key sites and actors at chosen locations, and then town hall meetings leading up to the televised events are organized. There may be an informal residue in specific communities, as participants continue to discuss the issues among themselves, but to date there has been no formal continuation of the deliberative process (other than the efforts noted above). As WTP moves on to the next topic, the informal connections among participants are all that remain.

The quality and reach of deliberation created by We the People can be summed up as a clear institutional success with wide recognition by an opinion-leading stratum of Madison. The deliberative process is limited, however, by a number of factors. Recognition among the general public is wide, but remains superficial. The project itself has purposely adopted a strategy of *weak deliberation,* in which the episodic airing of a topic is considered the deliberative limit.[17] Each organization has embraced WTP as central to its mission, but the investment in deliberation has been episodic and remains unintegrated into its daily or weekly news coverage.

Finally, a deliberative strategy, whether weak or strong, contains the inherent limits discussed in the first section of this chapter. Without linking deliberation to ongoing citizen problem-solving efforts, media-sponsored and induced deliberative efforts are more likely to fail, both in institutionalizing a wider discussion in the community, and in helping forge the links that lead from deliberation to civic problem solving. This is, of course, a choice that can be made consciously, as in the case of We the People. But we believe that it ultimately imposes limits on the deepening of deliberation proper.

Having explicated the limits of weak deliberation, we turn to City/ Schools of Hope as an opposite type, a project that is strongly and explicitly engaged in community problem solving. Before continuing, however, we briefly sketch the theory of community structure that we

17. For the distinction between strong and weak deliberation see Benjamin R. Barber, *Strong Democracy: Participatory Politics for a New Age.*

believe underpins both deliberation and problem solving, in order to make the basis for comparison more clear.

COMMUNITY STRUCTURE

Our research began with the hypothesis that the concerted effort of all of the most powerful media institutions in Madison to focus attention on a series of issues through the We the People project should 1) create a clear awareness of the effort itself; and 2) lead to some citizen action to address the issues that were raised, either through increased deliberation, community problem solving, or both. As we have just described, there is limited support for both propositions, but neither has been demonstrated clearly and unambiguously. In the course of our investigation, we have been led to revise our core theory of community structure, on which these two assumptions rest. While we cannot explicate this theory fully here, a brief sketch is necessary to make sense of our findings to date.[18]

The study of community can be very broadly divided into three types. First, studies have looked at communities from the standpoint of integration, the notion that communities consist of groups in relation to each other which are bound together into a more integrated whole. Second, studies have focused on conflicts among groups based on power and interest, often focused on the relation between local power structures and subordinate, linked groupings. Third, in the last twenty-five years, studies have emerged that look at communities from the standpoint of networks, or, more properly, networks of networks.

There are numerous differences, as well as overlaps, among these three broad divisions. Among the most important are those between theories that hearken back to the core sociological distinction between gemeinschaft and gesellschaft. In the tradition of gemeinschaft, the community is conceived of as a large, relatively bounded entity, with the groups within it being linked in some form of hierarchical unity, as subordinate parts to the whole. In the tradition of gesellschaft, groups are no longer bound to each other, other than through contractual ties. Both views tend to conclude that community is in "decline" if

---

18. For a more developed argument see Friedland, "Public Journalism: Deliberation and Social Capital," and Lewis A. Friedland and Jack M. McLeod, "Community Integration Reconsidered," in *Mass Media, Social Control, and Social Change*, edited by J. Demers and K. Visnawath, 1998.

not "lost" altogether. This loss can be seen as irretrievable, superseded by capitalist or bureaucratic development, or recoverable through a range of strategies for reinvigorating community life. In contemporary political discourse the latter position is represented by some forms of communitarianism on the one hand, and on the other hand by more conservative neo-Tocquevillian visions associated with the revival of civic virtue and the transfer of government power back to newly reinvigorated neighborhood and community-based associations.[19]

The vision of community as rent by power has a long and complex tradition, dividing primarily between those who proceed from C. Wright Mills to see the power structure of community as primary in determining the local distribution of power and resources, and the pluralist tradition represented by Dahl, which sees interest group competition resulting in long-term balance between in-groups and out-groups.[20]

The notion of community as a networked entity has emerged since the 1970s. Led by the work of Wellman and Fischer,[21] social network theory stresses the multiplicity of network connections among individuals and groups, making a primary distinction between local, or proximate, networks and more distant networks. Both Wellman and Fischer have found that individuals' network ties are more complex, multiplex in

19. For communitarianism see Amitai Etzioni, *The Spirit of Community: The Reinvention of American Society;* for conservative perspectives see Peter Berger and Richard John Neuhaus, *To Empower People: From State to Civil Society,* 2d ed., edited by Michael Novak (Washington D.C.: AEI Press, 1996).

20. For community power see Floyd Hunter, *Community Power Structure: A Study of Decision Makers* (Chapel Hill: University of North Carolina Press, 1953); Floyd Hunter, *Community Power Succession* (Chapel Hill: University of North Carolina Press, 1980); John R. Logan and Harvey L. Molotch, *Urban Fortunes: The Political Economy of Place* (Berkeley: University of California Press, 1987); Robert Dahl, *Who Governs? Democracy and Power in an American City.*

21. Claude Fischer, *To Dwell among Friends: Personal Networks in Town and City* (Chicago: University of Chicago Press, 1982); Claude S. Fischer, Robert Max Jackson, C. Ann Stueve, Kathleen Gerson, Lynne McCallister Jones, and with Mark Baldassare, *Networks and Places: Social Relations in the Urban Setting* (New York: Free Press, 1977); Barry Wellman, "The Community Question"; Barry Wellman, "The Community Question Re-evaluated," in *Power, Community and the City,* edited by Michael Peter Smith (New Brunswick, N.J.: Transaction, 1988); Barry Wellman, "Studying Personal Communities," in *Social Structure and Network Analysis,* edited by Peter V. Marsden and Nan Lin (Beverly Hills, Calif.: Sage, 1982), 61–80; Barry Wellman, Peter J. Carrington, and Alan Hall, "Networks as Personal Communities," in *Social Structures: A Network Approach,* edited by Barry Wellman and S. D. Berkowitz (Cambridge and New York: Cambridge University Press, 1988); Barry Wellman and Barry Leighton, "Networks, Neighborhoods and Communities," *Urban Affairs Quarterly* 14, no. 3 (March 1979): 363–90.

PUBLIC JOURNALISM AND SOCIAL CAPITAL

form and substance, and less proximate than implied by a more locally rooted view of community integration. In short, individuals have many sets of relations with local family, extended kin, in the workplace, and now via phone and e-mail that make generalizations about "community" more difficult.

Network research on community power structures by Laumann, Galaskiewicz, and Marsden in the 1970s and 1980s found the persistence of core networks of community leaders that were linked to each other through complex interlocking networks of information, communication, and resource exchange. Laumann et al. did not posit an a priori structure of community power. Rather, they investigated the empirical variation of these networks in multiple dimensions of power and opinion formation. Galaskiewicz found three dominant structures, the money network, the information network, and the support network, each dominated by different sets of elites and each using different media for establishing and maintaining influence. While conflict was central to each case study, so were efforts to work together to solve common problems.[22]

These findings led us to ask about the role of public journalism media in social networks. The question of media influence in social networks was first articulated in Lazarsfeld and Katz's *Personal Influence*. In a systematic review of the literature flowing from the opinion leadership tradition, Weimann observes that while the concept of opinion leadership was widely applied in the domains of health, marketing, and diffusion of innovations, it has only recently been resurrected in the study of politics. He attributes this renewed interest in part to the interest in social network analysis as a method for bridging micro- and macro-levels of politics. Understanding the local structures of both deliberation and social capital formation requires more complete mapping of local network structures, including problem-solving capacities or "community assets" (discussed later in this chapter).[23]

22. Joseph Galaskiewicz, *Exchange Networks and Community Politics;* Edward O. Laumann, *Bonds of Pluralism: The Form and Substance of Urban Social Networks* (New York: John Wiley and Sons, 1973); Edward O. Laumann and Franz U. Pappi, *Networks of Collective Action: A Perspective on Community Influence Systems* (New York: Academic Press, 1976); Peter V. Marsden, "Core Discussion Networks of Americans," *American Sociological Review* 52, no. 1 (1987): 122–31.

23. Elihu Katz and Paul Lazarsfeld, *Personal Influence* (New York: Free Press, 1955). Gabriel Weimann, *The Influentials: People Who Influence People* (Albany: State University of New York Press, 1994).

We can only suggest the relevance of this argument for research on public journalism here. The notion of the "two-step flow" presupposes a group of "opinion leaders" who pass on information to others in their circle of influence. But what has been somewhat obscured in the legacy of *Personal Influence* is the actual structure of opinion leadership posited. Beginning with *The People's Choice*, Lazarsfeld et al. had found a "molecular" level of opinion leadership, "persons who were influential in their immediate environments but not necessarily prominent within the total community."[24] Further, in contrast to the belief that opinions filtered down from elites to masses, they found that each social stratum generated its own opinion leadership, and that molecular leaders were likely to be attuned to media characteristics of their own groups, forming a horizontal structure of opinion leadership.

> The types of leader in which we are interested in this study—the ones we call opinion leaders—serve informal rather than formal groups, face-to-face rather than more extensive groups. They guide opinion and its changes rather than lead directly in action.
>
> What we call opinion leadership, if we may call it leadership at all, is leadership at its simplest: it is casually exercised, sometimes unwitting and unbeknown, within the smallest grouping of friends, family members, and neighbors . . . it is the almost invisible, certainly inconspicuous, form of leadership at the person-to-person level of ordinary, intimate, informal, everyday contact.[25]

It is this "lower"-level horizontal structure that interests us most in the investigation of the effects of deliberation and social problem solving within communities. Lazarsfeld and Katz based their research on early sociometric models of opinion diffusion and were concerned with the chain of information passed from small group to small group. In contrast, the later network community studies of Laumann et al. allow us to develop more comprehensive descriptions of community structure, in effect to begin to reunite the vertical and horizontal levels of influence in a single community, or, viewed from the standpoint of the media of influence, to trace the circulation of power and information.

24. Paul F. Lazarsfeld, Bernard Berelson, and Hazel Gaudet, *The People's Choice: How the Voter Makes Up His Mind in a Presidential Campaign*, 3d ed. (New York: Columbia University Press, 1944, 1968), cited in Katz and Lazarsfeld, *Personal Influence*, 3.
25. Katz and Lazarsfeld, *Personal Influence*, 138.

Our study of Madison has led us to rethink this interlocking set of relations. At the highest level of the community we find distinct yet interlocking leadership strata across a range of domains: political, economic, voluntary, and "grassroots" (including religious institutions).[26] Actors in this leadership group are most likely to be aware of public journalism projects in all of their dimensions. Indeed, as we shall see, in the case of City of Hope they were "called to the table" by the *Wisconsin State Journal* precisely because of their leading positions. It is important to emphasize that within each of these groupings there are distinct factions with competing and even antagonistic interests. For example, the Madison/Dane County political spectrum runs from independent left activists and a strong group of pragmatic progressive liberals who hold the offices of mayor and county executive (itself factionalized), to center-right conservatives, including the congressional representative, to rural conservatives who are prominent on the Dane County Board of Supervisors. Economic interests are divided among civic-oriented businesses, conservative businesses, real estate factions, and so on. We cannot detail this structure here, other than to suggest the complexity of this "leading" stratum. In the terms of *Personal Influence,* this group would function as both local elite and expert stratum, but also as the top rung of "opinion leadership."

At the next level are what we might call opinion leaders in the stricter sense used by Katz and Lazarsfeld. Structurally, these are actors with varied links to the leadership strata, generally multiple links that cut across both functional domains and factions. Prominent examples might be leaders of unions, religious and voluntary organizations, and so on. This group functions as both opinion leader in relation to those networks that it influences, and as molecular, in relation to the strata above.

Next are the moleculars who are two steps removed from the top strata. They are connected primarily (although not exclusively) through the second group. This group might include officers of organizations, active members, volunteers, the core of citizen activists found by Verba

26. We are tempted to call this stratum "elite" in the sense of leading strata. We do not use this term, not because we do not see concentrations of power in this stratum as a whole, which we do. Rather, although dominant power may be exercised by elite strata, it is spread across competing network cliques, none of which exercise decisive influence. This dynamic of competition and coalition formation is most relevant to our concerns here.

et al. These moleculars are influential within their circles, but these circles are somewhat more circumscribed.

Finally, we come to the group that Lazarsfeld and Katz call the "influencees" or, more simply, the influenced. We think that this term is unfortunate, because it tends to understate the degree to which the influenced remain reflective citizens and active influencers of others, and grossly understates the possibility for the generation of new ideas and conceptions from this group in a broad range of areas. In short, it associates a hierarchy of activity (which may exist) with a hierarchy of capacity. We think of this group in the strict empirical sense of those who report being civically inactive. They may still be influential in a broad array of cross-cutting networks in family and work life.

This structure begins to make the activities of deliberation and problem solving intelligible at a community level. We are *not* suggesting the revival of the oft-caricatured concept of the two-step flow. Rather, we suggest the need for a broader structural map of these multiple and cross-cutting networks through which opinion is formed and acted upon. In the case of We the People, we have found in our depth interviews that there is a strong and clear awareness of the project among the high leadership and opinion-leading strata. Awareness trails off among the third molecular stratum, and is extremely weak within the fourth. These results are supported by the adjusted figures of the Thorson/Denton and the Mass Communications Research Center studies. Thorson/Denton estimate 20 percent awareness controlling for misperception among the 51 percent reporting recognition. Our qualitative follow-up of the MCRC figure of 43 percent is similar, although less precise. The 12 rating for "Common Ground" is consistent with these figures. Verba et al. found a need to reduce their sample to 17 percent of the total to find a broadly defined activist core. We can estimate, then, that the activist core, which constitutes levels one through three in our typology, is roughly 15 percent of the population.

This is the core from which the closely attending audience for We the People is drawn. This structure begins to explain both the success and limits of the project as a form of deliberation. At the most basic level, this core has among the highest news readership/viewership of any group. Their percentages as "attenders" certainly extend beyond their raw numbers. Second, this core is by definition the most active in discussing public issues, both within each network, across network boundaries within the interlocking opinion-leading networks, and outside. Their active deliberation magnifies the success of the project in reaching beyond the core. Anecdotal reports of success and influence, whether to news managers or politicians, are most likely to come from this core.

We do not necessarily see this as antidemocratic or a sign of failure to reach out to the broader community. To the contrary, we believe that any media project oriented toward the reconstitution of public and civic life is likely to begin with this group, and to remain most firmly rooted within it. However, the limits of deliberation discussed above begin to be reached in discussions that are primarily restricted to this core. We do not believe that We the People necessarily tests these limits. It is a project that by choice does not move beyond weak deliberation and, further, has a statewide audience. We would not expect WTP to strongly mobilize public deliberation outside of this core. There is an implicit fallacy rooted in a mass audience concept of public action that media projects can reach relatively quickly beyond this activist core by concentrating their "fire," in effect, that concentrated media attention creates a hothouse environment for civic action. We do not find this effect from WTP. However, because the City/Schools of Hope projects have a more clearly defined mission of social problem solving, and a scope restricted to Dane County, we would expect to find stronger effects outside of the activist core.

CITY OF HOPE

Unlike We the People, which gained organizational momentum from successful cooperation in covering the 1992 primaries, City of Hope was oriented toward problem solving in Madison from the start. *Wisconsin State Journal* Managing Editor Frank Denton says he had not heard of the term "civic journalism," although he knew of the Wichita experiments and had been a Knight-Ridder editor in Detroit. City of Hope was triggered by the shooting death of a fifteen-year-old teenager after a drug deal went bad. According to Denton, "I came here, like a lot of people, largely for the quality of life. And for that stuff to suddenly be here, too, made me wonder if any place was going to be safe for me and my kids. And I also thought as a journalist, having lived in a number of places and now knowing Madison pretty well that if any city in America can attack these problems and do something about them while they're still manageable, it's Madison."[27]

27. Frank Denton, December 21, 1995.

Denton set out to do a news series on Madison's problems, but did not want to practice what he calls "hand grenade journalism" in which journalists "sit back in our fortress and throw these grenades and go out and count the bodies and then go back and do it again a few years later . . . I really didn't want that to happen this time. I really wanted something to result from it." Rather than beginning an investigation, Denton invited "community leaders" to come to the *State Journal* to discuss the range of problems that were surfacing in Madison. The leaders included the mayor, county executive, chancellor of the University of Wisconsin, director of the technical college, head of United Way, school superintendent, head of the chamber of commerce, police chief, and others.

The pattern that emerged was that the group would discuss one area, for example housing, and *State Journal* reporters would "cover" the discussion. The ideas were a starting point for an independent investigation of the issues. When the stories were published, the group was reconvened and asked, in Denton's words, "What are you going to do about it?" They were presented with the options uncovered by reporters, with the reporters there covering the leaders' responses.

The results were mixed. Part of the series led to a mapping of Dane County social services, with the expectation that there would be some overlap. When there was virtually no overlapping, the paper reported on this essentially positive finding. Another series on crime discussed one poor, isolated neighborhood on Madison's east side. Despite its high crime rate, a federally funded anticrime program had not been started there. When the mayor was confronted with the reporting, he became angry because he felt he had been ambushed. He sat down with the editors and reporters, and his views were reflected in the article. But he later told the *New York Times* that he was troubled by the methods of the project because the *State Journal* had been "wearing two hats" by reporting on a project that it had helped to create. He also expressed concern with the "top-down" nature of the process in which a group selected by editors rather than voters made decisions for the community.[28]

Denton does not deny that the power of the newspaper was used: "Part of the way that we can use our power is to get them [leaders] to the table. It's hard for them to say 'no' to the dominant newspaper

28. William Glaberson, "Press: From a Wisconsin Daily, a Progress Report on a New Kind of Problem-Solving Journalism," *New York Times,* February 27, 1995.

in town." Denton says that his definition of civic journalism means "taking responsibility for journalism beyond the door step," in contrast to Iverson's definition of "holding the door open." This is tied up with Denton's concept of leadership formation, which holds, in ways parallel to Putnam, that a widespread decline in leadership in American society has led to a vacuum. One of the ways that newspaper power can and should be used is to "take leadership" on community issues, in essence, to serve as a catalyst for existing leaders and to stimulate new forms of leadership.

As evidence, Denton points to the part of City of Hope that focused on jobs, which found that, while unemployment in Madison fluctuates around 2.2 percent, there is a great deal of underemployment, in part because of a lack of blue-collar jobs. Like many other communities in the United States, Madison has a bifurcated economy in which low-paying service jobs are relatively available, while an educated stratum of knowledge workers has access to high-paying jobs in the university, biotechnology, business services, and state government. The leadership group decided to address the lack of middle-level jobs by beginning a process that led to a countywide economic development plan, with an emphasis on career ladders in which local business works with social services, the technical college, unions, and the university to create a network of jobs and programs that lower-income residents can use to advance their careers. A Dane County Economic Summit Council was formed to do master planning for the county, and it began meeting in the fall of 1995.

ASSESSING CITY OF HOPE

The most significant criticism of City of Hope is that it has engaged in a form of top-down mobilization, using the convening and agenda-setting power of the newspaper to force leaders to the table who might otherwise not be there, on an agenda not entirely of their choosing. In various forms, these objections have been raised by local politicians, other local journalists, and those in the emerging public/civic journalism community who see Hope as having set a bad precedent by overstepping the bounds of legitimate action. We have already noted criticism by the mayor and WPT partner Iverson and *State Journal* editor Still that Hope has, at least in part, proceeded from the top down rather than the bottom up.

Denton responds that the distinction between deliberation and mobilization is valid, but that they are not at opposite ends of the spectrum. He sees a need for convergence in the process, in which journalists "ask the people what they want, go do the journalism that provides the factual basis for a range of options. And then you go to the leaders and say, 'This is what the people say. And here are the facts we found out.' "

Schools of Hope grew from City of Hope, but it reflects some of the lessons learned in the first project. Denton acknowledges that there "wasn't much of a public component" in City of Hope. After City of Hope, he received many requests to do something similar for the schools. Schools of Hope, initiated in late 1995, has three major components. The first is "traditional journalism," involving investigation. The second is "public involvement," which integrates We the People–style town meetings and issues polling. The third component is the involvement of a leadership group. The major differences between Schools and City of Hope is the higher degree of public involvement and mobilization on the one hand, and greater distance between the *State Journal* and the policy-making and leadership process on the other.

Beyond the question of the *degree* of involvement of the *State Journal* in community mobilization lies that of the *type* of mobilization. The Hope projects have mapped Madison primarily through what McKnight and Kretzmann have called a "needs-driven" approach to the community, which focuses on needs, deficiencies, and problems. They criticize needs-driven approaches to community problem solving for teaching people "the nature and extent of their problems and the value of services as the answer to their problems," which transforms lower-income neighborhoods into "environments of service." Further, the needs map often appears to be "the only neighborhood guide ever used by the members of the mass media," which leads to simplistic and sensational reporting on lower-income neighborhoods and tends to create a wall between these neighborhoods and the rest of society, a wall "built on the desire to help."[29]

McKnight and Kretzmann counterpose an alternative approach that they call "assets-based community development," which focuses on

29. John P. Kretzmann and John L. McKnight, *Building Communities from the Inside Out: A Path toward Finding and Mobilizing a Community's Assets* (Chicago: Center for Urban Affairs and Policy Research/Acta Press, 1993), 1–2. For a more complete critique of helping services as a form of community disempowerment see John McKnight, *The Careless Society: Community and Its Counterfeits* (New York: Basic Books, 1995).

developing the capacities, skills, and assets of lower-income people. They point to strong evidence that significant community-based development takes place only when citizens themselves invest their time and resources in the effort. They propose a method of mapping community assets that focuses on a systematic inventory of the capacities of individuals, citizens' associations, and local institutions, and a strategy of linking them together in a process of mutual deliberation and common problem solving.[30]

Discussion of community assets planning has been percolating through much of the leadership group convened by the *State Journal* for several years. Former Madison Mayor Paul Soglin and Community Development Director Tom Mosgaller have been engaging McKnight himself in a series of discussions, and the influential Madison Community Foundation has experimented with some community assets–based strategies in its giving in the past several years. The United Way, which has traditionally represented the needs-driven approach, has begun to incorporate an assets-based approach in its annual community mapping. Denton is also familiar with McKnight's work.

Despite this relatively lively discussion among key members of the leadership group convened by the *State Journal,* there is little evidence that these insights are being systematically incorporated into the City/ Schools of Hope projects. In no small part, this demonstrates the difficulty of moving from institutionally grounded professional strategies to community-driven ones, even when the questioning of professionalism and the recognition for civic revitalization is widespread among a group of ranking leaders. When recognized need for change confronts institutional routines, the routines usually triumph. It takes a long time and concentrated effort for routine to break down in any institution.

One piece of evidence demonstrates the difficulty of altering routine, despite the best intentions. The same Mass Communications Research Center study that measured public response to We the People also studied crime coverage in Madison. A content analysis found that both Madison newspapers, the *State Journal* and the *Capital Times,* and all local television stations, including City/Schools partner WISC, cover crime

30. The evidence for McKnight and Kretzmann's assertions is drawn from case studies cited in *Building Communities.* For many of these cases of citizen renewal, and others, see the Civic Practices Network, a citizen's learning collaborative on the Internet at http://www.cpn.journalism.wisc.edu.

at rates strongly disproportionate to its actual occurrence in Madison. Crime accounted for almost 50 percent of local television stories, and 85 percent of the crime stories dealt with violent crime.[31] Crime stories were featured in more than one-third of local newspaper stories, with almost half of these dealing with violent crime. This "imagined community" of Madison was, then, a crime-ridden and violent place, and this is how survey respondents perceived it, with more than 51 percent believing that crime was rising when in fact it was falling. At the same time, the *State Journal* featured prominent articles discussing these falling crime rates. However, respondents tended to *underestimate* the rate of crime in their own neighborhoods compared with Madison as a whole.

The irony in this finding is that despite a major effort to mobilize citizens to solve community problems, on one hand, the same media were so tied to daily news routines that they reported on crime in gross disproportion to its occurrence in Madison. Still, it is hopeful that citizens intuitively felt their own neighborhoods, which they knew from direct experience, to be safer than the city as a whole. This is a fitting place to end our story, a story in progress of the effort of a community and its leading news media to improve public deliberation and to mobilize to face problems similar to most communities in the United States.

DELIBERATION AND SOCIAL CAPITAL: LONG-TERM PROSPECTS

We have suggested some support for a revision of the theory of *Personal Influence* based on an empirically grounded theory of communities as structured by networks with specific leadership strata that operate through both horizontal linkages and somewhat porous vertical hierarchies.

This same structure allows us to generate additional empirical support for the findings of Verba et al. of an activist stratum, broadly defined, ranging from 15 to 20 percent of the population, and that, further, this stratum is divided among three different levels of civic leadership: high leaders, opinion leaders, and molecular leaders. We stress that these strata are *cross-cutting*. There is not a clear vertical structure, but a complex "honey-combing" of linkages.

31. Jack M. McLeod, Katie A. Daily, Zhongshi Guo, William P. Eveland, Jan Bayer, Seungchan Yang, and Hsu Wang, "Community Integration, Local Media Use and Democratic Processes," *Communication Research* 23, no. 2 (1996): 179–209.

We the People has become institutionalized among this combined leadership stratum. There is evidence that, among these groupings, it is known, respected, and anticipated, and that this group looks toward the "we-the-peopling" of a range of community issues. There is no clear evidence that this generalized awareness has reached much beyond this leadership stratum, though there is weak evidence of high recognition levels reported in two separate surveys.

We the People engages in a form of weak deliberation, in which there is no intention to *organize* deliberation beyond the presentation of individual projects. There is also no systematic follow-up of issues or topics once covered. Still, We the People appears to have stimulated awareness of specific issues among the relatively restricted but significant leadership group. It also has generated a broader discussion among these strata about the need for more firmly rooted deliberative institutions that has led directly and indirectly to the beginnings of local Study Circles and National Issues Forums groups. This may, in turn, lead to stronger institutionalized deliberation that can begin to develop citizen-driven rather than media-driven deliberative agendas.

The City of Hope project employed a strong mobilization strategy beginning from the top of that same leadership group. The initiative for the project has come from the newspaper, not the leadership group itself. Nonetheless, there is evidence that the process has set some significant communitywide initiatives in place that have had clear effects in galvanizing action on job development. The Schools of Hope project represents a combination of elements of We the People and City of Hope, and attempts to address the criticism that mobilization has been too restricted to the upper leadership stratum.

The City/Schools of Hope process also has paralleled a growing awareness in the same upper stratum of the need for an assets-based model of community problem-solving. Whether and how this will be translated into action, inside or outside the framework of the civic journalism projects, remains to be seen.

Civic and public journalism projects do not, in themselves, stimulate deliberation, although by setting a communitywide media agenda on a given issue they can create an environment in which deliberation is likely to be focused and intensified. This intensification in turn may lead to other forms of community action, as deliberation ripples through leadership networks. Our evidence suggests that this may be the case in Madison.

Likewise, civic journalism projects do not *create* social capital. News institutions are, in McKnight's phrase, central community assets. By stimulating leadership networks, creating environments for discussion, and focusing attention on issues, projects can, again, intensify the connections among networks that may lead to new connections and new forms of trust. But we want to stress that the process of building social capital occurs over long periods of time. We would not expect a project operating for four years to yield clear demonstrable results. There is some evidence from Charlotte that 1) a clear, consistent focus over a period of several years coupled with 2) community-assets mobilization strategies (whether called such or not) that involve communities and neighborhoods from the very beginning can perhaps create a kind of "hothouse effect" on social capital redevelopment.[32] Pending further evidence based on comparison of our case and others, we believe that the critical independent variable linking public journalism projects and social capital development is the existing network structure of deliberation and social capital in the community.

32. Esther Thorson, Lewis A. Friedland, and Steven H. Chaffee, "Evaluation of Civic Journalism Projects" (Philadelphia: Pew Charitable Trusts, 1996).

III

DELIVERING THE
POSSIBILITIES
OF PUBLIC
JOURNALISM

11

PUBLIC JOURNALISM IN THE 1996 ELECTIONS

Jennie Buckner on Giving Voters a Voice vs. Michael Gartner on Seeing Through the Gimmicks

JENNIE BUCKNER AND MICHAEL GARTNER

PUBLIC JOURNALISM—GIVING VOTERS A VOICE
BY JENNIE BUCKNER

"The biggest critics of press coverage of campaigns are in the press themselves," Howard Kurtz, *Washington Post* media reporter, said in the September 1996 *American Journalism Review.* "It's interesting that we rarely act on that hammering and self-flagellation of our performance every four years. . . . We have an awfully hard time weaning ourselves from the same sort of coverage we're used to."

Right you are, Mr. Kurtz. For tradition-loving journalists, change is hard. (Make that anathema to some.)

But in campaign '96, more journalists than ever decided that change we must.

From the *Virginian Pilot* of Norfolk to the *Seattle Times* of Washington, news organizations across the country made citizens, and their concerns, a key part of election coverage.

We listened to voters. Then we took voters' concerns to the candidates, asking them where they stood on the people's issues. We focused less on the inside stuff of strategy. Some of us even tried to kick the political junkies' toughest addiction and placed less emphasis on weekly horse race polls.

The *Charlotte* (N.C.) *Observer,* the newspaper I edit, is one of these reform-minded newspapers—and proud of it. We joined with five other North Carolina newspapers, six television organizations, and three radio stations in a project called "Your Voice, Your Vote." While we competed (sometimes fiercely) on most aspects of coverage, we cooperated to produce twelve special reports on issues that mattered most to North Carolinians.

The newspapers and commercial television stations shared the polling and administrative costs of "Your Voice, Your Vote." Only public television paid for its share of those costs through a foundation grant—thirty-five hundred dollars from the Pew Center for Civic Journalism. The station did this to avoid any direct expense to taxpayers.

The project began with two statewide surveys of citizens—one before the spring primary and one before the fall general election. The results were not all that surprising. Citizens wanted to know where the candidates stood on crime and drugs, taxes and spending, affordable health care, financial security, families and values, and education.

At least one critic has made much of the fact that the partnership limited to four the number of issues it would collaborate on in the fall election—crime and drugs, affordable health care, education, and taxes and spending. This critic missed an important point: The partnership's cooperative coverage was designed to *complement* the more comprehensive coverage of those races each media organization produced independently. The *Observer* covered every major issue in the poll, as well as others that reporters and candidates identified independently.

We invited all candidates for senator and governor for two three-hour-long interviews, first for the primary and then for the general election. The interviews were designed to be extended conversations that would get away from quick-hit, programmed responses. All candidates but one, Senator Jesse Helms, accepted.

These interviews became the basis for in-depth explanatory stories on each issue, accompanied by full-page graphics, or grids, distilling the positions of candidates on three questions about each issue. Each grid also included vignettes of people affected by the issue to give context to the questions.

Our approach generated enthusiastic responses from readers—and an almost hysterical level of criticism from some media elites. Opinion pieces in the *Washington Post,* the *New York Times,* and the *New Yorker* have denounced us as purveyors of the "insidious, dangerous idea" of public journalism. We've been charged with kowtowing to readers, evading our editorial responsibilities, and participating in a sinister, arrogant attempt to orchestrate the public agenda.

What is this supposedly evil thing called "public journalism"? First, a disclaimer. Labels are often imprecise. The label "Baptist," for example, applies to both Jerry Falwell and Martin Luther King, Jr. The label "public journalism" covers a lot of territory.

At the *Observer,* public journalism is simply this: When writing about public life, we try to provide readers with the information they need to function as citizens.

We expect politicians to address the issues that they, as leaders, consider important. But we also expect politicians to address issues the public considers important. We confine advocacy to the opinion pages. But on both opinion and news pages, we value citizen voices.

In a recent interview in the *Washingtonian,* David Broder of the *Washington Post* described the problem we're trying to address. Journalists often become so intent on reporting what goes on inside campaigns, he said, that they forget the campaigns belong "not to the candidates or their consultants or their pollsters, but to the public."

We've discovered that the more time we spend listening to voters, the better job we do. Not that citizens always ask better questions than journalists. But they often ask different questions—questions some journalists may regard as softball, even though they elicit basic information that helps voters understand how elections may affect them.

Many candidates bypass those basics. And in reportage that's too often centered on personalities, hot-button issues, and candidate marketing, many newspapers neglect basic issues too.

We have been lambasted for asking voters what issues matter to them. Our critics say this amounts to letting readers edit the newspaper. It does not. We still report what we think readers need to know, as well as what they want to know. We're not about to abdicate that responsibility. We're capable of being informed by polls without being slaves to them. And ignorance about citizen concerns is not bliss, we know; it's simply ignorance.

We don't think our coverage should be purely poll driven. And it hasn't been. "Your Voice, Your Vote" is less than 20 percent of our overall election coverage, we estimate.

We know our coverage wasn't perfect, and we're talking now about how to improve on it next time. Making issue stories interesting isn't always easy, and we need to get better at making them a more compelling read. We may want to refine our grids and expand them a bit so we don't risk oversimplifying candidates' stands.

We learned that sharing the writing of twelve stories among six newspapers took more management time than we ever imagined. But there were big pluses to the cooperative effort, chief among them: It's highly unlikely that candidates would have sat down for two lengthy interviews with each partner.

We know many readers in North Carolina got much broader and deeper information because of the partnership. And we know we focused the candidates, and ourselves, on issues that really mattered to people.

In the end, this was the most powerful lesson: We can do better political journalism. We can change—not just carp about the need for change.

We took a surprising amount of heat for it, but journalists here are as committed as ever to the notion that voters deserve a voice in political coverage.

When voters get a voice, the journalism gets much, much better.

PUBLIC JOURNALISM—SEEING THROUGH THE GIMMICKS
BY MICHAEL GARTNER

In July 1996, the *New York Times* ran a terrific series on Bill Clinton's record as president. It was in seven parts, and it was full of facts. It had graphics and time lines and charts, and it had results of a poll the *Times* had conducted to get people's views of how Clinton had handled various issues. It was just one of many highlights of a season of first-rate political coverage in the *Times*.

Throughout the summer and fall, the *Wall Street Journal* had wonderful reporting on politics. Fact-filled stories—especially on the front page and the back page of the front section—told of trends and personalities; columns by Albert Hunt and Paul Gigot laid out issues and laid into people. Polls conducted in conjunction with NBC provided data and insights.

As the election approached, my own tiny newspaper, the *Daily Tribune* in Ames, Iowa, wrote profiles on all the local candidates—from auditor and sheriff to congressman and senator. We covered all the speeches, looked at all the races, and ran editorials strongly in favor of some and against others.

It was all old-fashioned journalism at its best, with reporters and commentators following and interviewing candidates, poring over documents, commissioning polls, asking tough questions, and providing facts and views to enlighten and educate the readers. It led to an informed electorate.

It was what I call public journalism—journalism to inform the public.

Some of it even fits the definition of "public journalism," or "civic journalism," provided by that purveyor of this newly named trend, the Pew Center for Civic Journalism. "Civic journalism," it says in a fact sheet on its World Wide Web home page, "is an effort by print and broadcast journalists to reach out to the public more aggressively in the reporting process, to listen to how citizens frame their problems and what citizens see as solutions to those problems. And then to use that information to enrich their newspaper or broadcast report."

Strip away the jargon and it sounds like this: Public journalism means talking and listening to people and then reporting what the reporter heard and saw.

If that's what public journalism is, then public journalism did a great service for American readers and viewers in the 1996 election. No journalist, politician, or reader can dispute that.

But, alas, public journalism seems to be about much more. Ed Fouhy of the Pew Center and Buzz Merritt of the *Wichita Eagle* and other evangelists for the cause deny that it is journalism in which journalists set the agenda, but, in some places, that's what it is.

"I try to frame my stories to focus on what's real and relevant to people, on the things that *will encourage citizens to take action* [emphasis mine] rather than discourage them from caring," writes Karen Weintraub, a city hall reporter for the *Virginian Pilot*. Writing in the October 1996 issue of the Pew Center's *Civic Catalyst*, Weintraub says she feels she has a "burden" to "make clear when and how people can get involved."

Is that the role of a reporter?

Or listen to Merritt himself: One hallmark of public journalism, he says, is the "conviction that journalism has an obligation to public life beyond merely telling the news." It embraces, he says in the July/August 1996 issue of the *American Journalism Review*, "the obligation . . . to do our journalism in ways that are calculated to help public life go well by *reengaging people in it* [emphasis Merritt's]."

Is that the role of a newspaper?

Or look at North Carolina. In one of the more ambitious and outrageous examples of public journalism, six North Carolina newspapers—including the state's two largest—and five commercial television stations joined up with the state's public television and public television and public radio networks to—let's face it—set the agenda for coverage there. After common, but questionable, interpretation of a poll on what the public thought the issues were, the coalition set out on a joint course of coverage.

It was OK. The stories, at least as they appeared in the *Charlotte Observer*, seemed thorough and straightforward and fair, if a bit dull—at least to a person reading the newspapers from afar. They basically laid out what the reporter interpreted as the views of the senatorial and gubernatorial candidates on the issues the coalition had deemed important. The same stories, with some modifications and different accompanying pieces, appeared in all the newspapers.

And that's the catch. If five competing newspapers had gone after the stories, their reporters would have written the story in five different ways, held five sets of interviews, found five sets of facts. At least one of the five might have uncovered something startling, something contradictory, something new.

The newspapers were free to do supplementary reporting on their own. But the "Your Voice, Your Vote" project was so broadly based that it lulled North Carolinians into thinking they were getting broad coverage. The stories were identified by that tag line. The byline would read: "By John Wagner" and instead of identifying him as a staffer of such-and-such a newspaper, the italics line below the byline simply said "Your Voice, Your Vote." But maybe not your reporter.

The campaign manager for Harvey Gantt, who lost a bid to unseat Senator Jesse Helms, told the *New Yorker* that the experiment was "a bunch of crap, just nonsense, just bullshit, absolute bullshit." He added, "There are serious disagreements here, but all the disagreements are sanitized, everything is put through the washing machine, and it all gets blurred together."

Indeed, the stories did tend to read like a civics textbook. You had to read through more than a foot of copy on the Helms-Gantt views on education before you found Gantt on the jump saying, "I hope the voters of this state will disregard such stupidity." You had to go nineteen paragraphs into a budget story before you found a quote from either gubernatorial candidate.

Mightn't competing reporters have written the stories differently? Mightn't they have tried to elaborate more on this point, played down that one? One voice, even if it's a strong and somber voice, is just not as good as many voices. And this effort at community journalism—wildly misnamed "your voice"—was but one voice, a homogenized, poll-fed voice.

That's the problem with civic journalism, especially as it applies to politics. Media coalitions—there was one in Wisconsin, too—homogenize the news and reduce the number of voices gathering it. They cede editorial judgment to pollsters or, worse, to readers or viewers in focus groups who have no particular knowledge of a state, of politics, or of politicians.

They confuse the news pages with the editorial pages, serving up involvement and attachment instead of disengagement and detachment.

And there's an aspect of public journalism and political coverage that's even worse: What *isn't* being covered? What *isn't* being written? The "community involvement" takes up the time and resources of newsrooms. What would reporters and editors be doing if they weren't involved in this "civic" effort? What rocks would get turned over? What issues would be explored that didn't turn up in polling data?

Some of this new journalism, of course, is just semantics and packaging and gimmicks. The *Virginian Pilot* asked candidates to "apply" for the jobs they were running for, which is just a gimmicky twist on many op-ed pages' offer to let candidates write essays about why they should be elected. Others used graphics to tell stories. And still others, presumably wanting to please the bosses back at corporate headquarters, just did the same things they've been doing for years but put a "civic journalism" label on it.

Did they affect the outcome of any race in November 1996? Probably not.

Newspapers go through waves of experimentation, and nervous editors periodically listen to goofy professors or rich foundations. This civic journalism is no different, just the trend of the moment.

But if you look at a sample of the coverage of 1996 elections, you can reach only one conclusion:

"Public journalism" is a gimmick.

Public journalism is a blessing.

RESPONSE

Michael Gartner is among those critics attacking "Your Voice, Your Vote" for muting competition and limiting the range of reportorial voices. This might be a fair criticism if "Your Voice, Your Vote" were the only election coverage we offered. It was not—not even close.

The six participating newspapers (which comprise 13 percent of the dailies in North Carolina) shared only five stories, with accompanying sidebars, during the general election campaigns. We shared seven packages during the primary season. That's a total of twelve stories shared during a nine-month period—out of the many thousands of political stories run in these newspapers.

While we competed on most aspects of election coverage, we decided to cooperate and share the costs of two polls and a few major stories for a good reason: to give readers broader, deeper, more meaningful coverage. This effort didn't limit coverage. It expanded and improved it.

While Harvey Gantt's campaign manager criticized "Your Voice, Your Vote," saying we "blurred and sanitized" differences, many readers felt we clarified differences (and similarities) through the grids. On these pages each candidate answered three questions about a specific issue. The local League of Women Voters president has praised "Your Voice, Your Vote" for giving voters more information, more clearly.

Mr. Gartner belittles "public journalism" as a "gimmick." It is not. At our paper, public journalism has sought to give readers more of what they say they want: substance.

I have reached a troubling conclusion: that some members of the journalism establishment are so alarmed by anything called "public journalism" that they presume that anyone associated with it is guilty of corrupting the craft. No proof is necessary.

That was the prevailing ethic of the Grand Inquisition. It seems to be the ethic of some in the American journalism establishment, too.

—Jennie Buckner

RESPONSE

I have no real quarrel with Jennie Buckner. We both think newspaper stories should explore and explain, should contain facts and figures. She thinks they should also contain "citizen voices." I think they should contain "quotes." She simply uses the language of the academic; I use the language of the newsroom. Our differences are few—I think horse race coverage is important news, and I think strategy isn't always "inside stuff." But that's minor.

I don't think the coalition was a good idea, because I think many voices are better than one voice. I don't like the role of the Pew Center in this and other projects—would newspapers who take Pew money be willing to take money or put in their newsrooms "coordinators" paid by General Electric, say, or the United States Information Agency? What's the difference? Why is Pew money somehow not tainted?

I think some of this "public journalism" fever is simply a device used by editors who don't know their towns and states—editors transferred by chains who keep moving people from newspaper to newspaper. They need forums and meetings to learn what a resident editor would already know about people and issues and traditions. So that's why, perhaps, it is being embraced so heartily by the chains. That is not meant to criticize Jennie, though it is meant to criticize Knight-Ridder and Gannett.

Finally, I think—as I told Jennie when we were both on a panel together—that her readers and my readers would be better off if both of us quit appearing on panels about "public journalism" and quit writing articles in journals and instead paid more attention to our own towns and our own readers.

I think Jennie Buckner is a fine editor. If she wants to call what she does "public journalism," so be it.

—Michael Gartner

12

PUBLIC JOURNALISM AS CULTURAL CHANGE

EDMUND B. LAMBETH

The practitioners of public journalism may be forgiven if they had hoped to be seen as knights, parsons, or farmers on a Canterbury-like pilgrimage. But none should have been terribly surprised that the earliest tales of critics depicted them with Chaucerian scorn and satire as market-minded strays or walkers on slippery slopes.

After all, conceiving of one's goal as a change in the organizational culture of daily journalism—in short, altering an established way of occupational life—is more likely to generate hostility than patient support or encouraging curiosity. The challenge to the status quo felt by traditional journalism surfaced most clearly and candidly when pioneer public journalist Davis Merritt identified his own "biases." Near the beginning of *Public Journalism and Public Life: Why Telling the News Is Not Enough,* Merritt openly declared:

• Journalism in all its forms ignores its obligations to effective public life.
• That failure has been a major contributor to the resultant malaise in public life.
• Journalism should be—and can be—a primary force in the revitalization of public life.
• However, fundamental change in the profession—cultural, generational change—is necessary for that to occur.[1]

1. Merritt, *Public Journalism and Public Life,* 5.

This chapter attempts, first, to outline and illustrate the implications for news media leadership of public journalism's quest for a change in newsroom culture. Second, in so doing, it will try to show how such a cultural shift would represent, in effect, the embrace of a more demanding social ethic for journalism that would require new competencies. Third, it argues that the public and journalism itself have good reasons to want the investigative and narrative traditions to make an honorable peace with the very best of public journalism. Finally, it contends that public journalism poses a kind of challenge that could extend and deepen the relevance of professional ethics and media criticism.

Since at least the late 1970s, journalism has been occupied, in fact, with its own internal "ethics movement." The number of media ethics courses has tripled in recent years. Ethics is a staple topic at annual conventions of professional associations. Both the professional and academic literature have exploded. However, this concern for professional ethics has concentrated far more attention on the relationship of journalists and newsrooms to sources and subjects in the news than on what journalism's obligations to society are at the dawn of the twenty-first century. More precisely, the social ethics of the field—and, especially, the implications for the practice of journalism—have been neglected when compared to the attention given the professional ethics of individual reporters, editors, and photojournalists.[2]

LEADERSHIP OF A SPECIAL KIND

Arguably, no scholar has had a more significant effect on the goals of public journalism than Daniel Yankelovich. His book *Coming to Public Judgment* describes a process of public decision making that many of

2. The growth in the professional phase of the ethics movement is evident in Gene Goodwin and Ron F. Smith, *Groping for Ethics in Journalism.* Edmund B. Lambeth, Clifford Christians, and Kyle Cole, "Role of the Media Ethics Course in the Education of Journalists," *Journalism Educator* (autumn 1994): 20–26, describe the goals and content of media ethics courses at universities, which have tripled in recent years. Some studies that do focus on social ethics are Clifford G. Christians, John P. Ferre, and P. Mark Fackler, *Good News, Social Ethics and the Press,* and some of John Merrill's earliest and most recent work, most notably his *The Imperative of Freedom: A Philosophy of Journalistic Autonomy* and *The Dialectic in Journalism: Toward a Responsible Use of Press Freedom.* In some ways, the field of media social ethics is unavoidably indebted to the Commission on Freedom of the Press and its book, *A Free and Responsible Press,* and to Fred S. Siebert, Theodore B. Peterson, and Wilbur Schramm, *Four Theories of the Press* (Urbana: University of Illinois Press, 1947).

the most ambitious practitioners have assimilated as a framework for changes in the craft. In brief, Yankelovich documents a cycle in which the public is initially aroused to awareness of a problem, accumulates knowledge as it begins to "work through" an issue and, finally, comes to public judgment.

Yankelovich calls attention to the complexity of the process, emphasizing that for a public to reach a reasoned judgment entails cognitive and emotional as well as moral resolutions. "These facets of resolution are interrelated, but they each require hard work in their own right and are surprisingly independent of one another."[3] The indictment of journalism that emerges from Yankelovich's work is that the press does well enough—and often too well—in arousing awareness but usually poorly in helping a frustrated public work through and resolve issues.

The argument is that the traditional objective of the press—an "informed public"—is really inadequate. Mere information is not enough for citizens of a complex democracy. In a pluralistic society with contending stakeholders on public issues, the news media must cover the competing choices, the associated values and possible compromises, in ways that maximize the quality of public judgment. Moreover, the public—as polls and the animosity directed at journalists of most descriptions shows—is vexed at what it sees as the media's excessive focus on conflictual news coverage.

True, some of this angst may be triggered by deeper and parallel frustrations elsewhere, in the pocketbook, say, or in distrust of other institutions. Yet journalists need to pay heed to the disturbing finding that three out of four citizens say the press actually gets in the way of solving public problems. This formidable indictment will not be dissolved by journalists or executives of media conglomerates too proud, stubborn, or indifferent to seriously consider constructive change.[4]

It is one thing, of course, to analyze and critique news media performance in Yankelovich's terms but quite another matter to discuss his ideas in a newsroom. An even greater feat of leadership is to design journalistic approaches based on Yankelovich and deploy those, in turn, in tandem with a newspaper's overall strategy for news coverage.

3. Yankelovich, *Coming to Public Judgment*, 65.
4. Times-Mirror Center for the People and the Press, *The People, the Press and Politics*, 121.

In short, important as the conceptual heavy lifting may be, even more necessary in a new culture for daily journalism is a pragmatic imagination that can operationalize and evaluate the application of ideas such as those advanced by Yankelovich. It is not as though his thought has been fully explored, tested in newsrooms, and guaranteed to deliver a new culture for journalism. Far from it.

An important case study of such a shift in newsroom culture developed at the *Virginian-Pilot* and *Ledger-Star,* a daily and Sunday newspaper in the Norfolk-Hampton Roads area of coastal Virginia. Perhaps more than most, the management and staff at Norfolk have attempted to be explicit about how public journalism relates to publishing strategy and to reporters, editors, and photographers. As much as and maybe more than other news organizations engaged in public journalism, the *Virginian-Pilot* has held seminars for, and involved its staff in, the transition to a new organizational culture. Cole C. Campbell, the editor at Norfolk before he accepted the editorship of the *St. Louis Post-Dispatch,* said the *Virginian-Pilot* and *Ledger-Star* have spent "tens of thousands of dollars" on the transition in the form of seminars, retreats, and visiting specialists in public opinion formation and citizen education.[5]

An in-house "search conference" by editors and staff led to a quest for new ways to not only report the news most important to readers but also explain "what it means" to them. Their effort is related, in turn, to a concrete company goal of increasing the frequency of daily readership of the *Virginian-Pilot* by those who already read it once a week. Accompanying this new editorial emphasis on local "meaning," serious attention is paid to framing local events and issues in ways that will engage readers as citizens, help them participate in local affairs, and lift the level of public deliberation. The game plan is to increase readership among existing subscribers and use that momentum to pull new readers into the newspaper.

Although this intention may seem unexceptional, what appears to be new is the way the newspaper has conceptualized how it will deliver on the broader social ethic of actively assisting the public in "working through" and making more informed judgments on issues. To an important extent the newspaper is actually attempting to operationalize and test the key ideas in Yankelovich's *Coming to Public Judgment.*

5. Interview with Cole Campbell, executive editor of the *Virginian-Pilot,* February 2, 1996.

Its developing guidelines define different kinds of "stakeholders" in issues or events. Continuing stories are expected to identify and describe the stakeholders and the nature of their stakes. Editors are to aim for coverage that is proportionate to the needs of the stakeholders. Thus, in coverage of local schools major attention needs to be paid to the stakes of parents and children. Even more significant, the guidelines identify ways and standards that help clarify how to put more meaning into stories.

"Literacy" describes stories that will allow a reader to converse with others and pursue related information on a topic in the news. "Utility" stories help readers cope in their daily private lives, manage their personal affairs, and link with others in the community with similar interests. In public matters, "utility" stories help citizens form an opinion and connect with others that have a similar stake in an issue. They also provide enough background on which people can act. Finally, "mastery" stories equip people to explore and explain not only their own stakes but those of other citizens as well. They encourage reflection and considered judgments on public issues.[6]

Whether or not these particular standards of performance will be found successful, they still deserve to be tested and, if they work, saluted. That is because they represent the direction, imagination, and inventiveness a new culture of journalism needs. Their application could focus the intellectual attention of journalists on how they can assist citizens in judging public policies and public officials.

But the new culture requires not only the engaged intelligence of journalists. Reliable knowledge of how reporters and editors actually rank-order, define, and apply such standards in their daily work—and with what impact on readers, listeners, and viewers—requires practical and systematic research. Without such useful feedback, it is likely that the practitioners will slowly lose confidence in the process of change. Public journalism and its innovations would go the way of media action lines and the countless redesigns of news pages and newscasts. Thus, the logic and nature of public journalism implies much heavier reliance on clear and authoritative social science and humanistic research. Some such research, not often looked upon favorably by journalists, has been done by news media for years, usually by outside contractors

6. Interview and FAX communication with Dennis Hartig, deputy managing editor, *Virginian-Pilot*, February 9, 1996.

with little continuing responsibility for serving readers, listeners, and viewers, or educating journalists of the future. Given public journalism's continuing need for insights into public knowledge, opinion, and attitudes, it would seem wiser to build such a capacity into the newsroom itself.

If genuine public journalism is to succeed in commercial news media, managers and ultimately boards of directors of media conglomerates will have to be persuaded to invest in more in-depth assessment of media performance.[7] Mid-career training in leadership, management, and research and evaluation would be continuous. These are a few of the investments in the human capital of journalism that are clearly implied by a change in newsroom culture. They are necessary to make public journalism something other than a lengthy experiment. But newsroom culture cannot change unless the upper reaches of corporate culture change to provide the resources required.

Investments in education, training, and assessment are not the only demands on those fostering the new culture. They must take into account the continuing and persistent embrace by journalists of both the ethic of investigative reporting and that of traditional story telling. As Bare has shown in chapter 4, the latter beliefs are hardy perennials and are likely to continue in newsrooms that practice public journalism as well as those which, as yet, do not.

PUBLIC JOURNALISM AND INVESTIGATIVE REPORTING

Some critics see public journalism placing itself in an ethical bind such that it might not be able to do investigative journalism on or near the subjects on which it focuses. Thus, when Howard Schneider, managing editor of *Newsday,* appeared on a Walter Cronkite documentary, he specifically criticized the *Charlotte Observer*'s public journalism project, "Taking Back Our Neighborhoods," an anticrime effort centered on stimulating local initiative. After alluding dramatically to both journalism's informational and watchdog role, Schneider declared:

> I don't think Charlotte will be able to separate itself from the solutions that are being proposed for those communities. I don't think they will be able to probe whether those solutions are inclusive or whether they

7. This argument was first made in less extended form in Edmund B. Lambeth, "The News Media and Democracy."

are well done. I think they are going to be identified with the solutions, whatever their intentions.[8]

Asked to reply, *Observer* editor Jennie Buckner said the paper acted as a catalyst but did not try to tell neighborhoods what to do—just the opposite, and added: "We didn't put any solution out there. We don't feel we're 'identified.' Actually, we feel our role is to monitor whether people lived up to what they said they would do."[9] Before the eighteen-month project ended late in 1995, the *Observer* appeared to have been quite able to blow the whistle on a local group that had put itself on the list of organizations in need of assistance.

In a front-page story, *Observer* reporters John Hechinger and Gary L. Wright exposed "Fighting Back," an antidrug and neighborhood uplift organization financed half by Mecklenburg County and half by the Robert Wood Johnson Foundation. The reporters disclosed that in its first three years Fighting Back spent $1.6 million, almost half its county money, but only 14 percent of it went directly to drug- and alcohol-fighting programs. The balance, $1.3 million, went for administrative and staff expenses, travel to seventeen U.S. cities, rent, utilities, and food. One trip was a fifteen-thousand-dollar retreat for ninety people at Myrtle Beach. A neighborhood leader was quoted as saying, "They just haven't done anything except spend money, pay salaries and have meetings."[10]

In fairness, it needs to be pointed out that Fighting Back was not a creation of the *Observer*'s public journalism project. So the *Observer* did not need to "separate" itself in the sense intended by critic Schneider to expose its shortcomings. But the stated goals of Fighting Back are close enough to those of "Taking Back Our Neighborhoods" to show that a news organization practicing public journalism need not lose its independence. In fact, it may be required to conduct investigative journalism to protect the integrity of a public journalism project.

Proponents of public journalism frequently emphasize that they do not wish or plan to jettison investigative reporting and they certainly do not intend to discard compelling narrative. Yet, in their speeches and seminars, the leaders of the movement fail to emphasize how central to

8. Cronkite, "Is That the Way It Is?"
9. Telephone interview with David Craig, November 2, 1995.
10. "How Financial Mistakes Derailed Fighting Back, Mecklenburg's Anti-Drug Effort," *Charlotte Observer*, October 15, 1995.

public journalism investigative work can be and, in some places, actually is. The *Observer* conducted a computer-assisted analysis of city crime statistics, by neighborhood, and systematically asked citizens in the forty-two most violent neighborhoods what changes were needed. "They called," said Buckner, "for more community police, more parental involvement with kids, a crackdown on drug abuse and guns, more jobs and stronger neighborhood involvement."[11]

The *Observer* hosted nine town meetings with a cooperating TV station and two radio stations. Hundreds of residents attended. Later many residents took self-help initiatives in their neighborhoods. Often these took the form of crime watches and neighborhood development. United Way coordinated the donation of time, effort, and money generated from the newspaper's listing of community needs. Banks, churches, and businesses as well as individuals gave time and money. After the project finished late in 1995, the *Observer* reported that more than one thousand individuals and groups had volunteered help in "Taking Back Our Neighborhoods." A concluding *Observer* editorial acknowledged that "major problems still exist." It criticized city officials on several counts, including inadequate housing code enforcement, insufficient recreational facilities, and the persistence of crack houses in the neighborhoods.

But it asserted that the improvements, including new leadership developed in Charlotte's crime-ridden inner city neighborhoods, gave "reason for hope—and success if we make long-term commitments." Buckner pledged in a front-page note to "continue to report on the issues and the neighborhoods." In yet a third prominently displayed "look ahead" article, editorial writer Fannie Flono emphasized that "sustainable progress will occur only with government and private sector assistance and long-term commitment."[12] Together, the column, the editorial, and the article criticized key local institutions, praised the neighborhood residents and citizens for their responses, urged government and the private sector to commit for the long haul, and pledged the *Observer* to revisit the inner-city crime problem. It was as though the newspaper's top brass had taken their tune from the tone and content

11. Jennie Buckner, from a presentation to the first James Batten Award ceremony organized by the Pew Center for Civic Journalism, Decatur House, Washington, D.C., September 13, 1995, 3.

12. "Reason for Hope," Jennie Buckner, "Dear Readers," and Fannie Flono, "Next Step: A Long-Term Commitment," *Charlotte Observer,* December 3, 1995.

of the front-page wrap-up story by Liz Chandler and Gary L. Wright, the opening paragraphs of which read:

> The people of Seversville see a whole new world: Fewer prostitutes. Peaceful streets. And children playing at a new community center.
>
> About a mile away, the people of Druid Hills still see horror. Two people were murdered there last month alone. Families live in desolation and fear.
>
> For two years, Charlotte has waged a fresh attack on the crime and poverty ravaging the central city. No one can claim victory.
>
> But in rare circumstances, when courageous residents, outside volunteers, churches, businesses and focused government workers united, the swell of their commitment left a few neighborhoods safer.
>
> "You've got to get a lot of people involved," said Pat Garrett, whose nonprofit housing group helped revive Seversville. "You need the banks to play a bigger role. And the churches. And the neighborhoods themselves."
>
> Violent crime in Seversville has dropped 19 percent in two years. "A lot of things have changed. People are loving it," says resident Patsy Martin.
>
> That turnaround is an exception. Rescue efforts in other troubled neighborhoods either proved too brief or leaned too heavily on a government distracted by growing suburbs.
>
> Crime has leaped 30 percent this year in some central-city pockets, and is up 4 percent countywide. "It's as bad as it ever was," Gertrude Word, 71, says of her Druid Hills neighborhood.
>
> People on the front lines believe Charlotte's campaign to stop crime isn't intense or broad-based enough to loosen its grip.
>
> Elected officials put few new dollars into crime-prevention this year. Some touted campaigns to stop crime—such as a crackdown on crack houses—are fizzling.
>
> And though charities descended on a few neighborhoods, they eventually turned to other demands.
>
> "I guess you can never be aggressive enough—unless you're doing everything possible," Mayor Richard Vinroot says. "But there are a lot of other things we have to take care of . . . We must deal with our transportation system. We must deal with our educational system. There has to be a balance."[13]

This lengthy description of the *Observer*'s "Taking Back Our Neighborhoods" project was intended, first, to allow readers to make at least an initial assessment of its worth and, second, to show how investigative

---

13. "Hope amid Despair," *Charlotte Observer,* December 3, 1995.

work was linked to a broader social purpose. In my judgment, there was no substantial evidence in the neighborhood crime project to support the charge that seems easiest to make against public journalism: namely, that it "panders" to either the public or the power structure. The project's links to investigative journalism, however, require a bit more attention. Investigative journalism has become much more sophisticated in the past twenty-five years. True, journalism still makes room, and should, for hard-hitting exposés of wrongdoing by public officials. But there is a realization that complex urban problems cannot be reported effectively unless journalists examine them in depth and at the system level.

But what, journalists ask themselves, is "investigative"? Investigative Reporters and Editors has for years been debating an appropriate definition. Since its first outstanding reporting awards in 1978, IRE has followed a definition by investigative veteran Bob Greene, then of *Newsday* and, at the time, executive director of the organization. Rosemary Armao, herself a former head of IRE, said the agreement represented a "hard-won consensus from members" and required that winning contest entries:

• Must be substantially the product of the reporter's own initiative and efforts. (Coverage of Watergate was investigative; coverage of the Pentagon Papers was not.)

• Must be about matters of public importance to the circulation or broadcast area. (The president's sex life and his hemorrhoids may or may not qualify.)

• Must uncover facts or events that some persons try to keep secret or prefer be kept secret.[14]

As Armao said, the third requirement excluded from IRE competition at least two Pulitzer Prize winners. One was the 1983 *Philadelphia Inquirer*'s investigation of nuclear energy by Donald Barlett and James Steele. Another was *Washington Post* reporter Leon Dash's analysis of the effects on one family of poverty, crime, and AIDS. It won the 1995 Pulitzer for explanatory reporting.

Steve Weinberg, former head of IRE and a seasoned investigative reporter and biographer, has proposed revising IRE contest requirements

14. Rosemary Armao, "It's No Secret . . . or Is It?" *IRE Journal* (January–February 1996): 2.

to eliminate the stipulation that secrets must be uncovered. In support of this move, James Neff, IRE treasurer and Ohio State University professor, argued that computer-assisted reporting and insights gained from human and documentary sources now allow reporters to "shed light in new areas that the powers that be don't even know are areas of darkness."[15] Weinberg and Neff emphasized the importance of recognizing reporting that creates a mosaic of insight into public problems based on systematic searching of both documents and human sources.

Neither the Greene definition of the investigative craft nor the revision outlined by Weinberg should exclude investigative reporting from a possible and perhaps even pivotal role in any given piece of public journalism. That could happen in several ways.

First, and most obviously, an exposé of hidden wrongdoing can serve as the basis of follow-up stories that use public journalism techniques to engage the public and stimulate public deliberation. Second, as happened in Charlotte, investigative reporting may be required by story leads that are uncovered during the course of a public journalism project. Third, regular daily stories by public journalists may become so skillfully framed as to generate leads from citizens and key sources that serve as the basis for investigative initiatives.

Finally, and more generally, scholarship in the 1990s suggests that investigative journalists may have reason for the kind of serious introspection they recommend to public journalists. In a series of in-depth studies using both qualitative and quantitative methods, David L. Protess and his colleagues cast serious doubt that investigative reporting, as widely supposed, made its impact by directly mobilizing the public. Nor, their case studies concluded, is its impact felt through the policy outcomes of interest group conflict. Rather, investigative projects had most influence as a result of what the scholars called "coalition journalism."[16]

More specifically, in four of the six case studies, Protess et al. reported, the effects of investigative reporting resulted chiefly from "prepublication transactions between journalists and policy makers." That

15. Armao, "It's No Secret," 3.
16. Harvey D. Moltoch, David L. Protess, and Margaret T. Gordon, "The Media-Policies Connection: Ecologies of News," in *Political Communication: Theories and Cases,* edited by David Paletz (Norwood, N.J.: Ablex, 1987).

is, journalists collaborated with policy makers in the timing of their stories and/or policy agendas were set before publication or broadcast of investigations. In the words of the Protess group, "Specifically, coalitions were established that ensured both the nature and timing of the post-publication announcements of reforms."[17] How widespread such "coalitions" are and what possible negative impact they have on the health of investigative reporting is a topic, as yet, not addressed by scholars or media critics.

Protess and his colleagues concluded their study by noting that "present trends suggest the general public will play even less of an active policy-making role." Their assessment is supported by a wide range of previous scholarly work.[18]

Public journalists argue that if the public is engaged less and less in public life and public policy, the civic habits that historically created the need for a free press will erode. Logically, both investigative reporters and public journalists have a common ground in resisting and reversing that trend.

In any event, the proposal within IRE to expand the definition of the craft has a history all its own that predates the 1990s experiments in public journalism. However, such an expanded definition of its work could represent an important part of the cultural shift envisioned by public journalism.

The investigative expertise created over the past twenty years by IRE is a major resource not merely to practitioners of that craft but also to the public. Finding appropriate ways for IRE to relate to public journalism could enrich both practices by defining and demonstrating the possibilities of collaboration. After a frosty first reaction, IRE, to its credit, now appears to be examining public journalism more seriously and exposing its membership to an extended analysis.[19]

17. David L. Protess, Fay Lomax Cook, Jack C. Doppelt, James S. Ettema, Margaret T. Gordon, Donna R. Leff, and Peter Miller, *The Journalism of Outrage, Investigative Reporting and Agenda Building in America,* 246.

18. Ibid., 253. Benjamin Ginsberg, *The Captive Public;* Gladys Lang and Kurt Lang, *The Battle for Public Opinion* (New York: Columbia University Press, 1983); and, earlier, E. E. Schattschneider, *The Semi-Sovereign People* (New York: Holt, Rinehart and Winston, 1960).

19. See, for example, the November–December 1995 issue of the *IRE Journal* (vol. 18, no. 6), which included three in-depth articles on public journalism and its intersection with investigative reporting.

ETHICS, MEDIA CRITICISM, AND PUBLIC JOURNALISM

To understand the root fear triggered by the arrival of public journalism, it is helpful to revisit how contemporary journalists gained the autonomy and sense of independence that some now see as actually or potentially threatened. James Boylan, former editor of the *Columbia Journalism Review*, gave his colleagues a vivid sense of journalism's achievements in a memorable article in 1986 in *CJR*'s twenty-fifth anniversary issue.[20]

Aptly titled "Declarations of Independence," Boylan depicted a journalism that, from its status as a backwater of the 1950s, had within a decade transformed itself into a mountain rapids. To journalists and citizens alike, it gave a bracing shower rather than a Turkish bath. By the late 1960s, it had helped shake the lethargy of the Red-baiting era of Senator Joseph McCarthy. It began to heed the skepticism born of White House lying about the American U-2 spy plane. It reflected on how and why it had "blown" a preventive scoop on the CIA's (failed) plans to invade Castro's Cuba. Despite and, in a sense, in expiation for these events, the press more than rebounded with its aggressive and independent, though certainly not "all powerful," coverage of Watergate and the Vietnam War, to name only two major episodes. To protect themselves and build their profession's competence, journalists founded the Reporters' Committee for Freedom of the Press and Investigative Reporters and Editors. These institutions are evidence of the important organizational and educational achievements bequeathed by the reporters of that era.[21]

To underscore the theme of independence, Boylan noted that as early as 1965 Walter Lippmann asserted that journalism itself had at long last become an intellectual discipline. In a speech to the International Press Institute in London, Lippmann declared:

> This growing professionalism is, I believe, the most radical innovation since the press became free of government control and censorship. For it introduces into the conscience of the working journalist a commitment to seek the truth which is independent of and superior to all his other commitments . . .

20. James Boylan, "Declarations of Independence," 29–45.
21. Ibid., see especially 33–34. For a brief account of IRE's birth and early years, see Clark Mollenhoff, *Investigative Reporting* (New York: Macmillan, 1981), 339–44. For background on the activities of the Reporters' Committee, see Lambeth, *Committed Journalism*, 19, 133–34, 139, 166, 168.

PUBLIC JOURNALISM AS CULTURAL CHANGE

> As the press becomes securely free because it is increasingly indis-
> pensable in a great society, the crude forms of corruption which be-
> longed to the infancy of journalism tend to give way to the temptations
> of maturity and power. It is with these temptations that the modern
> journalist has to wrestle, and the unending conflicts between his duty
> to seek the truth and his human desire to get on in the world are the
> inner drama of the modern journalist's experience . . . [22]

Seemingly, much has changed in the more than thirty years since
Lippmann spoke. If the critics are right, newsrooms experimenting with
public journalism risk losing their independence. If the proponents
are right, such experiments are needed to ensure the indispensable
civic and public role for journalism that Lippmann, in his era, could
rightly celebrate. Today, however, many public affairs journalists believe
the health of journalism is at risk as a result of media conglomerates
that have reduced staffs and budgets to maintain profit margins at
unreasonably high levels. They believe the cutbacks only aggravate the
dwindling circulation of newspapers and the rising tabloid mentality
among both print and electronic news media.[23]

In the new era, both public journalists and those who are wary of their
experiments need a new form of media criticism whose evaluations
examine not only ethics but also the effectiveness of the journalism
under study. It would be media criticism that takes seriously both Lippmann's warnings about the pitfalls of being too close to power—whether
public or private—as well as the danger signals of public alienation
from politics to which public journalism is a partial response. Public
journalists, for their part, also need to recognize that the new techniques
they are testing do sometimes raise ethical questions.

That ethical questions associated with public journalism are neither
more nor less serious than those posed by investigative reporting or
dead-pan straight reporting is a point well worth making—or trying
to make—with critics of public journalism. But critics are correct in
that the new techniques do need continuing attention so that their
challenges can be anticipated and straightforwardly handled. Several
minor and major experiences in doing public journalism illustrate the
point.

22. Boylan, "Declarations of Independence," 34–35.
23. For a forthright description of this situation and how journalists are trying to
respond, see Ellen Hume, *Tabloids, Talk Radio and the Future of News* (Washington, D.C.:
Annenberg Washington Program, 1995).

In 1995 the newsroom of the *Columbia Missourian,* a daily and Sunday community newspaper affiliated with the University of Missouri School of Journalism, was beginning to examine Columbia's school-to-work program. For the *Missourian,* the story had begun in 1994 at a public forum the newspaper and public radio station KBIA held following a series on jobs and the local economy. The forum itself generated a question that the news media had not examined—whether the city's highly rated public schools were adequately serving the interests of students who did not plan to attend college.

As the newspaper reported the story, a Columbia school administrator suggested that the school system itself would conduct the expensive, systematic focus group interviews among teachers, parents, and local employers that the *Missourian* felt were necessary. A timely intervention, in which the school's dean-and-publisher was made aware of the situation, prevented a potentially harmful compromise of the newsroom's independence. The *Missourian* paid for its own focus groups and later published a series that sparked new discussion in the community.[24]

Newsrooms need to be prepared to pay for the greater precision that some of the tools of public journalism approaches—such as focus groups and polls—sometimes may require. Perhaps more important, the *Missourian* episode underscores that public journalism, too, requires the kind of detachment needed to protect journalistic independence.

To gain access to crime-ridden neighborhoods in Charlotte, the *Observer* hired former broadcast public affairs staffer Charlene Price-Patterson. During nine of her thirteen years in Charlotte she was on the air for two of the city's TV stations. That gave her recognition, acceptance, and standing in the inner city. As a "community coordinator" of the newspaper's "Taking Back Our Neighborhoods" project, she organized neighborhood meetings at which residents identified community needs.

The leader of one neighborhood organization, Grier Heights, bluntly refused to cooperate with the *Observer* or Price-Patterson. He claimed

24. The focus group interviews were conducted by independent consultant Jennifer LaFleur and paid for by Dean Mills, dean of the University of Missouri School of Journalism. The first ten-part series, "Making Education Work," ran in the *Missourian* from April 30 through June 4, 1995. A second, more thorough series, "A Look beyond the Classroom," appeared from November 12 through November 16, 1995. Ensuing community debate appeared in an op ed commentary by school board member Diane M. Calabrese (November 21, 1995) and in a story by Jennifer Baker, "Too Much Business?" November 27, 1995.

his neighborhood did not need to be "taken back." Yet the statistics indicated otherwise. Grier Heights ranked eleventh in violent crime among seventy-three central-city neighborhoods in 1993.[25] Its crime rate of 100 per 1,000 population compared to a city average of 22.8 per 1,000. Liz Chandler, one of the lead reporters on the project, said her editors made a mistake in not going ahead without the cooperation of neighborhood leaders. Said Chandler:

> It's one of our highest-crime places and there were some real high-profile killings out there this year and for us to have covered 10 neighborhoods and not hit this one is, to me, ridiculous . . . my argument was I don't think we know for sure what the whole neighborhood wants . . . If I was covering the government I would never let an official say, "Well, I don't want you to write a story," and for me not to write it.[26]

The neighborhood was the subject of a major drug sweep several months later. Rick Thames, at the time serving as public editor of the *Observer,* was not overseeing the project during the Grier Heights decision. However, retrospectively, he indicated he saw merit in Chandler's perspective. "If I had been in that position, I would have felt a particular burden at that point to still write about Grier Heights" using traditional interviewing and sourcing. Price-Patterson said she made it clear to the Grier Heights neighborhood leader that she and the *Observer* were not going to be a "P.R. firm" for the neighborhood. "I didn't look at Grier Heights as a major flaw in what we were doing," she said, adding, "I just felt bad they didn't take advantage of an opportunity that could have been helpful." *Observer* editors gave the work of the community coordinator high marks.[27]

Because the tool had never been used before in public service journalism and because the newspaper was perceived to risk a loss of independence, the *Observer* was criticized for employing a community coordinator. Yet, whatever the lapse in the Grier Heights episode, it had good reason, at least, to take unusual measures to try to stimulate a concerted community response to major crime. As the newspaper reported repeatedly to citizens, in 1993, Charlotte, thirty-fourth among

25. Liz Chandler, Ted Mellnik, and Gary L. Wright, "At Charlotte's Core, Violence a Daily Threat," reprint of *Charlotte Observer,* June 5, 1994.

26. Interview with David Craig, December 19, 1995.

27. Ibid. Interview with Edmund B. Lambeth, February 1996 and March 1, 1996. See also Kramer, "Civic Journalism," 4.

major cities in population, ranked eighteenth in the prevalence of violent crime. The sixty-six thousand people in central-city neighborhoods, representing 16 percent of the population, suffered 54 percent of the violent crime.[28] The *Observer*'s series and the prodigious effort it represented won recognition as a Pulitzer finalist in 1994.

Observer editors were candid when asked what they would have done differently. They said that they should have held more and better discussions of the goals and techniques of public journalism not only with the reporters directly involved in the project but with others in the newsroom as well. Because their discussions were not deeper and more inclusive, suspicion and criticism of the project developed early in the newsroom. "We just moved too fast," said Cheryl Carpenter, now assistant managing editor, adding, "We didn't give the necessary orientation. We were moving quickly and we had an ambitious project on our hands and they learned as they went and that never is a very gracious way to achieve your goals." But the *Observer* was not alone. Research commissioned by the Pew Charitable Trusts of public journalism in Charlotte; Madison, Wisconsin; Binghamton, New York; and San Francisco showed that in all but one newsroom the initiatives were "poorly introduced" and "were widely perceived as 'management gimmicks.' " Ed Fouhy of the Pew Center for Civic Journalism said that "perhaps the most vexing to me was that the four projects were more warmly received in the communities than in most of the newsrooms that produced them. Citizen responses were consistently enthusiastic. Newsroom responses were frequently ambivalent or even negative."[29] Clearly, newsroom leadership and management have lessons to learn if the rank and file are to find value and meaning in the practice of public journalism.

Interestingly, the *Observer*'s neighborhoods project received the highest marks from *Boston Globe* ombudsman Mark Jurkowitz in his study of public journalism projects in Charlotte, Spokane, San Jose, and Grand Forks, North Dakota. His conclusions may shed some light on why so many debates over public journalism slide unproductively into the equivalent of ideological "food fights." Wrote Jurkowitz:

28. For an exposition of the range and ethics of civic involvement by newspapers doing public journalism, see Edmund B. Lambeth and David Craig, "Civic Journalism as a Research Opportunity," *Newspaper Research Journal* 16, no. 2 (spring 1995): 148–60. Chandler, Mellnik, and Wright, "At Charlotte's Core."

29. Interview with Edmund B. Lambeth, February 2, 1996. "New Civic Journalism Research," *Civic Catalyst* (January 1997): 11, 1, respectively.

The mixed record of these projects suggests why partisans on both sides of the argument over public journalism have it wrong. Public journalism is neither inherently evil nor a panacea for the woes of the news media or democracy. It's all in the execution.

If in their efforts to carve a more interactive role for the media in the twenty-first century, proponents condone political advocacy and tolerate collaboration with institutions the press should be scrutinizing—business interests, municipal groups, government agencies—then public journalism will echo the journalism of the nineteenth century, before independence and objectivity became news priorities. But if done properly—by combining the aggressive reporting values of traditional journalism with effective mechanisms for tracking community concerns—then it offers a possible antidote to public frustrations with the news media.[30]

But rather than examining how best to combine entrepreneurial reporting with sensitive tracking of citizens' real problems and interests, practitioners of public journalism were caught off-balance for much of their first three to four years with having to defend themselves from attacks by the elite press. Unfortunately, their responses appear to have made little headway. Moreover, these public criticisms have created misperceptions that need to be addressed. To wit, polling by journalists to understand reader and viewer perceptions of public issues does not represent pandering. Stories conceived as a fit sequel to such polling require—and should be seen to require—independent and professional judgment by journalists to be effective. To "care about the consequences" of one's reporting need not represent an ethical lapse. It can reflect, instead, a justified and laudable concern about how journalists can better frame stories to communicate the complex realities of contemporary public affairs. Since when does an agnostic, "arrow in the air" attitude toward the destination and public reception of one's story constitute mental or intellectual toughness?

Jan Schaffer, executive director of the Pew Center, notes how editors shape the practice into different forms in different newsrooms, even though they start with the same basic concepts:

> Steven Smith in the *Colorado Springs Gazette-Telegraph* goes at it from the "inside out" with lots of civic journalism conversations about framing news stories, getting the "middle ground" into the coverage, getting the "essence" of the story, not just the facts. Dennis Hartig in the

30. Mark Jurkowitz, "From the Citizen Up," *Forbes Media Critic* (winter 1996): 75–83.

Norfolk Virginian-Pilot has created dedicated pages three days a week—
on public life, safety and education—that are getting amazing reader
response in satisfaction surveys. Glenn Ritt at the *Bergen Record* has taken
his civic journalism into the on-line world in a major way and into new
self-publishing opportunities for various sectors of the community.

To evolve and to mature in healthy directions, such public journalism
initiatives need systematic assessments, the design, execution, and results of which are given as much careful attention and necessary follow-
up as the initiatives themselves. If and when that happens, American
journalism can be said to have taken seriously the ethic of social responsibility. In fact, it will have embraced a more exacting social ethic
than currently prevails in most newsrooms. It will have truly done what
it could to help improve the quality of public deliberation in American
democracy. To achieve as much will require a commitment to cultivate
new competencies and new investments in human capital. The decade
ahead will likely tell whether contemporary news media conglomerates,
and, indeed, North American society, have either the staying power
to pursue or the "genes" to deliver such a bequest to the twenty-first
century. The risk of genuine public journalism may turn out to be not
so much that it "panders" to the public but that the news media leaders
may fail to commit the resources it requires to be successful.

13

IF IT WORKS, HOW WILL WE KNOW?

PHILIP MEYER

The topic is so vast and important that the usual perfunctory call for further research is insufficient. This time we really mean it—enough to get specific. We have therefore conceptualized this chapter as a call for papers for an idealized conference of researchers now and in the future. A hoped-for side effect is that it can serve as a guide for writing grant proposals, covering both theoretical justification and methodology.

THE PROBLEM OF DEFINITION

The first question about public journalism is simply, "What is it?" Other movements in journalism have been easy to define. "The new nonfiction" of the 1960s was the application to journalism of fiction techniques, including plotting for the creation and resolution of tension, descriptive scene and character creation, and the use of interior monologue. While the genre included a broad spectrum, from use of actual fiction disguised as fact, through composites, to merely colorful personality profiles, most of us knew it when we saw it, and some writers, such as Tom Wolfe, Jimmy Breslin, and Gail Sheehy, became permanently identified with it. "Precision journalism" was equally specific in definition: the application of social and behavioral science research methods to the practice of journalism. Although some observers have confused it with computer-assisted reporting, the fact that computing alone does not define scientific method makes the distinction easy enough.

But public journalism is another story. Its backers have refused to provide a definition and defended their refusal with the claim that a new approach to journalism is best defined by its practice. A definition, they say, would only limit its potential. Their reticence creates two problems. First, critics can build straw men to attack instead of finding fault with the real thing. Conversely, proponents of public journalism get an automatic defense whenever their creation is criticized, and so they echo the Prufrockian lament, "That is not what I meant at all. That is not it at all."[1] But what did they mean? It is up to us in the research business to find out, and we can thank them for presenting an interesting challenge.

The pursuit of a definition should follow two empirical streams, one quantitative and one more ethnological and historical. The latter should come first, because quantification without sound conceptualization is too easily biased toward what is conveniently observable, and it risks enumerating the irrelevant. So the first step toward a definition should be sorting out the sources and motivations of the idea. Carol Dykers (chapter 3), by tracing the public ruminations of one of the founding editors as he developed the concept, has taken an important step in this direction. Further steps might look at other actors in this process and show whether there are distinctions between "public journalism," as it is called by Knight-Ridder and the Knight Foundation; "civic journalism," the term favored by enterprises funded by the Pew Charitable Trust; or "citizen-based journalism" when the backing is coming from the Poynter Institute. Why so many names? Do they represent independent streams of thought with some common core? If so, how big is the core and what elements are specific to the independent streams? Is everybody trying to claim original invention of the concept, or are they all staking out independent terminology because they suspect the others of doing bad things with which they would rather not be associated?

This line of research should start with a trip to the library to find the historical roots of public journalism. In particular, it needs to be related to social responsibility theory and the Hutchins Commission report of 1947. That project originated outside the media while public journalism is probably more motivated from within. The Hutchins Commission recommendations were greeted with near unanimous skepticism by a

1. T. S. Eliot, *Collected Poems 1909–1962* (New York: Harcourt, Brace and World, 1963), 6.

fat and comfortable media establishment in that idyllic postwar period when the USA had a monopoly on atomic weapons and the existing order seemed the best of all possible worlds. It was a far different environment when Knight-Ridder Chairman James K. Batten gave the charge to his editorial writers at their 1989 meeting at Key Biscayne that launched their company's commitment to public journalism.[2] What happened in between? We need a historian to contrast and compare the social responsibility and public journalism movements and their historic environments to give us a better perspective and move us closer to a definition.

From earlier chapters in this book, the reader will have noticed two motivational elements that might be helpful in the problem of definition. The first is economic, and it comes directly out of the concern of the traditional media—newspapers and network affiliates— about the shrinking mass audience and the corresponding gains of more specialized media. James K. Batten, then CEO of Knight-Ridder, and John Gardner, former secretary of Health, Education and Welfare in the Kennedy administration and founder of Common Cause, addressed the Knight-Ridder editorial writers in 1988 and provided the ideological headwaters of this particular stream. Behind them was the work of an academic, Keith Stamm, who in turn had been funded by an organization whose motivation was explicitly economic, the American Newspaper Publishers Association (since consolidated with other newspaper trade groups into the Newspaper Association of America). Stamm broadened the conceptual connection between sense of community and newspaper readership, showing the dynamic interaction of the two factors.[3] The 1988 Knight-Ridder conference was historic on two counts: newspaper professionals took seriously a work of scholarship instead of guffawing at its obscure language; and they began to see the connection between the problems of their newspapers and the problems of their communities.

The second motivational element is social and political, and its main concern has been perceived flaws in the process of political communication. Jay Rosen and W. Davis Merritt, the leading academic and

2. Leigh, ed., *A Free and Responsible Press;* "Newspapers, Community and Leadership: A Symposium on Editorial Pages."

3. Keith R. Stamm, *Newspaper Use and Community Ties: Toward a Dynamic Theory* (Norwood, N.J.: Ablex Publishing Co., 1985).

professional advocates, respectively, of public journalism, have focused on flaws in the media system. Rosen's "six alarm bells" citing economic, technological, political, occupational, spiritual, and intellectual degeneration in the media system articulate the problem convincingly.[4] What remains to be articulated by researchers is an even broader view that connects the troubles of journalism to the troubles of society. One of the most important potential uses of the public journalism movement is that it can help us to see that a news medium and its community are parts of a single system, and that to repair journalism, it is necessary to try to repair the community. The damage to community is not just the fault of inadequate journalism, admirable as the mea culpas of editors like Merritt may be. Underlying social change, driven by information technology, is a more basic source of the problem.

For decades now, social scientists have noticed the increasing specialization of media and the resulting creation of artificial and isolated worlds that deplete the finite supply of attention that we can pay to the larger world.[5] Information and technology are supposed to make us free. That faith has been with us since the Enlightenment. Now some scholars are beginning to wonder. The implied equation goes something like this:

1) Information consumes the attention of those who receive it.

2) People who are information rich will therefore be attention poor.

3) Efforts to gain the increasingly scarce resource of attention will create a system that rewards the systematic violation of the social norms that define acceptable content.

4) These violations will increase in a cycle of competitive escalation until they trigger a backlash of authoritarianism or new cultural norms are established.

Both the backlash scenario and the projected shift in our culture are seen as antithetical to freedom. Amitai Etzioni founded the communitarian movement to head off the backlash. The fragmentation of interests, he argues, has led to replacement of "the democratic form of government with a government that largely heeds narrow, limited, self-serving groups."[6] His communitarian movement would shift our focus

---

4. Rosen, "Getting the Connections Right."
5. For early documentation of the rise of specialized media, see Richard Maisel, "The Decline of Mass Media," *Public Opinion Quarterly* 37, no. 2 (1973): 159–70.
6. Etzioni, *The Spirit of Community*, 226.

from rights to responsibilities and defragment political power at least enough to consolidate it at the community level.

Many recent scholars have ruminated about the notion that the Enlightenment's ideal of libertarian individualism has been overextended and grown into a dangerous caricature of itself, and they have done so through a variety of methodological perspectives. Robert N. Bellah and his colleagues argued from a moral philosophy point of view that America is in danger of losing the benefits of its collective-action tradition. Francis Fukuyama made a persuasive case that social virtues have an economic justification. And Robert Putnam, in a beautiful work that wove together different research methodologies, provided empirical confirmation that strong communities make strong democracy. His more recent work adds to the body of evidence that information technology, specifically television, is to blame for the decline of civic engagement in America.[7]

The ills that they describe sound very much like the problems that public journalism is trying to cure. There has not been much scholarship linking those goals to public journalism. Where to start? The economic concept of social capital was articulated in another context by Glen Loury in 1977 and picked up by James Coleman in 1990, before it was popularized as relevant to contemporary political systems by Putnam and Fukuyama.[8] Public journalism, through its emphasis on community, is trying to reverse the diminishing store of social capital, and clarifying that goal might help to conceptualize public journalism for its practitioners and justify it to its critics.

The media-as-destroyer-of-culture scenario comes from a different source. George Gerbner's career-long development of cultivation theory has resulted in a coalition of interest groups whose members fear that the creation of culture has shifted away from family and community to mass marketers and consequently has drifted out of democratic reach. Media conglomerates, in their desperate striving for our attention, says

7. Robert N. Bellah et al., *Habits of the Heart: Individualism and Commitment in American Life.* Francis Fukuyama, *Trust: The Social Virtues and the Creation of Prosperity* (New York: Free Press, 1995). Robert D. Putnam, *Making Democracy Work: Civic Traditions in Modern Italy* (Princeton: Princeton University Press, 1993). Putnam, "The Strange Disappearance of Civic America."

8. G. Loury, "A Dynamic Theory of Racial Income Differences," in *Women, Minorities, and Employment Discrimination,* edited by P. E. Wallace and A. LeMund (Lexington, Mass.: Lexington Books, 1977). Coleman, *Foundations of Social Theory.*

Gerbner, promote "practices that drug, hurt, poison, and kill thousands every day; portrayals that dehumanize and stigmatize; cults of violence that desensitize, terrorize and brutalize; the growing siege mentality of our cities; the drift toward ecological suicide; the silent crumbling of our infrastructure; widening resource gaps and the most glaring inequalities in the industrial world."[9]

Neither Gerbner, Etzioni, Putnam, nor Fukuyama is widely cited by proponents of the public journalism movement, but their concerns clearly fit the larger scene. All deplore the loss of community in America. All blame technology in general and the media in particular. A beauty of the public journalism movement is that it offers a nice symmetry: if media are part of the problem, perhaps they can be redirected toward being part of the solution. The participation of so many charitable foundations in this scene is evidence that there is more to the motivation than media profits. The common theme is to use the power of the media to fix something wrong in society, and to pay special attention to those wrongs that can be directly attributable to the media.

The proponents of public journalism who are motivated by economic concerns and those whose concern is more social and political no doubt overlap. But the prudent researcher will choose one perspective or the other as a basic framework and then look for the influence of the other within that frame.

The next important question is even broader: is public journalism a mere course correction in a media system gone temporarily adrift? Or is it the opening wedge in a radically new value system replacing those values that were born in the Enlightenment of the seventeenth and eighteenth centuries? The visceral opposition of some of the critics of public journalism may have resulted from a sense that the latter is true.

The Enlightenment was a reaction against authoritarianism in general and feudalism in particular, and its tool was reason, whose power was being demonstrated by rapid advances in science and technology. Information was viewed as a scarce but liberating resource. Milton's poetic defense of free speech in his *Areopagitica* (1644) was based on the notion that knowledge was a scarce good whose suppliers ought to be protected and encouraged. Now we are told by postmodern philosophers that information is less important than judgment, and

9. George Gerbner, *Prospectus*, Cultural Environment Movement, 1995. Scott Stossel, "The Man Who Counts the Killings," *Atlantic Monthly* 279, no. 5 (May 1997): 86–104.

that to find freedom, we must make use of other ways of knowing than reason.

In its extreme form, this line of thinking builds on a notion that originated with a collection of German philosophers known as the Frankfurt School in the 1920s. Drawing ideas from Karl Marx and Sigmund Freud, they declared that our ways of thinking about public policy questions are limited by the conceptual frames created by the domineering and coercive power holders of the status quo. In its most far-reaching extensions, as expressed by some of today's radical feminists, for example, the objective evidence in support of a proposition is less important than its usefulness in forming an ideology counter to the one propagated by the existing power holders. Some advocacy journalists buy into this idea when they color facts or even make them up to communicate what they perceive as a "higher truth" than one constrained by objective reality. If, as the German philosopher Immanuel Kant argued in the eighteenth century, truth is defined by the structures of our own minds as much as by the external world, then truth itself becomes a social construct and can legitimately be bent to serve agreed-upon social goals.

None of the advocates of public journalism that I know about have made such an explicit antireason argument, but one of their intellectual heroes, the contemporary German philosopher Jürgen Habermas, has advocated an "emancipatory mode" of knowledge as opposed to objective or scientific knowledge. As interpreted by Daniel Yankelovich, Habermas intends to supplement rather than replace traditional reason. Through public discourse that overcomes the barriers of culture, language, social class, and geography, members of a community can arrive at agreement based as much on intuition and judgment as linear, objective logic.[10] The advantage of this form of understanding is that it cleanses language and speech of their coercive aspects and leads to decisions on which people can take concerted action.

Habermas is a tough sell to journalists, and not just because he wants to get beyond objectivity. His goal is no less than to reinvent philosophy and produce a test of moral reasoning that would be as universally applicable as the categorical imperative of his home-country predecessor Kant. Toward that end he has read, seemingly, everything ever written in formal philosophy, and he writes with the apparent assumption that his readers have done so as well. But his ideas are creeping into the

10. Yankelovich, *Coming to Public Judgment,* 212.

debate, mostly through Yankelovich, who in turn inspired the Wichita editor W. Davis Merritt. And that at least opens the possibility that public journalism could be captured by the postmodernists who think that the individualistic values of the Enlightenment are flawed in today's context.

The notion of rejecting John Milton seems bizarre in view of his contribution to the thought that led to the First Amendment. But *Areopagitica* was conceived and written in a time of information scarcity. If John Milton were writing today, would he sound more like Habermas? Do the glut of information today and the corresponding scarcity of attention require an entirely new ethical system for journalists? And is that where public journalism is going? If redefining democracy is part of the agenda, that radical notion needs to be surfaced and openly debated. Serious efforts at researching and tracking public journalism and its related movements must be considered against the background of that larger question when the serious empirical work begins.

EMPIRICAL OPPORTUNITIES

If the desired end result of public journalism is increased social capital, and if that result is achieved, it ought to surface somewhere in the observable world. A necessary first step for empiricists is to prove that there are any results of public journalism at all. Such proof might come in three progressive steps: 1) Is public journalism real? 2) If so, does it have any visible output? 3) If it does, do those outputs make any difference in the minds, hearts, or observable behavior of the citizenry?

John Bare's work described in chapter 4 provides early empirical verification that there is such a thing as public journalism. By comparing the attitudes on basic journalistic values among the staffs of the *Wichita Eagle,* the *Raleigh News and Observer,* and the *Omaha World Herald,* he found convincing evidence that Buzz Merritt's leadership in Wichita had produced a value system that was palpably, if not radically, different. Public journalism exists, at least as a coherent concept in the minds of its adherents.

But so does the Loch Ness monster. The most interesting delusions are often coherent. To be convinced, we need to find the monster's spoor. In media studies, that means content analysis. In chapter 9 of this volume, Sally McMillan and coauthors have presented the first effort that we know about to find evidence of public journalism in the manifest content of news media. As a reading of that chapter shows, finding public journalism concepts tangible enough to be sighted and identified by independent judges is difficult, but it can be done. One problem is that content analysis is based on discrete elements—a sentence, a paragraph, a headline, a picture, or a story. Public journalism is defined by a more holistic concept. It involves the relationship of news elements or particular combinations of elements that might not be visible when any one element is observed in isolation from the others.

The problem is illustrated by a discovery that I made while I was the education writer for the *Miami Herald* (1958–1962). Management wisely wished to promote readership among the young, and so it conceived a weekly news summary called "Now" produced as a clip-out quarter fold directed at high school students. My job was to sit down on Saturday and write summaries of the week's national and international news for this audience. My first disillusioning discovery was that the summaries could not be written with the *Miami Herald* as the sole source. Not even the most important national and international stories were covered with a consistency that made it possible to write a continuing narrative describing the previous seven days. The *New York Times* helped some, but even it was not consistent. I finally had to arrange to have the spiked wire stories saved and sorted for my weekly chore.

The problem was that national and international stories were used as filler around the local stories and the ads. Nobody cared if they provided a consistent thread from day to day. But it is consistency, the duty of a journalist to answer the questions that he or she raises, that is one of the definitions of good public affairs journalism. And one way to tell whether it exists or not is to go through the exercise that I did and try to write a narrative from the daily reports that a newspaper gives its readers.

Here is another way. I call it the market basket method. Choose a topic in the news that is amenable to public journalism treatment. Immerse yourself in the topic so that you become the ideal informed citizen who understands the issue from a variety of interest perspectives, that is, you know how it affects you and also how it affects people whose situations are quite different from yours but whose interests deserve to be considered. Next, make a list.

The list should comprise a "market basket" of items of information whose possession would define a person who is capable of making an informed judgment about the issue. Now you are ready for content analysis. Look at every copy of the newspaper in the time period under study (or every broadcast videotape if TV news content is being studied) and count each appearance of one of the previously defined market basket items. Be sure to include multiple appearances. Public journalism allows, even encourages, redundancy as a way of ensuring that the important messages get through.

This methodology does not allow sampling. It requires a census of a given time period when the issue is up for public debate. But there are some aspects of public journalism in which content analysis based on a sample could be effective. The usual sampling model is the constructed week. From the time period under study, choose a random Monday, a random Tuesday, and so on until you have seven randomly chosen days, all different. Where the incidence of the phenomenon that you are looking for is suspected to be low, you might prefer to select two constructed weeks. Then you can look for concepts in whatever unit of analysis you have chosen. How to define the concepts? When you first have the ghost of a notion that you might want to do this, you should start keeping a notebook of operationalizations. To operationalize is to find a link between manifest content and the underlying concept you are trying to measure. It is best explained by example. Here are some operationalizations for content analysis to detect public journalism in an election campaign:

1) *Sources:* classify them as citizen-based or campaign-based and calculate the ratio.

2) *Tactics and strategy v. issues:* classify each unit (sentence, paragraph, or story) as to whether it deals mainly with tactics and strategy or the substantive issues of the campaign. Calculate the ratio.

3) *Horse race:* classify each unit as to whether its main purpose is to tell who is ahead at the moment—whether the source is a poll, campaign contributions, or the intuition of political insiders.

4) *Conflict v. agreement:* public journalism operations will have more references to agreement and fewer references to conflict than traditional efforts.

5) *Polls:* some editors use polling—or its absence—to define public journalism. But it really depends on how a poll is used. Horse race polls that merely give the standings of the moment are considered by some to be a distracter that keeps people from thinking about

issues. My own feeling, supported by some empirical evidence,[11] is that the horse race is interesting and a good way to draw a crowd whose attention can then be focused on issues. So a mere count of the number of polls is not sufficient. It is better to look for applications of polls that are specific to public journalism. Helping different subsets of the population to understand one another is one such application. Tracking the public's concern for the issues in the campaign is another. Polls that give feedback on how a candidate's tactics are working are of less relevance to public journalism.

In a 1997 study of twenty newspapers for the Poynter Institute, Deborah Potter and I succeeded in linking two of these constructs to staff intention to use public journalism techniques in the 1996 U.S. Senate and presidential campaigns. The public journalism–intending papers did have measurably more issue-oriented stories and fewer mentions of horse race polls. But those were the only effects we found, and those differences did not in turn seem to affect the citizenry in any direct way.[12] There were, however, effects traceable to the media's original intent. Just how that intention is realized through content remains a big mystery. Like McMillan and her coauthors, we had difficulty developing reliable measures of public journalism content, and that could be part of the problem. But it is also possible that our main problem is failure to have a clear enough idea of what signs to look for when the culture of the newsroom starts to change.

STUDYING THE COMMUNITY

If content is the spoor of the beast, and if it validates the existence of public journalism, a new and even more interesting area for research is opened. Does the existence of the beast matter to the community? The people who practice public journalism do so in order to have an effect on their community. So the ultimate measure is not what they put into their customers' hands but what ends up in their heads. And even then, it is only important if it affects behavior. The impulse of many

11. Philip Meyer and Deborah Potter, "Making a Difference: Covering Campaign '96, Report on the Poynter Election Project," paper presented at a National Press Club seminar, March 17, 1997, available on the Internet at http://www.unc.edu/~pmeyer/meyrpt1.htm.
12. Ibid.

evaluators of specific public journalism projects is to run a one-shot survey asking how many citizens had heard of the project. Affirmative answers can be gratifying, but they are hard to interpret. (In North Carolina, respondents are so anxious to please that 10 percent of them will claim to have heard of a fictitious candidate for governor.) As Thorson and colleagues demonstrate (chapter 8), message awareness is only a first step in detecting effects, and what we really care about is what the audience learned from the messages and what, if anything, it is doing about them.

When public journalism is applied to election coverage, one simple way to find an effect is to look at the election results. Public journalism ought to raise interest and that ought to be reflected in turnout. There was some premature self-congratulation among public journalism newspapers when the 1992 presidential votes were counted, because turnout was up. However, it was up just about everywhere, not just in the communities where public journalism was practiced. For reasons still not well understood, the long national trend toward declining voter participation was temporarily reversed in 1992.

More subtle effects can be teased out with survey research. Here is one example. Public journalism tries to make connections so that voters can see how one race affects another. If journalists succeed in forcing candidates and parties to offer coherent programs, voters will see that their choices for Congress and for the presidency are related, and there should be more coattail voting among independent or weakly partisan voters in public journalism media markets. This is not idle speculation. When political scientist Jeffery J. Mondak compared voter behavior in Pittsburgh and Cleveland in 1992, he found that weakly partisan and independent voters in Cleveland were more likely to make such internally consistent choices. This was not a test of public journalism versus conventional journalism, but a test of a campaign with newspapers compared to one without. The two Pittsburgh dailies were shut down by a strike throughout that campaign. Surprisingly, the loss of the newspapers did not have a visible effect on knowledge about the campaign. Voters in Pittsburgh knew as many isolated facts as those in Cleveland—television served them well enough in that area. But the weak partisans and independents among them were less likely to connect their congressional and their presidential votes by supporting candidates of the same party.[13] Print is better than TV at drawing such relationships.

Looking at one community at a time is a risky business. So many other things can happen to mask or exaggerate media effects, which are notoriously subtle. Mondak's brilliant use of the newspaper strike demonstrates the power of comparison across different communities and suggests a method for studying public journalism. To truly evaluate public journalism, we need a large-scale study in which the community itself is the unit of analysis. If we study enough communities simultaneously, their idiosyncratic differences will tend to cancel each other out and we might be left with a residue of effects traceable to public journalism. Consider the following idealized study design for evaluating public journalism in an election campaign:

1) Choose twenty to one hundred communities with as many similar characteristics as is feasible—especially size.

2) Measure their media's commitment to public journalism by surveying the managers of those media. While you are at it, survey the working stiffs, too, to get a sense of staff commitment to public journalism.

3) Content analyze those same media for a direct measure of whether they are doing public journalism.

With any luck at all, your sample of communities will show some interesting variance in their exposure to public journalism. If the researcher is very lucky, the variance will be normally distributed with some communities very low in public journalism, a few very high, and most bunched fairly close to the middle.

Small samples can give large statistical power when one is dealing with normally distributed continuous variables. Take the most obvious effect, voter turnout. For each community, one could develop a predicted election turnout based on its past voting record and its population growth. After the election, calculate the difference between the expectation and the actual turnout.

If public journalism has an effect on voting participation, there ought to be a correlation that can be visualized on a scatterplot— turnout residuals climbing ever higher with increasing degrees of citizen exposure to public journalism.

13. Jeffery J. Mondak, *Nothing to Read: Newspapers and Elections in a Social Experiment* (Ann Arbor: University of Michigan Press, 1995).

As described thus far, the proposed design is not outlandishly expensive. It includes a survey, but the sampled population is small. Election and population statistics are free. The next step is not so cheap.

To really nail down the connection between public journalism and what happens inside people's heads, we need to get directly into those heads with survey research. Some effects of public journalism could be visible right away. Others might take a very long time to form visible outcroppings. Here is a list of variables worth looking for, approximately in the order that we might expect them to appear.

1) *Political knowledge.* If public journalism is successful, more people will know who the candidates are and specific details about the issues. Asking voters about their subjective sense of being knowledgeable will produce a lot of affirmative answers, but it's best to test them as Esther Thorson and Frank Denton did in Madison (chapter 7) and as Thorson, Ekaterina Ognianova, James Coyle, and Ed Lambeth did in Columbia (chapter 8). In writing factual questions, it is easy to overshoot and create items that are interesting to journalists or graduate students but way over the heads of the general public. Some of the old standard items in political science research ask about such simple things as, "How many years does a U.S. senator serve?" or "How many justices are on the U.S. supreme court?" Ability to name one senator from one's own state also discriminates between those who are high and low in political knowledge.

The fact that there is variance on such simple items suggests that there is not much hope for detecting the much more sophisticated kind of knowledge needed to reach public judgment about complicated issues in a survey of the general public. Recent surveys by the Times Mirror Center for the People and the Press (from 1996 on, the Pew Center) show that the proportion of the public that follows news about public policy formation is quite small. Nevertheless, over time, the broad mass of voters does make decisions that appear to be both rational and based on information that has filtered down to them somehow.[14] For purposes of assessing public journalism at this basic level, all we require is that political knowledge vary across some measurable continuum. A knowledge scale that includes an array of items that vary in difficulty is likely to show the needed variance. In

14. V. O. Key, *The Responsible Electorate: Responsibility in Presidential Voting, 1936–1960* (Cambridge: Harvard University Press, 1966).

constructing it, the prudent researcher will see if he or she is in the ballpark by testing the items on some convenience sample such as a beginning newswriting class. In the analysis stage, education should, of course, be held constant.

2) *Political participation.* Voting is not the only way that people participate in the political process. It's not even the most important way. Those college kids who rang doorbells for Eugene McCarthy in New Hampshire in February 1964 were below the voting age at the time, but each of them was a far more effective participant than the typical adult, voter or not.

For a starter list of items that measure participation, from sporting a bumper sticker to working as a campaign volunteer, a good source is *Participation in America* by Sidney Verba and Norman Nie. Their survey work was first published in 1967, and has been twice updated, so it provides a nice historical baseline.[15] One form of participation that Mondak found related to newspaper use in his Cleveland-Pittsburgh comparison of 1992 was simply having conversations with friends about the election. If public journalism is contributing to political discourse, that is one variable that ought to show an effect right away. Other tried and true measures of participation can be found in the national election studies of the University of Michigan and the social indicator series of the University of Chicago's General Social Survey.

3) *Ideological consistency.* Citizens who have considered an issue and come to a coherent judgment will have more self-consistent views than those who look at each fragment of information in isolation. Political scientist Phil Converse has called this characteristic "ideological constraint" and its presence is indicated by high inter-item correlation on items that measure the same underlying political choices or attitudes.[16] If public journalism works, ideological constraint should increase.

4) *Attitude strength.* Daniel Yankelovich distinguishes between low-quality and high-quality public opinion. Opinions of high quality are not as sensitive to variations in question wording and represent considered responses to issues that respondents have thought about—which is one of the outcomes sought by public journalism. Stronger attitudes are a sign of progress in the process of developing public judgment on an issue. Yankelovich's "mushiness index" is only one of many ways to

15. Verba et al., *Voice and Equality.*
16. Converse, "The Nature of Belief Systems."

measure attitude strength. Richard E. Petty and Jon A. Krosnick have assembled a volume of essays on this concept that should serve as a starting point for discovering ways to measure this possible effect of public journalism.[17]

5) *Willingness to accept the consequences.* Another measure of quality in public opinion proposed by Yankelovich is whether the holder of the opinion accepts the implied consequences. Someone who favors greater government benefits but not the taxes to support them has failed to work through the process that molds casual and ill-considered opinion into judgment based on discourse and reflection.

6) *Coattail voting.* Mondak's 1992 work in Cleveland and Pittsburgh offers a promising model. People who vote for a congressional candidate because he or she belongs to the same party as their presidential choice are not necessarily less informed or sophisticated. In fact, the coattail effect has been found to occur less often among voters who do not read newspapers.[18] It shows up when voters read enough about the campaign and its issues to realize that the fate of their presidential choice, should he or she win, will have something to do with the kind of Congress that is elected. The coattail effect is not seen among the strongly partisan because their choices are consistent to begin with. For everybody else, it is a variable, and it might be connectable to public journalism.

LONG-TERM MEASURES

The long-term goal of public journalism is ambitious almost beyond belief. It seeks to reverse the damage to our national culture brought about by the atomizing forces of information technology. Cultural change, almost by definition, is slow. As the damage was gradual, so must be its repair. But we should start now to monitor the broad social indicators that public journalism aims to affect and try to find ways to link them to the exercise of public journalism. Here is a short list, in estimated order of the length of time it would take to detect effects if in fact public journalism is successful.

17. Yankelovich, *Coming to Public Judgment,* 34. Richard E. Petty and Jon A. Krosnick, eds., *Attitude Strength: Antecedents and Consequences* (Mahwah, N.J.: Lawrence Erlbaum Associates, 1995).

18. Mondak, *Nothing to Read,* 149–50.

IF IT WORKS, HOW WILL WE KNOW?

1) *Community ties.* Keith Stamm, building on work by John Kasarda and Morris Janowitz,[19] conceptualizes three levels of community identification—with a geographical location, with a community process, and with community structure. The works cited by Stamm provide specific operationalizations. Links between these ties and newspaper readership are so strong that the variables appear to decline in a vicious cycle. The newspaper is the informational glue that holds the community together, and when it fades, community belongingness fades, causing further deterioration in the newspaper. If public journalism can turn that around into a virtuous cycle—strong community ties driving people to the newspaper, which creates even stronger community identification—it should appear in survey attitudes and newspaper circulation almost simultaneously.

Some recent work by Richard C. Morgan, Jr. shows how to model the formation of such systems, including the conversion of a vicious cycle to a virtuous one, with a computer simulation.[20] Business-side newspaper simulations have long been used as a training tool, and a model that takes into account the community identification factor might lead to better understanding of its importance.

2) *Trust in people.* Public journalism aims to reverse the decline in social capital. As defined by Putnam and others, including Fukuyama, social capital is the reciprocal trust in a community of shared ethical values that facilitate cooperative action. Without such shared values, such action is still possible through the regulation provided by laws and contract. But these devices carry a heavy economic cost; drafting and enforcing a promissory note costs more than a handshake. Social capital, says Fukuyama, "can be embodied in the smallest and most basic social group, the family, as well as the largest of all groups, the nation, and in all the other groups in between . . . it is usually created and transmitted through cultural mechanisms like religion, tradition, or historical habit." It also is "much harder to acquire than other forms

19. John Kasarda and Morris Janowitz, "Community Attachment in Mass Society," *American Sociological Review* 39 (June 1974): 328–39.
20. Richard C. Morgan, Jr., *A Systems Thinking Paradigm and Learning Computer Simulation Model of the Positive and Negative Feedback Structures Underlying Growth, Competition and Displacement in the U.S. Mass Communication System* (Ph.D diss., University of North Carolina at Chapel Hill, 1994).

of human capital, but because it is based on ethical habit, it is also harder to modify or destroy."[21]

The absence of social capital is *anomie,* the state of normlessness or lack of social structures. Social psychologists have developed measures for it and some of them, including the trust-in-people questions, can be found in the General Social Survey and the national election surveys of the Michigan Survey Research Center. One question in the series asks for agreement or disagreement with the statement, "Most people really don't care what happens to the next fellow." Faith in others has generally declined since the 1960s.

3) *Trust in institutions.* Trust in government and other institutions has been declining more sharply than trust in people. Seymour Martin Lipset and William Schneider (the CNN commentator) have documented this decline through 1986.[22] The surveys that they cite, including those of the universities of Michigan and Chicago, still do their periodic measures, so that recent national benchmarks are continually being created. If public journalism succeeds in empowering citizens and bringing them closer to their political leaders, trust in political institutions should rise again.

In sum, we are not talking about wispy and hard-to-measure abstractions when we discuss the hoped-for effects of public journalism. The variables of trust and alienation in the general population have been successfully measured and studied for half a century. If public journalism is successful, and these trends turn a corner, we'll know about it. And we'll know it sooner if we focus on long-term projects like those described by Lewis Friedland and his coauthors in Madison (chapter 10). We'll also save time if we can answer the "compared-to-what" question by running large-scale multiple-market projects like the one funded by the Poynter Institute in the 1996 elections. Making markets the unit of analysis is a good way to get the attention of the editors and publishers who serve those markets and can find themselves in the scatterplots.

THE COSTS OF PUBLIC JOURNALISM

That's the good news. The bad news is that the effects of public journalism are likely to be slow and incremental. The costs, on the other

21. Fukuyama, *Trust,* 26–27.
22. Seymour Martin Lipset and William Schneider, *The Confidence Gap: Business, Labor, and Government in the Public Mind* (Baltimore: Johns Hopkins University Press, 1987).

hand, are visible and immediate. As the effects of public journalism become more susceptible to measurement, the next obvious research questions are:

1. What is the cost of a given level of effect?
2. Is it worth it?

Unlike other research goals discussed here, cost-benefit analysis of editorial innovation is a particularly difficult area. It is nevertheless important because media managers are under great pressure to make decisions on the basis of short-term benefits. Public journalism has several parallels with the newspaper management fad of the 1970s, market research.

Newspaper editors and publishers first became concerned with the decline in their audience in the early 1970s after several years of consistent decline in average daily readership, the indicator most closely watched by advertisers. They turned to market researchers for guidance, recognizing that a reader who buys a paper on any given day is making a business transaction, and a better understanding of that person's needs and motivations might help editors to improve the product. These efforts were widely criticized by traditional news-editorial people, who derided the concept of the newspaper as a product and the community as a market. Their arguments had the same ring as those made by today's critics of public journalism. It is the responsibility of the journalist, they argued, to give readers not what they want, but what they need. Pandering to readers' tastes—which, in the minds of the critics, is what market researchers did by definition—would lead to frivolity and entertainment at the expense of enlightenment.

These critics greatly underestimated the taste and intelligence of their readers and overestimated the ability of editors' intuition to assess their needs. Media market researchers prospered despite the criticism— for a time. But they never realized their full potential because newspaper owners and managers were interested only in solutions that could be implemented cheaply and that would pay off quickly. Redesigns of newspapers are relatively cheap because one typeface costs no more than another, and so market research often led to new designs.

Expensive innovations did not fare as well. One suggested by market research was to set aside a substantial amount of space for children because it was known that childhood reading habits tend to persist in later life. At Knight-Ridder, a kids' page was produced and tested for six months but finally dropped when no child-oriented advertising could be sold to pay for the newsprint consumed. The long-term benefit, raising a generation of newspaper-habituated young people, was too far in the future and too difficult to predict to be put into a cost-benefit analysis. (A new generation of Knight-Ridder editors is trying with better results. "Yak," a daily feature for kids produced by the *Detroit Free Press* and syndicated elsewhere, uses long-term reader recruitment rather than current advertising as its justification.)

Public journalism's failure to show immediate economic benefits could prove a major disadvantage. Some of its tools, such as public opinion polls, focus groups, and community meetings, are expensive. So are some of its structures, like the reorganized newsroom used by the *Columbia State* (see chapter 5). The traditional newsroom, with beats ordered by news sources and agencies, is efficient at generating copy, and it is easy to administer in a daily routine. Organizing the newsrooms into teams of writers and editors dedicated to broad themes can certainly stimulate creativity, but the underlying economies of the traditional beat system may prove a relentless force pushing them back toward the old structures.

Because there is more than one way to do public journalism, it will be important to know what ways do the most at the least cost. The search for synergy effects through multimedia efforts in Columbia and Madison (chapters 7 and 8) represent a good start in this direction. Other recent work, by Russell Neuman and his colleagues,[23] provides a convincing justification for more cooperative efforts between newspapers and TV stations. But while such joint endeavors are becoming fairly common, they are not always managed in the most effective way. Newspapers dominate in content, and they sometimes force deals that prevent their broadcast partners from being first with the news—in the mistaken notion that letting TV launch a joint project amounts to getting beaten on the story. What Neuman, Just, and Crigler have shown is that the reverse strategy works better. Breaking the attention barrier is television's main strength, and it can lead the audience to seek out the interpretation and the nuances in the newspaper that it would otherwise ignore. A newspaper that insists on being first with the news is losing a promotion opportunity.

Research aimed at finding the cheapest way to get a public journalism effect is likely to be popular and relatively well supported. But it could

23. Neuman, Just, and Crigler, *Common Knowledge*.

easily degenerate into theory-starved minutiae like the old marketing studies on whether color ads sell more than black and white and whether sans serif type is easier to read than Roman. Such tidbits might be useful in short-term editorial decision making, but without being woven into a larger picture, they are not very interesting.

THE ULTIMATE RESEARCH QUESTION

At the start of this chapter, we considered the question of whether public journalism is a conservative force preserving the values developed from the Enlightenment or whether it is a radical search for something to replace those values.

If the traditional values of journalism do need replacing, it is not because the eighteenth-century thinkers were flawed but because information technology has created an entirely different playing field.

The Enlightenment grew out of the development of scientific method and respect for reason. Its roots were in the Renaissance and the Protestant Reformation. What these movements had in common was a struggle against authority, first of the church and then of the state. If George Gerbner and some of the postmodern philosophers are right, the authority representing today's greatest threat to freedom is neither church nor state but the collective effect of advertising-driven mass media. It (in Gerbner's imagery, the media are a de facto monolith and therefore deserve the singular pronoun) is controlling our culture, and it has, in Gerbner's words, "drifted beyond democratic reach." That is a startling proposition, but one of the justifications of public journalism is or can be that we can bring media content back into democratic reach by making it more audience participatory.

So the ultimate question for researchers on public journalism is, simply, how can it be paid for? In the long run, can it be supported by media that depend on advertising as their primary revenue source? Or will we have to find some other way to pay for information about public life and how it is going?

This question does not assume any conspiracy or predictable attempt by advertisers to control content in their direct interests. It does assume the obvious: that as attention becomes increasingly scarce, advertisers will tailor their strategies in response to that scarcity. Logically, they can react in one of four ways. Only one of the four is good for journalism as we know it.

1) They can seek to associate themselves with editorial content that gains attention with its shock value, often by being outrageously deviant and countercultural.

2) They can support increasingly narrow messages directed at highly specific subgroups.

3) They can become primary providers of editorial content and blend their advertising with that content.

4) Or they can gravitate toward whatever broad-based medium is the most trusted and respected in its community and hope to share in its influence.

The first of these three strategies is already in place and accounts for the increasing emphasis on sex, violence, and oddball personal revelations in the media. It is the scramble for attention that is "defining deviancy down," as Senator Daniel Patrick Moynihan has put it in another context. The second is also being implemented, as a trip to any large newsstand will demonstrate. (There are, for example, multiple magazines directed at bow-and-arrow hunters or people with tattoos.) Specialized information sources are efficient at meeting individual needs, but at a cost to a broad sense of community. The other cost is reduced independence for the editorial side. The narrower the advertising market, the more the advertisers can dictate editorial content. The third strategy exists in experimental mode with businesses paying to have their products appear in movies and letting commercials blend seamlessly into TV drama. Product placements in news stories may lie further down this slippery slope. The fourth model is the traditional one, and the reason for its success is that it has enabled news media to find economic value in integrity and trust. It is hard to envision any other model that will be able to accommodate advertiser-supported public journalism without damaging both journalism and the communities it serves. Public journalism could be its last, best hope.

Research on the links between advertiser support and public journalism might provide the missing element in the cost-benefit analysis. Neuman has argued that news media will look for new sources of monopoly power as the physical means of production becomes cheaper and less of an entry barrier. He sees their best hope in content.[24] Creation of

24. W. Russell Neuman, *The Future of the Mass Audience* (Cambridge: Harvard University Press, 1991). For my extrapolation of this idea to the newspaper case, see "Learning to Love Lower Profits."

credible, authenticated content could be the new bottleneck in the information production process—and therefore a potential source of near monopoly power in the media forms of the future. If true, that would create an opportunity for public journalism. If information overload makes credibility scarce, those who can provide it might capture enough critical mass of the public's attention to attract advertisers who seek a trustworthy, and therefore influential, editorial environment.

The traditional economics of the newspaper business bear this out. Eighty percent of a newspaper's value is what accountants call "good will" rather than physical plant or inventory. Goodwill is nothing more tangible than the public's willingness to trust the medium enough to use it as an information exchange for both social and commercial benefit. Public journalism might be a way that a news medium, whatever its delivery mode, can capture enough goodwill to hold the main position of trust and responsibility in its community. Build that, and the advertisers will come in the hope that the medium's societal influence will result in commercial influence for them. If such a thing is possible, the sooner we all know about it, the better. It would be a nonradical way of maintaining media power within democratic reach.

SELECTED BIBLIOGRAPHY

BOOKS

Abramson, Jeffrey R., F. Christopher Arterton, and Gary R. Orren. *The Electronic Commonwealth.* New York: Basic Books, 1988.

Altschull, J. Herbert. *Agents of Power: The Role of the News Media in Human Affairs.* New York: Longman, 1984.

———. *From Milton to McLuhan: The Ideas behind American Journalism.* New York: Longman, 1990.

Anderson, Charles W. *Pragmatic Liberalism.* Chicago: University of Chicago Press, 1990.

Bagdikian, Benjamin J. *The Media Monopoly.* 5th ed. Boston: Beacon Press, 1997.

Barber, Benjamin R. *Strong Democracy: Participatory Politics for a New Age.* Berkeley: University of California Press, 1984.

Bellah, Robert N., Richard Madsen, William M. Sullivan, Ann Swidler, and Steven M. Tipton. *The Good Society.* New York: Alfred A. Knopf, 1992.

———. *Habits of the Heart: Individualism and Commitment in American Life.* Berkeley: University of California, 1945.

Black, Jay, ed. *Mixed News: The Public/Civic/Communitarian Journalism Debate.* Mahwah, N.J.: Lawrence Erlbaum Associates, 1997.

Bogart, Leo. *Preserving the Press: How Daily Newspapers Mobilized to Keep Their Readers.* New York: Columbia University Press, 1991.

Carey, James W. "The Dark Continent of American Journalism." In *Reading the News,* edited by R. K. Manoff and Michael Schudson. New York: Pantheon, 1986.

————. "The Press, Public Opinion and Public Discourse." In T. L. Glasser and C. T. Salmon, *Public Opinion and the Communication of Consent*, 403–16. New York: Guilford Press, 1995.

————. "A Republic If You Can Keep It: Liberty and Public Life in the Age of Glasnost." In Raymond Arsenault, *Crucible of Liberty: 200 Years of the Bill of Rights*. New York: Free Press, 1991.

Charity, Art. *Doing Public Journalism*. New York: Guilford Press, 1995.

Christians, Clifford G., John P. Ferre, and P. Mark Fackler. *Good News: Social Ethics and the Press*. New York: Oxford University Press, 1993.

Clark, Roy Peter. *The American Conversation and the Language of Journalism*. Poynter Papers No. 5. St. Petersburg, Fla.: Poynter Institute for Media Studies, 1994.

Coleman, James S. *Foundations of Social Theory*. Cambridge: Harvard University Press, 1990.

————. *Individual Interests and Collective Action*. Cambridge and New York: Cambridge University Press, 1986.

Dahl, R. *Who Governs? Democracy and Power in an American City*. New Haven: Yale University Press, 1961.

Dewey, John. *The Public and Its Problems*. Denver: Swallow Press, 1927.

Dionne, E. J., Jr. *Why Americans Hate Politics*. New York: Simon and Schuster, 1991.

Etzioni, A. *The Spirit of Community: The Reinvention of American Society*. New York: Simon and Schuster, 1993.

Fallows, James. *Breaking the News: How the Media Undermine American Democracy*. New York: Pantheon Books, 1996.

Fishkin, James S. *Democracy and Deliberation: New Directions for Democratic Reform*. New Haven: Yale University, 1991.

————. *The Voice of the People: Public Opinion and Democracy*. New Haven: Yale University Press, 1995.

Galaskiewicz, Joseph. *Exchange Networks and Community Politics*. Beverly Hills, Calif.: Sage, 1979.

Garreau, J. *Edge City: Life on the New Frontier*. New York: Anchor Books, 1991.

Ginsberg, Benjamin. *The Captive Public*. New York: Basic Books, 1986.

Goodwin, Gene, and Ron F. Smith. *Groping for Ethics in Journalism*. 3d ed. Ames: Iowa State University Press, 1994.

Graber, Doris. *Processing the News: How People Tame the Information Tide*. 2d ed. New York: Longman, 1988.

Greider, William. *Who Will Tell the People? The Betrayal of American Democracy.* New York: Simon and Schuster, 1992.

Habermas, Jurgen. *The Structural Transformation of the Public Sphere: An Inquiry into a Category of Bourgeois Society.* Trans. Thomas Burger. Cambridge: M.I.T. Press, 1989.

Herr, Michael. *Dispatches.* New York: Alfred A. Knopf, 1977.

Hovland, C. I., I. L. Janis, and H. H. Kelley. *Communication and Persuasion.* New Haven: Yale University Press, 1953.

Huckfeldt, R., and J. Sprague. *Citizens, Politics and Social Communication.* Cambridge and New York: Cambridge University Press, 1995.

Hunter, James D. *Culture Wars: The Struggle to Define America.* New York: Basic Books, 1955.

Iyengar, Shanto. *Is Anyone Responsible? How Television Frames Political Issues.* Chicago: University of Chicago Press, 1991.

Kosicki, Gerald M., and Jack M. McLeod. "Learning from Political News: Effects of Media Images and Information-Processing Strategies." In *Mass Communication and Political Information Processing,* edited by Sidney Kraus. Hillsdale, N.J.: Lawrence Erlbaum Associates, 1990.

Kurtz, Howard. *Media Circus: The Trouble with America's Newspapers.* New York: Times Books, 1993.

Lambeth, Edmund B. *Committed Journalism: An Ethic for the Profession.* 2d ed. Bloomington: Indiana University Press, 1992.

Lappe, Frances Moore, and Paul Martin DuBois. *The Quickening of America.* San Francisco: Jossey-Bass, 1994.

Leigh, Robert D., ed. *A Free and Responsible Press: A General Report on Mass Communication.* The Commission on Freedom of the Press. Chicago: University of Chicago, 1947.

Lemert, James B. *Criticizing the Media: Empirical Approaches.* Newbury Park, Calif.: Sage, 1989.

————. *News Verdicts, the Debates and Presidential Campaigns.* New York: Praeger, 1991.

Lippmann, Walter. *The Phantom Public.* New York: Harcourt Brace, 1922.

————. *Public Opinion.* New York: Harcourt Brace, 1922.

McGuire, W. J. "Theoretical Foundations of Campaigns." In *Public Communication Campaigns,* 2d ed., edited by R. E. Rice and C. K. Atkin, 43–65. Newbury Park, Calif.: Sage, 1994.

McManus, John H. *Market-Driven Journalism: Let the Citizen Beware?* Thousand Oaks, Calif.: Sage, 1994.

SELECTED BIBLIOGRAPHY

Mathews, David. *Politics for People: Finding a Responsible Public Voice.* Urbana: University of Illinois Press, 1994.

Merrill, John. *The Dialectic in Journalism: Toward a Responsible Use of Press Freedom.* Baton Rouge: Louisiana State University Press, 1989.

——. *The Imperative of Freedom: A Philosophy of Journalistic Autonomy.* New York: Hastings House, 1974.

Merritt, Davis. *Public Journalism and Public Life: Why Telling the News Is Not Enough.* Hillsdale, N.J.: Erlbaum, 1995.

Miller, Edward D. *The Charlotte Project: Helping Citizens Take Back Democracy.* St. Petersburg, Fla.: Poynter Papers No. 4, 1994.

Milton, John. *Areopagitica.* Folcroft, Pa.: Folcroft Press, 1969.

Moriarty, S. "Theories of Integrated Communication." In *Integrated Communications: Synergy of Persuasive Voices,* edited by Esther Thorson and Jeri Moore, 333–53. Mahwah, N.J.: Lawrence Erlbaum Associates, 1996.

Neuman, W. Russell. *The Paradox of Mass Politics: Knowledge and Opinion in the American Electorate.* Cambridge: Harvard University Press, 1986.

Neuman, W. Russell, Marion R. Just, and Ann N. Crigler. *Common Knowledge: News and the Construction of Political Meaning.* Chicago: University of Chicago Press, 1992.

Postman, Neil. *Amusing Ourselves to Death: A Public Discussion in the Age of Show Business.* New York: Viking, 1985.

Protess, David L., Fay Lomax Cook, Jack C. Doppelt, James S. Ettema, Margaret T. Gordon, Donna R. Leff, and Peter Miller. *The Journalism of Outrage, Investigative Reporting and Agenda Building in America.* New York: Guilford Press, 1991.

Putnam, Robert D. *Making Democracy Work: Civic Traditions in Modern Italy.* Princeton: Princeton University Press, 1993.

Rawls, John. *A Theory of Justice.* Cambridge: Harvard University Press, 1971.

Robinson, John P., and Mark R. Levy. *The Main Source: Learning from Television News.* Beverly Hills, Calif.: Sage, 1986.

Rosen, Jay. *Getting the Connections Right: Public Journalism and the Troubles in the Press.* New York: Twentieth Century Fund, 1996.

——. *The Impossible Press: American Journalism and the Decline of Public Life.* Ph.D. diss., New York University.

Rosen, Jay, and Davis Merritt. *Public Journalism: Theory and Practice.* Dayton, Ohio: Kettering Foundation, 1994.

SELECTED BIBLIOGRAPHY

Schudson, Michael. *The Power of News.* Cambridge: Harvard University Press, 1995.

Seib, Philip M. *Campaigns and Conscience: The Ethics of Political Journalism.* Westport, Conn.: Praeger, 1994.

Seibert, Frederick S., Theodore Peterson, and Wilbur Schramm. *Four Theories of the Press.* Urbana: University of Illinois Press, 1969.

Thomas, W., ed. *Synergy Access: A Global Newsletter on Futuristic Communications, Media and Networking.* Twenty-First Century Media, 1973.

Thorson, E., and J. Moore, eds. *Integrated Communication: Synergy of Persuasive Voices.* Mahwah, N.J.: Lawrence Erlbaum Associates, 1996.

Tocqueville, Alexis de. *Democracy in America.* New York: Vintage Classics, 1990.

Toffler, Alvin. *The Third Wave.* New York: Bantam Books.

Tuchman, Gaye. *Making News: A Study in the Construction of Reality.* New York: Free Press, 1978.

Underwood, Doug. *When MBAs Rule the Newsroom.* New York: Columbia University Press, 1993.

Weaver, David H., and G. Cleveland Wilhoit. *The American Journalist.* Bloomington: Indiana University Press, 1991.

Yankelovich, Daniel. *Coming to Public Judgment: Making Democracy Work in a Complex World.* Syracuse: Syracuse University Press, 1991.

ARTICLES AND REPORTS

Achenbaum, A. A. "Effective Exposure." *Journal of Media Planning* (fall 1996): 11–13.

Albers, Rebecca Ross. "Going Public: Going Public Unites Some Publishers and Newsrooms in a Controversial Mission." *Presstime* (September 1994).

Archie, Michele. "Framing Issues: Building a Structure for Public Discussions." Dayton, Ohio: Kettering Foundation, 1995.

Austin, Lisa. "Public Journalism: A Progress Report." Research report from New York University's Project on Public Life and the Press.

Avis, Ed. "Where's the Money Going? Bigger Newspaper Profits Don't Mean More Jobs." *Quill* (April 1995): 20–22.

Bales, Michael. "Tuning In to Public Concerns." *APME Readership Committee* (August 1994): 10–14.

Bare, John. "Case Study—Wichita and Charlotte: The Leap of a Passive Press to Activism." *Media Studies Journal* 6, no. 4 (fall 1992): 149–60.

Batten, James. "Public Journalism: Fulfilling Our Responsibility." Report on the American Press Institute Seminar, 1993.

Bogart, Leo. "The American Media System and Its Commercial Culture." *Media Studies Journal* (fall 1991).

———. "Who Pays for the Media?" *Journal of Advertising Research* (March/April 1994): 11–18.

Boylan, James. "Declarations of Independence." *Columbia Journalism Review* 25, no. 4 (November–December 1986): 29–45.

Bramlett-Solomon, Sharon, and Bruce Merrill. "Newspaper Use and Community Ties in a Model Retirement Community." *Newspaper Research Journal* 12, no. 1 (fall 1991): 60–67.

Brewer, Marcus, and Maxwell McCombs. "Setting the Community Agenda." *Journalism and Mass Communication Quarterly* 73, no. 1 (spring 1996): 7–16.

Bridges, Janet. "Daily Newspapers Managing Editors' Perceptions of News Media Functions." *Journalism and Mass Communication Quarterly* 68, no. 4 (winter 1991): 719–28.

Broder, David. "A New Assignment for the Press." Riverside, Calif., *Press-Enterprise* Lecture Series, February 12, 1991.

Budiansky, Stephen. "The Media's Message: The Public Thinks the National Press Is Elitist, Insensitive and Arrogant." *U.S. News and World Report* 118, no. 1 (January 9, 1995): 45–47.

Carey, James W. "The Press and Public Discourse." *Center Magazine* (March 1987): 5.

Case, Tony. "Public Journalism Denounced." *Editor and Publisher* (November 12, 1994): 12.

Charity, Arthur. "What Readers Want: A Very Different Model." *Columbia Journalism Review* (November/December 1993): 45–47.

"Citizens and Politics: A View from Main Street America." Harwood Group: Kettering Foundation, 1991.

Dennis, Everette E. "On People and the Media: Raising Questions about Public Journalism." *Communique* 9, no. 10 (June 1995): 2.

Denton, Frank, and Esther Thorson. "Civic Journalism: Does It Work?" Washington, D.C.: Pew Center for Civic Journalism, 1995.

Dill, Sherie. "Wichita Reverses a Trend." *Civic Catalyst*. Pew Civic Journalism Newsletter. Washington, D.C., March 7, 1995.

Dykers, Carol Reese. "A Critical Review: Re-Conceptualizing the Relation of 'Democracy' to 'News.' " Paper presented to the Association for Education in Journalism and Mass Communication. Washington, D.C., August 1995.

Eberly, Don E. "The Quest for a Civil Society." *National Civic Review* (spring 1995): 119–25.

Faber, Ron, and M. C. Storey. "Recall of Information from Political Advertising." *Journal of Advertising* 13, no. 3 (1984): 39–44.

Faber, Ron, A. R. Tims, and K. G. Schmitt. "Negative Political Advertising and Voting Intent: The Role of Involvement and Alternative Information Sources." *Journal of Advertising* 22, no. 4 (1993): 67–76.

Fallows, James. "Why Americans Hate the Media." *Atlantic Monthly* (February 1996): 45–64.

Foughy, Ed. "The Dawn of Public Journalism." *National Civic Review* (summer/fall 1994): 259–66.

Frankel, Max. "Fix-It Journalism." *New York Times Magazine*, May 21, 1995.

The Freedom Forum Media Studies Center. *Religion and the News: A Conference Report.* New York: Columbia University, 1994.

Friedland, Lewis A., and Carmen J. Sirianni. "Critical Concepts in the New Citizenship." Philadelphia: Pew Charitable Trusts, 1995.

Garramone, Gina. "Voter Response to Negative Political Ads." *Journalism Quarterly* 61 (summer 1984): 250–59.

Gartner, Michael. "Give Me Old Time Journalism." *Quill* (November/December, 1995): 66–69.

Hoyt, Michael. "Are You Now, or Will You Ever Be, a Civic Journalist?" *Columbia Journalism Review* (September/October 1995): 27–33.

———. "The Wichita Experiment: What Happens When a Newspaper Tries to Connect Readers and Citizenship?" *Columbia Journalism Review* (July/August 1992): 43–47.

Hunter, James Davidson. "Before the Shooting Begins." *Columbia Journalism Review* (July/August 1993): 29–32.

Kramer, Staci D. "Civic Journalism: Six Case Studies." Edited by Jan Schaffer and Edward D. Miller. Washington, D.C.: Pew Center for Civic Journalism and Poynter Institute for Media Studies, July 1995.

Lambeth, Edmund B. "A Bibliographic Review of Civic Journalism." *National Civic Review* (winter/spring 1996): 18–21.

———. "Good News: Social Ethics and the Press." Review and essay in *Media Development* (winter 1995): 50–51.

———. "The News Media and Democracy." *Media Studies Journal* 6, no. 4 (fall 1992): 161–75.

Lambeth, Edmund B., and James Aucoin. "Understanding Communities: The Journalist as Leader." *Journalism Educator* (spring 1993): 12–19.

Lambeth, Edmund B., and David Craig. "Civic Journalism as Research." *Newspaper Research Journal* (spring 1995): 148–60.

Levine, Peter. "Public Journalism: A Philosophical Profile." Institute for Philosophy and Public Policy: University of Maryland, 1995.

Luttbeg, Norman R. "The Structure of Beliefs among Leaders and the Public." *Public Opinion Quarterly* 32, no. 3 (fall 1968): 398–409.

McCombs, Maxwell E., and Donald L. Shaw. "The Agenda-Setting Function of the Press." *Public Opinion Quarterly* 36 (1992): 176–87.

Mathews, David. "Community Change through True Public Action." *National Civic Review* 83, no. 4 (fall/winter 1994): 400–404.

Merritt, Davis. "The Misconceptions about Public Journalism." *Editor and Publisher* 128, no. 26 (July 1, 1995): 80–82.

Meyer, Philip. "Defining Public Journalism: Discourse Leading to Solutions." *IRE Journal* (November/December 1995): 3–5.

———. "Learning to Love Lower Profits." *Columbia Journalism Review* (December 1995).

Morton, John. "When Newspapers Eat Their Seed Corn." *American Journalism Review* (November 1995).

Neuman, W. Russell. "Patterns of Recall among Television News Viewers." *Public Opinion Quarterly* 40, no. 1 (1976): 115–23.

"The New Political Landscape." Report of the Times Mirror Center for the People and the Press, Washington, D.C., October 1994.

Overholser, Geneva. "Learning from 'Civic Journalism.'" *Washington Post,* September 17, 1995.

Picard, R. G. "Institutional Ownership of Publicly Traded U.S. Newspaper Companies." *Journal of Media Economics* 7, no. 4 (1994): 49–64.

Putnam, Robert D. "Bowling Alone: America's Declining Social Capital." *Current* 373 (June 1995): 3–10.

———. "The Prosperous Community: Social Capital and Public Life." *American Prospect* 24 (winter 1996): 35–42.

———. "The Strange Disappearance of Civic America." *American Prospect* (spring 1993): 35–42.

———. "What Makes Democracy Work?" *National Civic Review* (spring 1993): 101–7.

Rosen, Jay. "Beyond Objectivity." *Nieman Reports* (winter 1993): 48–53.

————. "Community Action: Sin or Salvation?" *Quill* (March 1992): 30–33.

————. "Community Connectedness: Passwords for Public Journalism." Poynter Papers No. 3. St. Petersburg, Fla.: Poynter Institute for Media Studies, 1993.

————. "Cynicism and the Faltering Public Will: What Should We Be Doing?" *IRE Journal* (November/December 1995): 6–8.

————. "Forming and Informing the Public." *Kettering Review* (winter 1992): 60–70.

————. "Making Journalism More Public." *Communication* 12 (1991): 267–84.

————. "Making Politics Work: Journalists and the Public Share Responsibility." *Media and Values* 58 (spring 1992): 10–12.

————. "Making Things More Public: On the Political Responsibility of the Media Intellectual." *Critical Studies in Mass Communication* 11, no. 4 (December 1994): 363–88.

————. "The Media Is the Mess." *Nation* 262, no. 5 (February 5, 1996): 25–28.

Rosen, Jay, and Davis Merritt, Jr. *Public Journalism: Theory and Practice.* Kettering Foundation, 1994.

Sandel, Michael J. "America's Search for a New Public Philosophy." *Atlantic Monthly* 277, no. 3 (March 1996): 57–74.

Schooler, C., J. Flora, and J. W. Farquhar. "Moving toward Synergy." *Communication Research* 29 (1993): 587–610.

Schudson, Michael. "The Sociology of News Production." *Media Culture and Society* 11 (1989): 271.

Shepard, Alicia C. "Buying Press Coverage: How Pew's Civic Journalism Projects Put Newspapers, Radio and Television Stations on the Payroll." *Foundation Watch* 1, no. 7: 1, 3–7.

————. "The Pew Connection." *American Journalism Review* (April 1996): 24–29.

Smorada, C. K. "The Personal Development Seminar: Probing Disciplinary Perspectives." Paper presented at the meeting of the National Endowment for Humanites. Glenside, Pa., July 1982.

Stamm, Keith, and Doug Underwood. "The Relationship of Job Satisfaction to Newsroom Policy Changes." *Journalism Quarterly* 7, no. 3 (autumn 1993): 528–41.

Starobin, Paul. "A Generation of Vipers: Journalists and the New Cynicism." *Columbia Journalism Review* (March/April 1995): 25–32.

SELECTED BIBLIOGRAPHY

Stevenson, R. L. "The Disappearing Reader." *Newspaper Research Journal* 15, no. 3 (1994): 22–31.

Tharp, Tony. "The Media's New Fix." *U.S. News and World Report* (March 18, 1996): 72–73.

Thorson, Esther, Frank Denton, and James Coyle. "Effects of a Multimedia Public Journalism Project on Political Knowledge and Attitudes." Paper presented at the Association for Education in Journalism and Mass Communication. Washington, D.C., August 1995.

Thorson, Esther, and Edmund B. Lambeth. "An Evaluation of the Cognitive, Attitudinal and Synergistic Effects of a Multimedia Civic Journalism Project." Paper presented at the Association for Education in Journalism and Mass Communication. Washington, D.C., August 1995.

Weaver, David H., and G. Cleveland Wilhoit. "Daily Newspaper Journalists in the 1990s." *Newspaper Research Journal* 15, no. 3 (summer 1994): 2–21.

Wellman, Barry. "The Community Question." *American Journal of Sociology* 84 (March 1979): 1201–31.

Winn, Billy. "Public Journalism—An Early Attempt." *Nieman Reports* (winter 1993): 54–56.

Winship, Tom. "Civic Journalism: A Steroid for the Press." *Editor and Publisher* (October 7, 1995): 5, 37.

Yankelovich, Daniel. "A Conversation about Our Public Priorities." *National Civic Review* 83, no. 4 (fall/winter 1994): 389–99.

INDEX